DISABILITY AS DIVERSITY

# ACADEMY OF REHABILITATION PSYCHOLOGY SERIES

**Series Editors**

Bruce Caplan, *Editor-in-Chief*
Timothy Elliott
Robert Frank
Barry Nierenberg
George Prigatano
Daniel Rohe
Stephen Wegener

**Volumes in the Series**

# Disability as Diversity

DEVELOPING CULTURAL COMPETENCE

Erin E. Andrews, PsyD, ABPP

OXFORD
UNIVERSITY PRESS

# OXFORD
UNIVERSITY PRESS

Oxford University Press is a department of the University of Oxford. It furthers
the University's objective of excellence in research, scholarship, and education
by publishing worldwide. Oxford is a registered trade mark of Oxford University
Press in the UK and certain other countries.

Published in the United States of America by Oxford University Press
198 Madison Avenue, New York, NY 10016, United States of America.

Library of Congress Control Number: 2019949803
ISBN 978-0-19-065231-9

*In loving memory of my brother, Vinh Michael Andrews:*
*February 29, 1972–March 23, 2013.*

# Contents

# Preface

THE CONTENTS OF this book are personal, professional, and political. I am both a rehabilitation psychologist and a disabled woman. Within these pages is the history of our people and evidence of our strength and determination to forge an identity and culture despite persistent devaluation by society.

Although I write from the perspective of a disabled person, I cannot claim to speak for our entire heterogeneous group. The perceptions in this book are mine alone, as are any mistakes or misconstructions. I have tried to present a balanced viewpoint, but the limitations of my own experience and my biases as an upper middle-class, highly educated, White, heterosexual, physically disabled, cisgender woman should be noted.

I intentionally chose to alternate between person-first and identity-first language in this book. Similarly, I elected to use both the words *patient* and *client* synonymously to refer to disabled people receiving care from disability and rehabilitation professionals and providers. In a way, this reveals my two minds; I know what it is like to be both the provider and the patient.

My hope is that this book will affect readers even a fraction as much as disability scholarship has impacted me. I hope these pages can help bridge the chasm between those who are serving and those who are being served. I hope that more disabled people will be afforded the opportunity to become service providers, and that non-disabled providers will learn and grow as true allies.

# Acknowledgments

AS AN UNDERGRADUATE at Michigan State University, two important things happened to me. First, I lived in one of the only accessible dormitories on campus, where all the physically disabled students were assigned to the first floor; suddenly, disabled peers surrounded me. Ever since that time, I have made countless friends and colleagues with disabilities who have enriched my life. Second, I discovered disability scholarship. I read *No Pity* by Joseph Shapiro, whose writing about disability history energized me and made me feel proud. By this time, I had changed my major to psychology and came across a new book called *What Psychotherapists Should Know About Disability* by Rhoda Olkin, a disabled psychologist. Her writing about disability resonated with me profoundly. That's when I decided that I too wanted to become a psychologist.

I was fortunate to have strong mentors in my psychology education, in particular, Nancy Crewe at Michigan State University and Julie Williams at Wright State University. I remember reading journal articles by rehabilitation and disability researchers and imagining what it would be like to meet them one day. I am indebted to my senior colleagues, especially Tim Elliott and Dana Dunn, who took a chance on me by inviting me to work and write with them. I am humbled when I reflect on the opportunities I have been given to serve, represent, and advocate. This book would not have been possible without the disabled trailblazers who have taken this path before me; it is because of them that I have been afforded so much opportunity. I want to express my appreciation to the fellow disabled psychologists and professional colleagues who have become my support system and sisterhood—in particular Linda Mona and Carrie Pilarski.

I want to thank Nancy Rich-Gutiérrez, not only for reading and editing each chapter draft but also for being the most loyal and true friend I could ever imagine. Thank you to my family—especially my parents and Paul—for their support and encouragement. I am grateful to my husband, Todd, and my children Gavin and Schuyler, for their patience and unconditional love which helped me create the space to write this book.

The hard reality is this. Society in every nation is still infected by the ancient assumption that people with disabilities are less than fully human and therefore, are not fully eligible for the opportunities which are available to other people as a matter of right.

—JUSTIN DART

.....................................................................................................................................................

# 1    History

DESPITE THE LARGE volume of people who are affected by disability, directly or indirectly, the history of the disability rights movement is little known and not well represented in popular culture. It is essential to understand important historical developments in the disability rights movement—most of which are not in U.S. history books or taught in school—to grasp how disability culture has developed and how disabled people come to form their identities. The most impactful work historically has been done by people with disabilities themselves; some of the earliest activism is attributable to communities of Deaf[1] and blind individuals. This history is powerful; some of it is disturbing, and some is encouraging. Without this history, it is impossible to appreciate the foundation of disability culture and identity and effectively interface with disabled people. This chapter will provide an overview of the some of the crucial events in U.S. history that were driven by people with disabilities and their fight for equal rights. Although these stories are rarely told, disabled Americans have always advocated for their human rights (Burch & Sutherland, 2006).

Disability history has largely existed on the fringes of the mainstream narrative, but in this chapter, U.S. history will be unpacked with disability squarely in the center. There are too many important people and events in U.S. disability history to cover them all, but I will capture some of the most influential history that has led

---

[1] The word deaf with a lowercase 'd' is used to refer to the condition or impairment of inability to hear. The word Deaf with a capital 'd' is used to denote those with the inability to hear who identify with the distinct cultural and linguistic Deaf community.

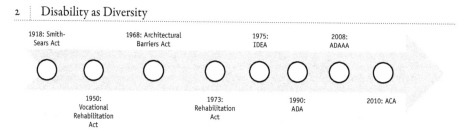

FIGURE 1.1. Timeline of important U.S. disability-related legislation. ACA, Affordable Care Act; ADA, Americans With Disabilities Act; ADAAA, ADA Amendments Act; IDEA, Individuals With Disabilities Education Act.

to current disability struggles. Throughout, it is clear that social change for people with disabilities has almost always been preceded by war and the needs of veterans. A timeline of the most important disability-related legislation is shown in Figure 1.1. The story of civil rights for disabled persons in the United States is not particularly positive until the late 20th century, but those changes could not have occurred without the foundation built by the earliest American disability activists.

## Early Activism

In the early 1800s, a blind French man named Louis Jean-Philippe Braille began to invent the raised-point alphabet system known as Braille that was introduced in the United States in the 1860s and officially adopted in 1932 (National Federation of the Blind [NFB], 2009). Braille became widely used and universally accepted as the most effective system for reading and writing for the blind (NFB, 2009). Braille has been modified for most written languages, mathematics, music, and computer codes, all of which are based on Louis Braille's original system of six by three dot cells (NFB, 2009). Even at its inception, Braille was controversial; most of those teaching literacy to blind people in the 19th and 20th centuries were nonblind instructors who favored print and held biases against Braille including assumptions that it was difficult to learn, slow, and alienating for the blind. Contemporary prejudices persist, and the NFB (2009) estimates that now only 10% of blind children are taught Braille, and a lesser proportion of blind individuals of all ages are Braille proficient. Blind disability advocates blame functional illiteracy and high rates of blind unemployment in the United States on this endemic trend (NFB, 2009). In addition to these concerns, the NFB (2009) suggests that decreased use of Braille may adversely affect the development and maintenance of blind culture.

Following the Fair Labor Standards Act of 1938, blind Americans and those with other types of disabilities were sent to "[sheltered] workshops" to provide labor, usually for very low or no pay. These workshops were often developed under the pretense of protecting disabled workers or helping them prepare for competitive employment, but exploitation was rampant (Longmore & Goldberger, 2000). Typical work was simple sorting, folding, assembling, packaging, or other light tasks. Despite organized efforts, these disabled workers did not have the same benefits and protections as those with employee status or collective bargaining rights; even so, strikes did occur (Longmore & Goldberger, 2000). For example, blind employees led a sit-down strike at a Pittsburgh workshop in 1937. Other concerns were around worker well-being as a result of lax health and safety standards (Hoffman, 2013).

Most Americans learned about Alexander Graham Bell as an inventor, who was credited with the invention of the telephone. Born to a deaf mother, he was familiar with the deaf community and became a deaf educator; he also married a non-signing deaf woman (Christiansen & Barnartt, 2003). Less well known are Bell's eugenic views: he expressed opposition to the creation of a "deaf race" (Lane, 2002). A staunch advocate for oralism, or teaching deaf people to speak verbally, Bell was in opposition to the use of American Sign Language (ASL); he sought to discourage marriage between deaf individuals by separating deaf people from one another so as to prevent the proliferation of deaf children (Baynton, 2006). His advocacy helped oralism become the dominant method of teaching deaf students, but grassroots community organizations fought to promote ASL, the "natural language of the deaf" (Lane, 2002). The U.S. Deaf community has had to fight fiercely to preserve their language and culture (Burch & Sutherland, 2006).

Activism among blind Americans came to prominence in the 1920s with the establishment of the American Foundation for the Blind. Helen Keller, an author and advocate who was both blind and deaf, gained worldwide fame (Nielsen, 2009). Keller's family was advised by Alexander Graham Bell, so unsurprisingly she was taught in the tradition of oralism (Crow, 2000). Despite her persistent and iconic childlike image as a "little deaf-blind girl" who overcame her disabilities, Crow (2000, p. 845) points out that Helen Keller was a real woman, whose beliefs were quite radical. Keller was a suffragette and a Socialist, and she was quite savvy in the ways that she used her celebrity status to advance her causes (Crow, 2000). She was one of the original founders of the American Civil Liberties Union and an advocate for racial desegregation (Crow, 2000). Keller fell in love, but her family and her famous teacher, Anne Sullivan Macy, interfered to prevent her from marrying (Nielsen, 2009).

The Connecticut Asylum for the Education and Instruction of Deaf and Dumb Persons was established in Hartford in 1817. Later renamed the American School for the Deaf, it was the first permanent Deaf school in the United States. The *American Annals of the Deaf* began publication in 1847, making it the oldest publication exclusively focused on deafness. The Columbia Institution for the Instruction of the Deaf opened in 1856 and would later become Gallaudet University, considered to be the preeminent Deaf cultural institution in the United States (Gallaudet University, n.d.). The National Association of the Deaf was established by and for Deaf people in 1880. The focus of these early advocacy efforts was solidarity, access to communication, and the freedom and encouragement to use ASL. The National Association of the Deaf (n.d.) issued a position statement that asserts that Deaf schools both provide quality education and foster Deaf culture, heritage, and language. These "schools for the Deaf, including charter schools founded to serve Deaf children, are uniquely capable of providing the necessary visual learning environment and the ideal conditions for language development for Deaf children" (National Association of the Deaf, n.d., para. 4).

As persons with sensory disabilities were fighting for their rights to communication, education, and employment, Americans with physical disabilities were also forging their way.

## Freak Shows

Freak shows in 19th-century America are an uncomfortable aspect of disability history that is rarely discussed. Rosemarie Garland Thomson (1996) published a thorough history about the ways in which disabled people became spectacles in American freak shows and in museums and circuses, such as P.T. Barnum's American Museum. The public would pay to stare at disabled individuals who were exhibited to highlight the ways in which their bodies were different or strange—the complete objectification of people with disabilities (Thomson, 1996). Those with congenital disabilities, considered "born freaks," were seen as particularly authentic and taboo in terms of monstrosity (Hadley, 2008).

Sideshow performances remain controversial, because it is unclear how much agency disabled performers had. Some evidence suggests they led a difficult and unhappy existence, exploited without real alternatives for livelihood (Hayes & Black, 2003). Other scholars contend that freak show participation enabled disabled people greater independence and freedom than was otherwise possible at that time, and that some performers developed successful and prosperous lives (Bogdan, 1988; Hadley, 2008). Although no more positive, in contrast to the traditional attitude of pity, freak shows were a much different form of attention toward disability—that of curiosity, because performers were marketed as an attraction (Bogdan, 1988). Church (2011, pp. 3–4) explained how the tradition of American freak shows exists today:

In normative society, freakery is premised on unequal viewing and social relations. A nondisabled audience retains the power to subject a non-normative body (traditionally, that of a person with disabilities) to the ableist gaze as entertaining spectacle, enjoying a mixture of shock, horror, wonder, and pity.

Although it has taken many different cultural forms throughout history, freakery's viewing dynamic is still very much with us in contemporary society, allowing non-normative bodies to remain largely inseparable from the specter of freakery in the popular consciousness. People with disabilities are frequently silenced, placed on display, curiously examined, and subjected to hostile, embarrassed, or pitying reactions from non-disabled people.

Freakery was used to define normality, by emphasizing bodies and minds that looked and functioned in unexpected ways; as a result, disabled people of color were particularly exploited (Thomson, 1996). For example, disabled people with dark skin were showcased as strange and unusual in multiple ways, as if they were exotic animals. Sideshows are widely considered to have set the stage for the further dehumanization of people with disabilities, displayed as neither human nor animal (Cook, 1996).

The production company MGM recruited little people in large numbers to play munchkins in the film *The Wizard of Oz* in 1938 (Hogan, 2014). Theatrical roles for people with disabilities including dwarfism were (and still are) rare, so it was unique to have so many individuals employed together in this way. Specifically, MGM sought "proportionate" little people, many of whom came from carnivals, circuses, or vaudeville acts (Hogan, 2014). Some went on with careers in show business, whereas others returned to their non-Hollywood lives following *Oz*. These actors and actresses were not particularly well paid (some reports indicate that the dog who played Toto was paid more than the people who played the munchkins) and were treated, at best, condescendingly (Hogan, 2014). Demeaning stories were told and embellished for decades afterward by *Oz* cast members (including star Judy Garland) about "midgets" who fell and got stuck in toilets, pretended to be schoolchildren to sit on female teachers' laps, participated in orgies, and otherwise acted in raucous and grotesque ways (Hogan, 2014). Needless to say, they were nevert treated with the respect received by nondisabled performers in Hollywood.

Far from the world of show business and entertainment, civil strife between the North and South United States would change the future of America, and for no one was this truer than those who were injured in the war, returning home with various acquired disabilities.

## Mid- to Late 1800s

The American Civil War resulted in extensive injuries and resulting disability, most prominently amputations and psychological problems like "soldier's heart" (Nielsen, 2012, p. 84; Reznick, Gambel, & Hawk, 2009). The Civil War also marked the beginning of the American tradition of community philanthropy toward disabled veterans and organized governmental efforts to help reintegrate disabled soldiers into civilian society. The U.S. Sanitary Commission was developed to facilitate placement of disabled service members, with their families in homes or at institutions called soldiers' or sailors' homes, which were meant for short-term stays leading toward full community reintegration (Reznick et al., 2009). Nielsen (2012) noted that the tradition of institutionalization began when war veterans, especially those with the fewest resources and lowest social status, were placed in hospitals. Perhaps originally intended to rehabilitate, these institutions essentially became prisons that kept disabled people away from the public at large and propagated abuse and nonconsensual medical experiments (Nielsen, 2012).

Blanck and Millender (2000) point out that the ways in which Civil War veterans utilized legal representation and established grassroots advocacy movements to effect change in governmental policies are often overlooked. The veterans and their families played a significant role in convincing medical providers and policymakers to broaden the notion of disability and provide appropriate "invalid pensions" (Reznick et al., 2009).

During the same time period, Americans increasingly acquired disability from participation in industrial labor, and disability became viewed as both a social and economic problem. Institutionalization expanded, and the so-called ugly laws were developed to keep disabled and poor people out of sight (Siebers, 2003; Schweik, 2009). Many U.S. cities legally banned people with disabilities; an 1881 Chicago law read: "Any person who is diseased, maimed, mutilated, or in any way deformed, so as to be an unsightly or disgusting object, or an improper person to be allowed in or on the streets, highways, thoroughfares, or public places in this city, shall not therein or thereon expose himself to public view, under penalty of a fine" (Schweik, 2009, p. 2). Disabled applicants for immigration into the United States were generally declined on the basis of their presumed inability to work and the assumption that they would become burdensome to American society (Baynton, 2006; Burch & Sutherland, 2006). Meanwhile, some philanthropists took a medical or charitable approach and created rehabilitation centers to assist disabled people to become less dependent through medical and rehabilitative interventions (Byrom, 2001). For a time, progress related to disability seemed to stall, but soon another war would again propel disability issues into American consciousness.

## World War I and Its Aftermath

In U.S. history, civilian disability policy invariably follows trends established by legislation originally enacted for veterans; this continues in contemporary society so that the fate of disabled civilians is inextricably linked to that of disabled veterans (Elliott & Andrews, 2016). In the aftermath of World War I, disability issues again came to the forefront as U.S. society absorbed over 4,000 service members who sustained disabilities in the war (Hickel, 2001). During the early 1900s, there was no promise beyond the dates of service that veterans would receive any ongoing support or benefits from the military. Much like the activism after the Civil War, World War I veterans too spoke out for their rights. During the Depression in 1932, nearly 20,000 unemployed veterans—disabled and nondisabled—demonstrated in Washington, DC. These veterans were advocating for cash payment for the wartime military bonuses that had been promised to them by Congress, for which they held only certificates; regrettably, the demonstration ended in violence against the veterans (Longmore, 2000).

Blackie (2014) explored the experiences of unemployed veterans with disabilities who applied for pensions and found that their families often rented out rooms to boarders for additional income and took other measures to support the disabled male head of household (Blackie, 2014). Disabled female civilians faced a tougher challenge: They were considered unable to fulfill roles designated for women in the workplace and the home, such as the coordination of housework (Jennings, 2006). Disabled women have traditionally been discouraged from or not permitted to marry and have children, as they are stereotyped as incapable caregivers for children and inadequate nurturers (Andrews & Ayers, 2016); disabled women who did reproduce were considered a burden on society.

By this time, medical and charitable organizations had become the authority on disability and so began the modern roots of occupational therapy, physical therapy, and vocational rehabilitation (Friedland, 1998). One such institution was the American Red Cross Institute for Crippled and Disabled Men in New York. Funded through both federal appropriations and philanthropy, the goal was purportedly to empower the disabled veteran to "win his own way to self-respect and self-support." However, according to Carden-Coyne (2007), veteran patients and treating professionals often disagreed on the extent to which recovery to prewar employability was possible.

Changes from an agricultural-based to an industrial-based U.S. economy made it more difficult for many veterans to find suitable work (Elliott & Andrews, 2016). Industrial capitalism tended to marginalize people with disabilities, who were forced to compete against nondisabled workers (Lawrie, 2018). In 1918, the Smith-Sears Veterans' Rehabilitation Act was the first federal legislation to offer rehabilitation services to injured service members. Shortly after, the Smith-Fess Act, also known as the Civilian Vocational Rehabilitation Act, allowed the federal government to match state funds to provide rehabilitation services to disabled people whose injuries were not sustained during military service (Elliott & Andrews, 2016). Disabled Black Americans were routinely denied the same opportunities as Whites in vocational rehabilitation, and there is strong evidence that racial discrimination occurred in the distribution of benefits (Lawrie, 2018). Over time, rehabilitation centers' focus on war veterans decreased, and advocacy groups such as Disabled American Veterans, the American Legion, and Paralyzed Veterans of America emerged, championing better public services for disabled veterans (Galer, 2016).

Post–World War I, the pervasive assumption that disability universally meant inability to work was challenged, as the rehabilitation movement publicized the skills obtained by disabled people through rehabilitation. Jennings (2016) noted that disability activists and labor unions found common ground in their quest to dispel emasculating myths about disabled veterans and injured industrial workers to reduce victimization and improve public perception. In 1935, the Congress of Industrial Organizations (CIO) was founded and organized thousands of laborers; although several labor leaders had disabilities themselves and a high number of workers were disabled, there was not yet an organized disability rights labor movement (Longmore, 2000). Baynton (2006) found that some industrial leaders (e.g., Henry Ford) hired many disabled workers and enacted an antidiscrimination policy for their company. Similarly, some industrial efficiency designers promoted modified accommodations to assist disabled workers to function (Baynton, 2006). Rather than a progressive approach to diversity inclusion, finding roles for disabled workers was most likely a means of economic gain; assembly lines created positions that required less physical capability, and people with disabilities typically were less costly employees because of government-sanctioned disparities in pay (Miralles, Garcia-Sabater, Andres, & Cardos, 2007).

## FDR

President Franklin D. Roosevelt was long believed to be a polio survivor, but sophisticated contemporary analyses suggest that he more likely had Guillain–Barré syndrome (Goldman et al., 2003). Roosevelt consistently concealed his lower extremity paralysis by hiding his lower body from view when possible, standing with assistance of a cane and/or a person next to him, and ambulating short distances using leg braces that simulated walking (Burch & Sutherland, 2006; Houck & Kiewe, 2003). He had to minimize the impact of his disability to appear fit for the role of president, because disability was considered incongruent with masculinity and strength, characteristics highly sought in the political climate (Houck & Kiewe, 2003). The press was complicit and never photographed him when his disability might be apparent (J. P. Shapiro, 1994).

Roosevelt cocreated the organization the March of Dimes, and he also invested his own resources into a rehabilitation center for polio survivors in Warm Springs, Georgia (Rose, 2016). As president, his legacy in terms of disability advocacy was variable. In 1935, FDR signed the Social Security Act, which expanded funding for vocational rehabilitation programs and care for the elderly and disabled children (Houck & Kiewe, 2003). However, hundreds of people were turned down for jobs on the basis of physical disability under Roosevelt's Works Progress Administration (WPA; Longmore, 2000). In New York City, the League for the Physically Handicapped formed in May 1935 to protest employment discrimination. Members conducted a 9-day sit-in at the Home Relief Bureau, which, instead of forwarding their job applications to the WPA, stamped them "PH" for physically handicapped, to indicate to the WPA that they were unhirable. The league opted to do a sit-in after the director refused to meet with them. The group later held a brief sit-in at the WPA headquarters and ultimately prevailed by garnering press and public attention that resulted in thousands of WPA job placements for workers with disabilities (Longmore, 2000). This important work set the foundation for decades of disability rights activism.

Out of the public eye, however, Americans with disabilities were quietly being stripped of their civil rights; the medicalization of disability had dire consequences for individual liberties and freedom.

## Eugenics, Compulsory Sterilization, and Systematic Extermination

Even Americans who are aware of the country's history of compulsory sterilization are probably unaware of how widespread the practice was, or that the United States was the first country to legalize compulsory sterilization for eugenic purposes (Iredale, 2000). The primary targets of the practice were those with intellectual disabilities ("feebleminded") and mental illness ("insane"), but secondarily, many state laws allowed for involuntary sterilization of people who were deaf, blind, or physically "deformed," and those with epilepsy (Sofair & Kaldjian, 2000). In 1907, Indiana was the first state to legalize compulsory sterilization, and by the 1920s, 24 states had passed laws allowing involuntary sterilization (Tilley, Walmsley, Earle, & Atkinson, 2012). An estimated 20,000 legal sterilizations were completed by the mid-1930s, and another 22,000 were performed in 27 states between 1943 and 1963 (Sofair & Kaldjian, 2000). At least 60,000 Americans are believed to have been involuntarily or coercively sterilized in total (Burch & Sutherland, 2006; Lombardo, 2003).

The opinion of renowned Judge Oliver Wendell Holmes Jr. in the landmark involuntary sterilization case of *Buck v. Bell* summarized the American sentiment toward those with intellectual disabilities in the early 20th century: "three generations of imbeciles are enough" (Lombardo, 2003, p. 14). The case of Carrie Buck and her family illustrates the realities faced by people considered socially inferior; eugenic laws explicitly stated that sterilization was a legitimate means to decrease or eliminate people labeled as undesirable (Sofair & Kaldjian, 2000). The U.S. Supreme Court upheld the constitutionality of these laws in 1927 (Lombardo, 2003).

Carrie Buck was a young White woman from Virginia, one of several illegitimate children of her mother, Emma Buck, born into poverty, and raised by foster parents (Lombardo, 2003). Carrie Buck reported that she became pregnant after she was raped by a family member of her foster parents; because of the shame surrounding pregnancy among unmarried women and the desire to protect the identity of the rapist, Gould (1985) hypothesized that the pregnancy was the real reason Carrie was sent away to an institution. Indeed, evidence suggests that many women were sent to institutions under the guise of being "feebleminded" because they were viewed as sexually promiscuous or became pregnant outside of marriage (Carey, 1998). Sometimes women were even sterilized covertly while they happened to be in the hospital (Gould, 1985; Lombardo, 2003). Women of color were disproportionately represented among those who were involuntarily sterilized (Carey, 1998).

Upon admission to a state institution, both Carrie Buck and her mother, Emma, were labeled as "feebleminded" through early use of the Stanford-Binet Intelligence Scales; their scores reportedly placed them in the range of "imbeciles" ("idiots" were those with lower intellectual functioning, and "morons" had higher, but still subpar, intellectual abilities). The intelligence of Carrie's daughter, Vivian, was assessed in a dubious fashion by comparative observation to another infant made by a social worker (Lombardo, 2003). The Buck family example was used to illustrate the supposedly hereditary nature of intellectual disability, and the case set precedent to enact compulsory sterilization laws in other states.

In the 1980s, records surfaced from the Virginia hospital where Carrie Buck was sterilized confirming that more than 4,000 sterilizations had been performed, the last one as late as 1972 (Gould, 1985). Carrie Buck was still alive and able to provide details about her history. Her sister Doris was reportedly sterilized without her knowledge or consent during an operation she believed was for appendicitis (Lombardo, 2003). Other records indicated that the publicly paid lawyer for Carrie Buck actually colluded with the state attorney to maintain the sterilization law (Gould, 1985). Gould (1985) obtained school report cards from Carrie's daughter, Vivian, which listed her as an "honor roll" student, contradicting the testimony that she was "feebleminded."

The practice of sterilization is widely thought to have been inspired by the belief of heritability of these disabilities, but Tilley and colleagues (2012) pointed out that even after scientific evidence disproved this theory midcentury, involuntary sterilization was still carried out well into the 1970s (Gould, 1985). The rationale was merely reframed away from eugenic purposes toward the perceived unfitness of disabled women to raise children and the cost and burden of disabled people on society (Tilley et al., 2012). In fact, compulsory sterilization was even spun as therapeutic: Proponents argued that the practice would actually liberate disabled women and allow for deinstitutionalization, which was further supported by the economic case. Tilley and colleagues (2012) argue that contemporary law and practice reflects this same motive (Iredale, 2000); indeed, today the children of parents with disabilities are involved with the child welfare system and removed from their care at disproportionate rates (National Council on Disability, 2012).

It is important to understand that eugenic sterilization in the United States predated such practices under Nazi rule in Germany. In fact, it is widely accepted by scholars that some of the very acts condemned by American judges at Nuremberg were modeled after the practices of American eugenicist physicians and repeatedly sanctioned by the U.S. Supreme Court (Kendregan, 1966; Sofair & Kaldjian, 2000). People with disabilities were considered inferior and a burden to society, and they certainly did not embody the Nazi ideal of a master race (S. E. Evans, 2004). Hitler and his cabinet passed a law on July 14, 1933, ordering sterilization of disabled people, or *lebensunwertes leben* ("lives unworthy of life"), authorizing the use of force to do so (Bock, 1983). The political climate of Nazi Germany allowed their eugenics program to develop into the systematic extermination of disabled people (Sofair & Kaldjian, 2000).

People with cognitive, psychiatric, and physical disabilities were the first targets of state-sanctioned murder in Germany at the beginning of World War II (Bryant, 2017). In all, Adolf Hitler's Aktion Tiergartenstrasse 4 (T-4) program carried out the extermination of tens of thousands of children and adults with disabilities (Bryant, 2017; S. E. Evans, 2004). In fact, a program called the "Children's Operation" was specifically designed to kill mentally and physically disabled children (Bryant, 2017, p. 29). Hitler's own physician, the top medical official in the Third Reich, testified at the Nuremberg trials that efforts to eliminate disabled children were a natural extension of earlier sterilization laws (Sofair & Kaldjian, 2000).

Although initially referred to as a "euthanasia" or "mercy-killing" program, T-4 was never limited to those with terminal illness or poor quality of life; conversely, children and adults with a wide range of disabilities and functional limitations were exterminated (Sofair & Kaldjian, 2000; U.S. Holocaust Memorial Museum, n.d.). The Reich Ministry of the Interior issued a decree in 1939, the "Requirement to Report Deformed etc. Newborns," that mandated the report of newborns or children under 3 presumed to have any number of congenital disabilities, including blindness, deafness, microcephaly, hydrocephaly, missing limbs, and paralysis (Bryant, 2017). Included in these war crimes was extensive medical experimentation conducted on disabled adults and children without their consent (S. E. Evans, 2004).

Initially, Nazi physicians murdered disabled people by lethal injection (Sofair & Kaldjian, 2000). Later, these patients were transferred to one of six gas chambers where they were poisoned to death by carbon monoxide, with their bodies burned in crematoria (U.S. Holocaust Memorial Museum). Toward the end the Holocaust, disabled people under Nazi captivity were starved to death (S. E. Evans, 2004). Because the medical profession largely condoned and committed these heinous acts, it is hardly a surprise that the disability community developed a deep distrust of the medical profession. Nevertheless, some scholars contend that the crimes committed against disabled people during the Holocaust have been forgotten or overlooked in the retelling of history (S. E. Evans, 2004). In some respects, the horrific genocide committed against Jews overshadowed the persecution of disabled people, but the history of eugenic harm against people with disabilities did not begin or end in Nazi Germany; these traditions have deep roots in the United States.

## Rosemary Kennedy

The story of President John F. Kennedy's sister Rosemary illustrates attitudes toward disability in early 20th-century America and highlights the ways in which disability was handled in private. Rosemary experienced anoxia during her birth, causing some developmental delays that hampered her academic performance; also, she reportedly had significant mood swings that made her behavior difficult to manage (Larson, 2015). Rosemary was sent to a boarding school for children with cognitive deficits at age 11 and then changed schools numerous times because of her behavioral difficulty. (Koehler-Pentacoff, 2015).

Rosemary's own writings reveal her as a somewhat immature teen who was insecure and also cared deeply for her family (Larson, 2015). Her parents consented to a series of experimental injections for hormonal imbalances to treat what her father referred to as "backwardness" (Larson, 2015). In her late teens, Rosemary struggled with angry outbursts and began to experience violent seizures (Koehler-Pentacoff, 2015). After learning their daughter was sneaking out of her residential school at night and reportedly meeting up with men at taverns, the Kennedys became alarmed and looked to the medical establishment for help (Koehler-Pentacoff, 2015).

Joseph Kennedy elected to have his daughter undergo a prefrontal lobotomy in 1941, a procedure labeled by the American Medical Association as having cosiderable risks (Larson, 2015). The brain surgery resulted in permanent and significant disabilities, and Rosemary was institutionalized until she died (Larson, 2015). Neither of her parents was a consistent presence in her life. However, her siblings remained involved and made meaningful contributions to disability philanthropy and policy. Her sister, Eunice Kennedy Shriver, was a founder of the Special Olympics, and her brother John F. Kennedy established government support for childhood disability, including the Maternal and Child Health and Mental Retardation Planning Amendment to the Social Security Act. Nearly 50 years after her surgery, Rosemary's younger brother Ted sponsored the Americans With Disabilities Act (Koehler-Pentacoff, 2015; Larson, 2015).

Disability would emerge from private family life to the public stage once again in the aftermath of World War II.

## Post–World War II

Dr. Howard Rusk was an Army physician who took a novel approach to rehabilitation with World War II veterans (Gelfman, Peters, Opitz, & Folz, 1997). He espoused a holistic model of recovery that encompassed more than just physical and medical aspects (Diller, 2005). Rather than the traditional military-style formal disciplinary approach, Rusk described the first Air Force rehabilitation center in Pawling, New York, as "a combination of a hospital, a country club, a school, a farm, a vocational training center, a resort, and a little bit of home as well" (Reznick et al., 2009, pp. 31–32).

Rusk, who enthusiastically engaged psychologists as essential providers in his program and emphasized an interdisciplinary approach to care, helped establish some of the foundational principles of rehabilitation (Diller, 2005; Elliott & Andrews, 2016). Following World War II, he joined the faculty at the Institute of Rehabilitation at New York University Medical Center, an institution that—largely through his efforts—had tremendous national and international impact on the field. The facility was later named in his honor (Atanelov, Stiens, & Young, 2015).

As in previous conflicts, philanthropy and policy both played important roles in the rehabilitation of disabled World War II service members (Reznick et al., 2009). The Vocational Rehabilitation Act of 1950 required that vocational rehabilitation be provided for both combat and noncombat veterans. Increasingly, service members with serious disabilities survived because of improved medical evacuation procedures, advanced medical interventions, and better-quality care facilities (Blanck & Millender, 2000). Veterans Health Administration (VHA) medical centers across the country began developing comprehensive rehabilitation programs that included physical therapy, occupational therapy, psychotherapy, recreational activities, and vocational rehabilitation (Elliott & Andrews, 2016). A World War II combat veteran, George Hohman, who sustained a spinal cord injury and used a wheelchair, pursued his PhD in psychology and went on to advocate for rehabilitation services throughout the VHA system (Elliott & Andrews, 2016).

Disabled veterans using their GI educational benefits pushed for equal access on college campuses. For example, a group of veterans at a branch campus of the University of Illinois sought to transfer to the main campus at Urbana-Champaign, which was inaccessible for wheelchair users. To get the university to provide necessary accommodations, the veterans took their protest to the governor and ultimately succeeded (McCarthy, 2003). These early victories were small but crucial; in the next decades disabled college students would lead the way toward expanding civil rights.

## Civil Rights Movement of the 1960s

The 1960s witnessed the increasing efforts of Black Americans to gain civil rights. Discussion of groundbreaking activism for racial equality and women's rights is familiar content in history books, but the important disability rights work being done at the same time is usually overlooked (Nielsen, 2012; J. P. Shapiro, 1994). The Civil Rights Act of 1964 prohibited discrimination on the basis of race, religion, sex, or national origin. However, there were no provisions to protect people with disabilities from discrimination, despite the efforts of senator and later vice president Hubert H. Humphrey, who had a grandchild with Down syndrome (Davis, 2015). Many would argue that disability rights were more complicated than those of racial or gender equality: In addition to adjusting attitudes, implementing disability rights meant infrastructural changes, which were deemed too expensive (J. P. Shapiro, 1994). Instead, the National Commission on Architectural Barriers to the Rehabilitation of the Handicapped was created in 1965 to address limited accessibility in federal buildings; this set the precedent for states to provide construction grants and laid the foundation for the Architectural Barriers Act of 1968 that set initial accessibility standards (Goldman, 1982; Winter, 2003).

The epicenter of many types of civil rights advocacy was in the San Francisco Bay Area, and it was no different for disability rights. In 1962, a young polio survivor named Ed Roberts enrolled at the University of California at Berkeley, but because he required an 800-pound negative pressure ventilator or "iron lung," he could not live in the dormitories (Pelka, 2012; J. P. Shapiro, 1994). Instead, the university allowed Roberts to reside in the student health service building (Nielsen, 2012). When other families learned that Roberts had obtained these accommodations, increasing numbers of disabled students enrolled in the university and joined

Roberts living in the health center. They called themselves "the Rolling Quads" and started a disabled students' program at UC Berkeley; they went on to pioneer the independent living movement (J. P. Shapiro, 1994).

## The 1970s and the Independent Living Movement

In the 1970s, many important events converged to become what can be viewed as the most productive decade in the struggle for civil rights for people with disabilities in the United States. In the early 1970s, Ed Roberts and the Rolling Quads took their activism into the community and established the very first Center for Independent Living (CIL) in Berkeley, California (DeJong, 1979; J. P. Shapiro, 1994). Roberts has been called the "father of independent living," and he attracted other important disability activists like Judy Heumann to grow the CIL into what became the model for every such center in the United States (McDonald & Oxford, 1995). The hallmark of the CIL paradigm is the rejection of the medical model and emphasis on peer support, advocacy, and skills training (DeJong, 1979; Winter, 2003). The goal of the CIL movement was to work toward full participation for disabled people in all aspects of community life and to eliminate the systematic institutionalization of people with disabilities (McDonald & Oxford, 1995; J. P. Shapiro, 1994). Independent living advocates shed light on the deplorable conditions in state hospitals and nursing homes and began demonstrating how community-based living was far less costly in both human and financial expense (McDonald & Oxford, 1995; J. P. Shapiro, 1994). Roberts is well known in the disability community for his many contributions, but he is possibly most admired because 15 years after he was deemed too physically impaired to be employable, the governor of California appointed him head of the California Department of Rehabilitation, the very agency that had completely discounted him as a candidate for vocational rehabilitation (McDonald & Oxford, 1995; J. P. Shapiro, 1994). His story captures the spirit of disability culture: that people with disabilities can be successful and powerful despite the assumptions of nondisabled people.

Several federal legislative advances took place around this time, starting with the 1973 passage of the Rehabilitation Act. However, Secretary of Health, Education, and Welfare (HEW) Joseph Califano declined to sign Section 504, the part that disallowed discrimination against disabled people, as it was originally written. Instead, an HEW task force composed of nondisabled members revised the language of 504, weakening its enforcement. On April 5, 1977, a group of over 100 disabled people occupied the San Francisco offices of the HEW department to protest these changes, staying for almost 1 month, the longest occupation of a federal building in U.S. history (Longmore & Goldberger, 2000). The sit-in was successful, and the Section 504 regulations were finally issued—as originally written—on May 4, 1977 (Longmore & Goldberger, 2003).

Disability scholars believe the movement succeeded for a few reasons. First, activists also occupied the other regional offices throughout the United States. Second, the participants were all involved in decisions and planning, so the government had difficulty identifying a distinct leader of the occupation. Finally, because of their commitment to social justice across various identities, advocacy groups dedicated to racial and sexual equality supported the disability group by bringing needed supplies (Longmore & Goldberger, 2003; J. P. Shapiro, 1994).

At the same time, Califano signed the Education for All Handicapped Children Act, requiring schools to provide "the best possible public education" to students with disabilities in "the least restrictive environment" (J. P. Shapiro, 1994). In 1978 an amendment passed that federally funded CILs and required that disabled people be involved in the oversight and direction of the centers (Winter, 2003). This legislation was particularly meaningful because it mandated what had become the disability civil rights movement credo: "Nothing About Us Without Us" (Charlton, 1998). Disability activists did not stop there, not with so much human rights ground left to cover.

## ADAPT Action

One of the greatest struggles for people with disabilities in the United States involves transportation. Many impairments make it difficult or impossible to drive, and adaptive equipment is expensive, and thus prohibitive for a population with disproportionately high rates of poverty (Kraus, Lauer, Coleman, & Houtenville, 2018). In the latter part of the 20th century, people with disabilities had greater opportunities for education and employment, but many remained hampered by a lack of accessible public transportation. In Denver, Colorado, disability activist Wade Blank and 19 associates swarmed a brand new city bus; people in wheelchairs blocked both the front and back of the bus so that it could not move (Hershey, 1994). Blank's group, at that time called Atlantis, had advocated for wheelchair lifts for the new city buses, but none of the new fleet was fitted with lifts (McDonald & Oxford, 1995). The protesters stalled traffic and ignored police orders to disband; they stayed for 2 days until Denver agreed to become the first U.S. city to provide accessible bus transit for disabled residents (J. P. Shapiro, 1994). The grassroots group changed their name to American Disabled for Accessible Public Transit (ADAPT), and they are considered one of the most radical and militant advocacy groups in the disability community; their trademark is called a national ADAPT "action," which is marked by nonviolent civil disobedience that routinely results in arrests (Hershey, 1994). These protests have involved disabled people chaining themselves to the White House fence and being forcibly dragged away by police (J. P. Shapiro, 1994). In a 1980 ADAPT action, protesters used sledgehammers to break curbs to convince legislators to make Colorado the first state to require curb cuts on public sidewalks to create access for wheelchair users. In October 1983, ADAPT held an action in Washington, DC at the American Public Transit Association (APTA) Convention where advocates blocked entrances with their bodies and assistive devices, requiring attendees to climb over them (Hershey, 1994; McDonald & Oxford, 1995). Achieving federal enactment of accessible transit was a profound accomplishment; regulations that required lifts on new buses were passed back in 1970 but were not implemented until the spring of 1990. The fact that they were implemented at all was a result of the hard work and action of ADAPT.

Following their success with public transportation, ADAPT shifted its focus to the need for personal care assistants for disabled people to keep them out of institutions and living in the community; ADAPT now stands for Americans Disabled for Attendant Programs Today (Hershey, 1994; McDonald & Oxford, 1995). ADAPT is no less active now; in fact, their protests gained national media attention in January 2018 for holding actions and getting arrested in congressional offices in an effort to protect health care for disabled Americans under the Affordable Care Act (ACA).

During this same period, social justice work was also occurring in the realm of education and cultural institutions. Disability advocates forcefully challenged the tradition of demanding ownership of disabled bodies and lives when it was extended to taking control of the institutions meant to be theirs.

## Deaf President Now

In 1988, students at Gallaudet University in Washington, DC argued vehemently that the time had come for the Deaf school to employ the first Deaf president in its 124-year history (Christiansen & Barnartt, 2003). In 1857, the Columbia Institution for the Deaf and Dumb was established near the U.S. Capitol (J. P. Shapiro, 1994). President Abraham Lincoln signed legislation to permit the institution to offer baccalaureate degrees in 1864 (Christiansen & Barnartt, 2003). The college became the National Deaf Mute College, later Gallaudet College, and eventually Gallaudet University (Christiansen & Barnartt, 2003). Gallaudet is the only liberal arts college for the Deaf in the world (Gallaudet University, n.d.).

In 1987, the president of Gallaudet University resigned, and there was significant lobbying by student organizations and Deaf interest groups encouraging the board of trustees to choose a Deaf president, given a preponderance of well-qualified

Deaf individuals (J. P. Shapiro, 1994). The board of trustees narrowed the candidates to three Deaf candidates and three hearing candidates (Christiansen & Barnartt, 2003). When word spread that a hearing applicant was selected, protesters blocked all entrances to the Gallaudet campus and held marches in the capital (Pelka, 2012). There were numerous rallies, press conferences, and media interviews, which attracted national attention (J. P. Shapiro, 1994). Advocates also took their grievances to members of Congress; their involvement was important, given that Gallaudet is reliant in large part on federal funding (Christiansen & Barnartt, 2003). After almost a week of protesting, the university finally acceded to the protesters' demands: The new hearing president resigned after only 2 days and a Deaf president, I. King Jordan, was named (Christiansen & Barnartt, 2003). The chair of the board that had elected a hearing president was removed, and a 51% Deaf majority was guaranteed on the board of trustees (Pelka, 2012). Part of the agreement was that no retaliation could be taken against any faculty, staff, or students involved in the protest (Pelka, 2012; J. P. Shapiro, 1994).

By the time Deaf President Now was over, the pressure and momentum of the disability rights movement had reached its peak. However, disabled people still had no federal civil rights legislation protection, and the status quo could not hold much longer.

## The Americans With Disabilities Act and Its Impact

When Vice President George H. W. Bush met with disabled activist and lawyer Evan Kemp Jr., he took notice of Kemp's perspective that people with disabilities sought independence and employment (J. P. Shapiro, 1994). Kemp was the original "Jerry's Kid," or poster child for the Muscular Dystrophy Association (MDA); like many poster children over the years, Kemp ultimately condemned the demeaning objectification of disabled people and pity evoked by charities in order to raise money (Pelka, 2012; J. P. Shapiro, 1994). In 1990, Kemp would sit next to Bush as he signed the Americans With Disabilities Act (ADA), the only civil rights legislation to protect people with disabilities. Justin W. Dart, Jr., who was part of the team that drafted the bill, is widely credited as the father of the ADA; his creative and progressive approach to unified advocacy involved co-authoring white papers on the issues and conducting nationwide tours to talk with consumers and other stakeholders about their experiences and opinions (Frank & Beane, 2015; Pelka, 2012).

The ADA was both monumental and at the same time underwhelming. No doubt, it is the most important legislation ever passed in disability history and has drastically improved the lives of disabled people in the United States (Pelka, 2012).

Nonetheless, the ADA has significant weaknesses that have truncated its practical effect on social justice. Symbolically, the ADA validated the disability rights movement and disability culture by identifying disabled people "a discrete and insular minority who have been faced with restrictions and limitations, subjected to a history of purposeful unequal treatment" (ADA, 1990). The ADA was indeed a vast improvement upon earlier policies and promised to cease "employment, access, housing, and educational discrimination against people with disabilities" (ADA, 1990). Advocates for its passage had to make clear that the ADA would benefit more than just disabled people and would not overly burden society with cost (J. P. Shapiro, 1994). Again, ADAPT had to stage a protest (as they had for the 504 sit-in) to demand disabled civil rights in the United States in the form of the ADA (Pelka, 2012). ADAPT members crawled out of their wheelchairs and up the steps of the U.S. Capitol Building (J. P. Shapiro, 1994). The signing of the ADA was indeed a triumph in disability advocacy that created new opportunities. As time has passed, however, ADA judicial outcomes have skewed in favor of defendants in contrast to appellate findings from other civil rights legislation; in other words, it is harder to win disability discrimination suits based on the ADA than it is for other minority discrimination cases (Colker, 2001). Numerous clauses in the ADA are widely considered to be loopholes. For example, if a defendant can prove that providing access is an "undue hardship," the entity need not act, and if an employee needs an accommodation to work that is not "reasonable," the employer is under no obligation to grant the request (ADA, 1990; Colker, 2001). This underscores the fundamental difference between disability civil rights and those of other minorities; equality for disability can mean physical and structural changes, and under the ADA, cost factors into these decisions (M. Johnson, 2007). Finally, there is no real mechanism for justice under the ADA unless a lawsuit is filed. For employment claims, the Equal Employment Opportunity Commission will take up strong cases (M. Johnson, 2007). In other areas of discrimination, if the disabled party is without means to sue, a case can be opened with the U.S. Department of Justice, but it is unlikely to result in meaningful action and can take years to traverse the bureaucratic process. In no case may a disabled party receive damages from an ADA suit, only attorney fees and injunctive relief wherein the violation is corrected (ADA, 1990). The ADA Amendments Act of 2008 (ADAAA) corrected some problems identified with the original ADA; for example, the ADAAA broadened and clarified the definition of disability, which had been criticized as too vague (Long, 2008). The ADAAA also specifies that mitigating factors such as assistive devices cannot be used in the determination of disability. To illustrate, an amputee cannot be denied as disabled simply because he can walk with prosthetics. The new law allows for conditions that can wax and wane or are episodic, rather than considering only the person's functioning at the time of a possible ADA infraction (Long, 2008). These and other changes improve the ADA but do not completely ameliorate the aforementioned problems (Mackelprang & Salsgiver, 2016).

### Convention on the Rights of Persons With Disabilities

The United Nations enacted the Convention on the Rights of Persons With Disabilities (CRPD) in 2008. The United Nations CRPD was largely modeled after the ADA, affirmed the personhood of people with disabilities, and stated that disabled people are entitled to the same human rights and freedoms as nondisabled people (Mackelprang & Salsgiver, 2016). Going further, the CRPD acknowledges the diversity of disability, and it explicitly discusses the right of people with disabilities to societal inclusion, respect, and identity preservation (Mackelprang & Salsgiver, 2016). Even though the United States signed the CRPD in 2009, Congress elected not to ratify it in 2012, with the justification that to do so would endanger national sovereignty. Despite significant advocacy efforts, the U.S. Congress has yet to ratify the CRPD.

## Disability Studies

Following the rise of the disability rights movement and some legislative gains, a new field of study began to emerge in the United Kingdom and in the United States. Disability studies is an interdisciplinary academic area encompassing social sciences, humanities, rehabilitation, technology, and engineering (Albrecht, Seelman, & Bury, 2001). The field of disability studies is the formal intellectual examination of disability as a phenomenon (Davis, 2006). Lennard Davis (2006) noted that early disability studies scholarship was largely anthropological, whereas contemporary writing is influenced by cultural and feminist studies, postmodernism, and an emphasis on the relation between the body and power. Disability scholarship has not historically witnessed the same development as have parallel academic studies focused on race, class, and gender (Albrecht et al., 2001). The development of this new field dovetailed with the rise of the social and diversity models of disability (see Chapter 2). The academic focus perhaps offered increased legitimacy to the concept of disability as a culture (see Chapter 4).

The disability studies field is a product of English-speaking countries, primarily the United States and the United Kingdom (Shakespeare, 1998). Although the U.K. focus has been predominantly on the social model and sociopolitical factors affecting disability, U.S. disability studies emphasized the importance of disability culture and history (Shakespeare, 1998). At some point in the United States, perhaps in the 1970s, disability inquiry seems to have taken two separate paths—one medical and rehabilitative, and the other academic (disability studies) and cultural (Finkelstein, 1998). In the United States, the Society for Disability Studies (SDS) was founded in 1982 as the Section for the Study of Chronic Illness, Impairment, and Disability (SSCIID), and renamed in 1986. One of the founding members of the SDS was Irving Kenneth Zola, an American sociologist and the founder-editor of *Disability Studies Quarterly*.

Many, if not most, disability studies scholars are disabled themselves, a stark contrast to the fields of rehabilitation medicine and psychology, where disabled professionals represent a minority incommensurate with the representation of disability in the population (Davis, 2006; Shakespeare, 1998). Davis (2006) cautions that when disabled scholars focus on helping nondisabled people understand the experience of disability, they risk playing into the inherently unequal power differential between disabled and nondisabled communities. In other words, the onus is then on disabled people to play the stereotypical and often exhausting role of educator and representative of the disability community, relieving nondisabled people of the labor burden of seeking to educate themselves about disability.

An important development in disability studies discourse is the integration of intersecting diverse identities, called critical disability studies. Critical disability studies essentially align disability cultural and political movements alongside those of other marginalized communities, such as racial and ethnic minorities and lesbian, gay, bisexual transgender, and queer-plus (LGBTQ+) communities (Goodley, 2016). Finkelstein (1998) criticized the academic disability studies field for being a small group of elite academics, with little relation and of little importance to average disabled citizens. The philosophical writings and abstract theories often witnessed in disability studies scholarship are indeed limited in their applicability to the broader disability community.

## Conclusion

Today, the disability rights community continues to face significant challenges. Threats to the ACA mandate of health care coverage for disabled people with pre-existing conditions and diminished eligibility for Medicaid have inspired action among disability advocates (Block & Friedner, 2017). The frontier of reproductive justice and parenting rights has started to take hold; parents with disabilities have their children removed from their care at astronomical rates, without culturally informed, accessible evaluation procedures and without adequate adaptations (Andrews & Ayers, 2015; National Council on Disability, 2012). Several U.S. state statutes include disability itself as grounds for termination of parental rights, but activists are challenging these laws (National Council on Disability, 2012).

On January 23, 2017, disability history went mainstream when Google featured "Ed Roberts's 78th Birthday Today" for their Google Doodle in tribute to the disability rights movement leader. Following the 2018 death of legendary scientist Stephen Hawking, disability activists took to social media to protest the portrayal of Hawking in death as "freeing," and a meme of him standing, having walked away from his wheelchair, looking up at the stars. Keah Brown, a disability activist and writer, stated that these representations signify to "other disabled people that we should be excited for the opportunity to be 'free' of our bodies, but it also reduces Stephen Hawking, one of the greatest intellectuals ever, to his disability and nothing more" (K. Brown, 2018).

Young disability rights activists like Brown, who never knew life in America before the ADA, and who understand the importance of intersectionality of multiple identities, are making history today. The modern disability rights movement has flourished with the ease of access to online platforms and social media, because the internet allows disabled people access to one another and to promote ideas without having to physically attend a rally or a march. The presence of disabled activists is more prominent than ever, evidenced by trending hashtags like #cripthevote and #iamapreexistingcondition (Block & Friedner, 2017). The traditional barriers that isolated disabled people from one another have been reduced, and despite very real civil rights threats, people with disabilities continue to rally together, generation after generation.

Politically and psychologically our power will come from
celebrating who we are as a distinct people.

—GILL (1995, p. 49)

# 2 Models of Disability

DISABLED PEOPLE HAVE been treated in different ways throughout history as
illustrated by the rich history of disability rights described in Chapter 1. Various
models of disability have shaped the way in which persons with disabilities have
been conceptualized, and subsequently treated, in society. Models simply provide
a framework for understanding the complex relationships among individuals, disabilities, and outcomes at both the personal and the societal level (Wang, Badley, &
Gignac, 2006). Indeed, these ideas and theories regarding the nature and definition
of disability influence how disability is discussed and addressed. In this chapter, five
significant disability models are described: the moral model, the medical model, the
rehabilitation model, the social model, and the diversity model. I will discuss biopsychosocial models—those that consider a combination of biological, psychological, and social factors—that encompass the strengths of the historical models before
them. Finally, implications for these models in the lives of disabled people will be
explored.

## Moral Model

The oldest model of disability is the moral model, which assumes that disability is
a result of a moral failing or sin on the part of the individual or his or her family
members (Olkin, 2017). This model is grounded in the tension between good and
evil; unfortunate situations are attributed to evil (Devlieger, 2005). For example,

it may be concluded that the birth of a child with physical anomalies results from immoral behaviors on the part of his or her parents (Mackelprang & Salsgiver, 2016). Moral model proponents interpret disability as a source of shame; as a result, many disabled people were historically hidden at home or institutionalized. The concept of disability as a burden to families and to society was heavily influenced by religious dogma (Andrews & Elliott, 2014; Mackelprang & Salsgiver, 2016). Biblical references include disability as punishment for wrongdoing and as a blemish on the divine image of human beings (Mackelprang & Salsgiver, 2016; Otieno, 2009).

Attitudes of pity and shame are prominent in moral model language. Although considered offensive today, common expressions used to refer to people with disabilities included "gimp," "cripple," or "imbecile" (Olkin, 1999). Externally, moral model conceptualizations offer no meaningful social or occupational role for those with disabilities; internally, moral representations may breed self-pity or self-hatred.

Conversely, another moral model interpretation of disability is that of disabled people as righteous, selected to be used for God's work and to teach others lessons of virtue (Devlieger, 2005). Certain charities are one example of how pity can be used to fundraise; disabled children are prominent in television ads and other campaigns for donations. These organizations often herald disabled people as "inspirational," becoming the object of sympathy or a means to remind nondisabled people of their inherent life advantages (Mackelprang & Salsgiver, 2016).

Although the moral model views the concept of disability as a punishment, it can also define disability more positively such as a gift or a challenge given to special people (Landsman, 1999). These ideations are commonly expressed among parents of children with disabilities. Although the moral model is less modern than other ideas, remnants remain ingrained in our societal fabric.

## Medical Model

The medical model evolved from global advances in rationality and modern societal development (Devlieger, 2005). Like the moral model, the medical model views disability as intrinsically negative (M. Dunn, 2011). However, the widespread adoption of the medical model challenged the dominance of religious ideology to explain disability (Devlieger, 2005). As medicine developed, the medical model emerged in the early part of the 20th century. Replacing moral explanations for disability, society came to understand people with disabilities as having biomedical problems (Mackelprang & Salsgiver, 2016). Early medical model uses were to address military injuries. The medical model explains disability impairment as a problem in need of a remedy or cure (Kaplan, 2002). In the words of Paul Longmore (1987), "the medical model defines disability as the inability to perform expected social roles because of chronic medical pathology. . . . It presents disability as a social problem, but it makes deviant individual bodies the site and source of that problem" (p. 355).

The medical model defines disability as impairment. Impairment is viewed as the problem, so that structures and functions that do not work as expected or that differ from some presumed norm are the focus of intervention (Mackelprang & Salsgiver, 2016). The medical model persists and remains influential today. In the medical setting, it is not uncommon for patients to be referred to by their impairments or conditions; a clinician may describe a patient as "the severe TBI [traumatic brain injury] admitted last night." Medical model interventions focus on treating or curing impairment, with scant attention paid to other factors, including environmental and attitudinal barriers or cultural and political influences (Mackelprang & Salsgiver, 2016).

The function of people with disabilities in the medical model is to assume the sick role, which releases them from the typical responsibilities within their families and communities (Mitra, 2014). As a result, they are required to comply with the directives of expert medical providers. Critics would argue that the medical model deprives disabled people of full involvement in and contribution to society. They assert that those with disabilities are usually capable of participating in their communities, and that the sick role promotes the confinement and institutionalization of disabled people. Contemporary examples make it clear that the medical model has significantly guided public policy approaches. That the U.S. Social Security Administration (SSA) defines disability as the incapacity for employment deters some with disabilities from seeking work due to concern they could lose a reliable, albeit low, income source and access to health care. The SSA Ticket to Work and Self-Sufficiency program was introduced in 1999 and intended to address several major work disincentives to disabled people receiving benefits. The program was meant to help disabled people, most of whom would prefer to work, become employed while keeping their health insurance coverage. It is important to note that people with disabilities in the program are closely monitored by the SSA and must meet certain benchmarks within specific timeframes with the goal of decreasing the amount of assistance received from the SSA. In any case, activists argue that although disabled people can require medical intervention, the medical system should not be the catalyst for the development of disability-related policy issues.

Other champions of the medical model—with roots in the moral model—are many charities, whose missions are to fundraise toward the cure or eradication of particular disabilities. Donors typically expect that their contributions will enhance the lives of people living with the specific disability. In common practice, charity funds often emphasize the identification of genetic markers associated with impairment, prioritizing detection and elimination (Brock, 2005). Disability rights advocates posit that many disabilities will never be cured, opposing both the collection of money utilizing the medical model ideology that disability is a personal tragedy and the funneling of resources toward the elimination of disability instead of supporting those currently living with disability.

## Rehabilitation Model

The rehabilitation model is a descendant of the medical model, and it is the most common framework in medical rehabilitation settings. In this paradigm, disabled people are considered to have potential to contribute societally; however, they require interventions from rehabilitation professionals to help them learn to develop compensatory strategies for disabilities. After World War II, the rehabilitation model emerged as a way to meet the needs of injured and disabled veterans. The model was also influenced by the supportive efforts of people with disabilities. The League of the Physically Handicapped initially used the mantra "We Don't Want Tin Cups. We Want Jobs" (Longmore, 1987). In contrast to the medical model approach of the federal social security system, many state-funded vocational rehabilitation programs in the United States are based on the rehabilitation model. As a derivative of the medical model, the assumption of the rehabilitation model is that physical impairment is the problem; unlike the medical model, the rehabilitation approach postulates that rehabilitative efforts can reduce or help the individual compensate for disability-related limitations (Mackelprang & Salsgiver, 2016). Rehabilitation model proponents argue that disabled people need not be excluded from employment, but require specific compensatory tools or adaptations (Longmore, 1987). Disability activists criticize the rehabilitation model as insufficient, as it fails to address the sociopolitical and cultural issues related to disability. In addition, disabled people continue to be expected to acquiesce to medical rehabilitation specialists, maintaining a steep power differential between professionals and consumers (J. Evans, 2004).

## Social Model

The emphasis of the social model is on external barriers such as physical obstacles to access and attitudinal issues like prejudice and discrimination (Oliver, 2013; Shakespeare, & Watson, 1997). The development of the social model of disability was revolutionary because it was the first model in which neither the individual nor the impairment was identified as the crux of the problem (Oliver, 2013; Shakespeare, & Watson, 1997). The social model was the first to acknowledge the effects of external factors (e.g., social and environmental issues) on the lives of people with disabilities (Barnes, 2014; Oliver, 2013). Disability defined by the social model is a neutral quality, not an inherently negative attribute. The social model focus is not on cures or moral failings, as it shifts the source of difficulty away from the individual and impairments. Disability is instead considered a social construction and the social model centers on the environmental, structural, and attitudinal barriers that hinder people with disabilities from full participation in society (Olkin, 2017). Within the fields of philosophy and bioethics, the social model views disability as a mere difference that does not inherently make one worse off (Barnes, 2014).

One early advocate of the social model was social psychologist Beatrice Wright, who objected to language that dehumanized people with disabilities and ignored their other identifying characteristics. Her work led to a shift in psychology, reducing the acceptability of equating people with impairment. Wright argued that the focus should be placed on the person, who comes before his or her disability. This concept, known as person-first language, literally emphasizes the person rather than impairment. In practice, this means that the phrase *person with a disability* should be used rather than *disabled person*. Wright argued that this approach preserved humanity while promoting individuality (Wright, 1983). Disability language will be discussed in greater depth in Chapter 5.

The social model was well received by activists in the disability rights and independent living movements, as it was congruent with their regard for disability as a normal aspect of life, with problems created primarily through artificial means such as prejudicial behavior toward disabled people (Altman, 2001; Oliver, 2013). This was a paradigm shift—the social model was the first model that did not conceptualize problems as inherent to impairment. The social model was not without its critics, however. The main weaknesses of the social model of disability relate primarily to measurement; there is no differentiation between who does and does not meet criteria for the label of disability because disability is ambiguously identified (Peterson & Elliott, 2008).

Crow (1996) argues that highlighting the negative impact of social and environmental factors on disabled people does not deny the real consequences of impairment. In reality, some disabled bodies function with difficulty, require significant assistance, or involve pain. Social model proponents suggest that the view that a disabled person's body and worth are inferior is a socially constructed interpretation (Crow, 1996). However, the social model can be criticized for minimizing the objective concept of impairment, focusing almost completely on the phenomenological aspects and the impact of the social and environmental contexts in which impairments occur. As such, Crowe (1996) argues that exclusion and discrimination are what debilitate people with impairments, but these processes are not inevitable and immutable.

## Diversity Model

An evolution of other the social model, the diversity model (sometimes called minority model) extends the importance of the sociopolitical experience of disability (Altman, 2001). The diversity model is associated with the emergence of the academic field of disability studies, which considers disability a unique, diverse, cultural identity. As with other demographic characteristics such as race and sexual orientation, the diversity model positions disability as a central and valued aspect of one's identity (Andrews et al., 2013). Diversity model proponents argue that disability is an individual difference within the normal spectrum of diversity; this characteristic has been largely overlooked as a form of diversity. Like the social model, the diversity model theorizes that the primary encumbrance for people with disabilities is attitudinal and that "ableism"—discrimination against and prejudice toward disabled people—is the culprit of disability-related disparities in society (Mackelprang & Salsgiver, 2016).

There are some differences between the social and diversity models of disability. The diversity model extends beyond mere acceptance of disability to explicit expressions of disability pride (Olkin, 2002). Diversity model proponents often reject the person-first language that developed out of the social model, instead electing to identify as "disabled people," describing with pride their identification with disability culture (Andrews et al., 2013). In an effort to represent fidelity to disability culture, some scholars have promoted the use of the term *Disabled* with a capital "D," borrowing a custom from Deaf culture (Gill, 1995).

Contrasting ideologies among these models has resulted in dissidence among stakeholders across disability fields. Medical model proponents remain largely focused on cure and the amelioration of impairment, whereas social and diversity model advocates converge around the importance of human rights and social justice (J. Evans, 2004). Although the overt influence of the moral model has diminished (as observed by decreased prominence of pity-based charity fundraisers such as the Muscular Dystrophy Association telethon), there remain subtle and underlying moral model messages about disability throughout mainstream culture. Contemporary developments have led to more nuanced disability models that address some of the shortcomings of traditional discourses.

## Biopsychosocial Models

The World Health Organization (WHO) developed the International Classification of Functioning, Disability, and Health (ICF), a biopsychosocial model that incorporates strengths from other models of disability (WHO, 2001). The WHO originally intended to offer a coherent alternative and a more balanced perspective on disability than either the medical or social model. The original WHO model and its latest iteration distinguish among disability, health, and functional impairment, distinctions with important implications for health promotion and disease prevention.

The original WHO model (WHO, 1980) was called the International Classification of Impairments, Disabilities, and Handicaps (ICIDH). In the ICIDH, the WHO defined *impairment* as a significant deviation or loss of bodily function or structure. Bodily functions are physiological functions of body systems, including psychological and personality factors, whereas body structures are anatomical parts. Examples of impairment include absence of a limb, loss of bowel or bladder control, and the experience of persistent hallucinations. In the ICIDH, *disability* was considered to be a limitation in activity or a restriction in participation—for example, the inability to walk or difficulty establishing social relationships. Finally, *handicap* was designated to represent the interaction between a person with a disability and his or her environment that affected the person's role fulfillment; this was an early effort to account for the idea of disability as a social construct.

In 2001, the WHO published the ICF, the most recent version of the model, wherein functioning is considered a "dynamic interaction between a person's health condition, environmental factors and personal factors" (WHO, 2013, p. 5). Although some aspects of the ICF are consistent with definitions in its predecessor, the ICIDH, the ICF offers several important updates that correspond to evolving disability ideologies. The ICF continues to describe *impairment* as an alteration in bodily function or structure. One important difference, however, is that the WHO no longer denotes impairments themselves as problematic (WHO, 2001). Impairments can result from injury or disease or may be anomalies present at birth.

*Activity limitations* are interpreted by the ICF as difficulties an individual may experience in executing a wide range of tasks or activities. These may include barriers to mobility, communication, learning, or self-care (WHO, 2001) and may or may not be affected by the use of assistive devices or environmental modifications. The ICF uses performance and capacity qualifiers to distinguish between actual performance of tasks or actions in one's current environment and context versus activity limitations that are inherent consequences of one's impairment (WHO, 2001).

The ICF eliminated the term *handicap*; in the ICIDH, the concept of handicap resided in the person ("the person is handicapped"), but more contemporary paradigms emphasize the role of the social and physical environments in either restricting or enabling participation ("the person requires assistance to bathe"). As a result, the

ICF introduced the term *participation restriction* to describe life activities and roles including interpersonal relationships, education, employment, financial autonomy, recreation and leisure, religion and spirituality, and political advocacy. Examples of participation restriction are limitations on attending school, maintaining gainful employment, or pursuing romantic relationships.

Among the most important elements of the WHO ICF are the *contextual factors* that influence the overall functioning of the individual. The contextual factors are divided into two categories. *Environmental factors* consist of the physical, social, and attitudinal environment in which people conduct their lives. These external elements affect the experience of the individual by either facilitating or inhibiting one's functioning. The ICF includes an exhaustive list of categories that could be considered environmental factors such as technology, climate, attitudes, services, and policy. Environmental factors that could *enable* activity and participation are assistive devices and technology, personal care attendants, physical alterations to the environment, supportive relationships, social policy or legal protections, or inclusive social milieus. Conversely, environmental factors that could *impede* functioning of the individual might include the experience of abuse, inaccessible infrastructures, extreme temperatures, unaffordable housing, lack of access to health care, or employment discrimination.

*Personal factors*, though gaining importance, are the least well-developed aspect of the ICF; they have yet to be classified or coded. Essentially, personal factors encompass attributes of the individual that are not accounted for elsewhere in the ICF model. These may include intersecting aspects of the self, such as gender identity, age, sexual orientation, socioeconomic status, education level, or personality characteristics. The personal factors have the potential to cover concepts emphasized in the social and diversity models of disability, thereby acknowledging the ways in which identities and circumstances may influence the experience of disability. Examples include important life events and specific developmental stages. For the field of psychology, the personal factors are particularly salient. Indeed, research on psychological responses to disability supports the idea that one's type of disability is less salient in terms of adjustment than individual differences, including psychological aspects (Rath & Elliott, 2012).

*Disability*, then, is an overarching term in the ICF for impairments, activity limitations, and participation restrictions that describes the dynamic interaction between an individual and that individual's contextual factors including environmental and personal characteristics. For example, an individual with a missing digit may have impairment yet minimal disability. In contrast, those with craniofacial abnormalities may have little impairment but significant disability due to the reactions or attitudes of others.

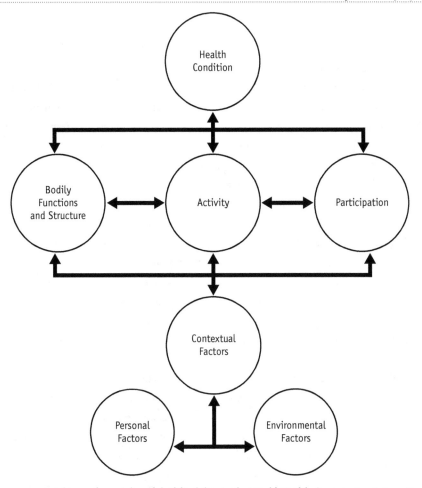

FIGURE 2.1. A biopsychosocial model of disability in the World Health Organization International Classification of Functioning, Disability, and Health framework.
*Credit:* Figure adapted from WHO (2002).

The WHO ICF model can be applied to the full range of disabilities resulting from spinal cord or brain injury, amputation, stroke, burn injuries, depression, anxiety, and most other acquired and congenital physical, cognitive, and sensory, emotional conditions. The ICF discourages linear and causal inferences among impairment, functioning, and disability. It is clear in the ICF framework that impairment does not necessarily result in any functional limitations and that environmental factors have profound effects on activity limitations and participation restrictions. The complex nature of disability is better reflected in this model than in earlier, more narrowly focused conceptualizations. Figure 2.1 illustrates the dynamic relations in a biopsychosocial model with ICF elements. Table 2.1 includes examples, using the WHO ICF framework, of the interface among health conditions, impairments,

TABLE 2.1

Example Chart of Factors and Functioning Using the WHO ICF Model of Functioning, Disability, and Health

| Health Condition | Impairment | Activity Limitation | Contextual Factors | Participation Restriction |
|---|---|---|---|---|
| Fibromyalgia | Chronic pain | Difficulty ambulating long distances | Limited coping strategies | Reduced recreation |
| Spinal cord injury | Tetraplegia | Unable to toilet independently | Lack of affordable personal care attendants | Cannot attend college out of state |
| Intellectual disability | Moderate difficulty learning | Struggles to learn in typical classroom setting | Inclusive school system with strong special educational programming | None |
| Moebius syndrome | Facial paralysis | None | Bullying | Social isolation and withdrawal |
| Alzheimer's dementia | Deficits in memory | Gets lost driving | Has no family or close support network nearby | Stops trying to go to church weekly |
| Posttraumatic stress disorder | Heightened arousal | Trauma triggers cause anxiety and anger | Lives near a military base | Avoids going into the community with family |
| Blindness | Unable to see | Cannot drive | Resides in urban setting with excellent public transportation | None |
| Deafness | Cannot hear | None | One of only few Deaf people in community | Unemployed as a result of discrimination |
| Traumatic brain injury | Expressive aphasia | Unable to express self verbally | Low self-esteem | Difficulty making friends |
| Crohn's disease | Frequent diarrhea | Must be close to restroom | Experiences severe anxiety about having an accident | Forgoes social outings with friends |

activity limitations, contextual factors, and participation restrictions, highlighting how environmental factors mediate functioning in ways that both enable and hinder people.

The ICF was a groundbreaking development in disability theory and research in several ways. First, the ICF promotes the premise of universalism, whereby disability is a fully human trait. Universalism acknowledges that by nature, humans are vulnerable to the acquisition of impairments and are inherently interdependent on one another (Bickenbach, 2012). Some could argue that universalism contradicts the concept of disability as a culture; however, universalism merely highlights the difference in the nature of disability as opposed to other diverse groups that are discrete minorities, something disability culture advocates have acknowledged. More important, universalism underscores the wisdom in allocating resources or accommodations to enhance participation of disabled people, a group anyone can join and a condition nearly everyone will eventually experience. Fundamentally, the ICF promotes the concept of justice in the allocation of resources, requiring equal consideration of all people, including those with disabilities who have the same rights as everyone else (Bickenbach, 2012). This same premise makes the ICF a call for human rights for people with disabilities; in other words, it is an expression of the intrinsic worth of each human being. The ICF conclusively defines disability as interactive relations among the human body and mind and aspects of the physical, social, and attitudinal environment (Bickenbach, 2012). The ICF acknowledges that disability is a complex function of physical, social, attitudinal, and environmental factors. The interactional nature of the ICF promotes social justice for persons with disabilities:

> It is as much an injustice to ignore the fact that disability is grounded, both conceptually and in fact, in the physiology of the body and the neurophysiology of the brain, as it is to ignore the fact that features of the physical, social, political, cultural, and attitudinal environment, both conceptually and in fact, determine the existence, the characteristics, and the severity of disadvantage associated with disability. (Bickenbach, 2012, p. S166)

The ICF offers etiologic neutrality in that the same disability can result in differing lived experiences, contingent upon environmental factors (Bickenbach, 2012). The ICF also reduces the importance of the supposed distinction between physical and psychological conditions by focusing less on etiology and more on functioning and participation. Together, these developments advance the understanding of disability as deriving from medical or social determinants to a much more comprehensive and complex picture. This paradigm shift in the global conceptualization of disability allows for more effective advocacy for social justice and human rights (Bickenbach, 2012).

A criticism of the ICF is the omission of choices and resources. The ICF fails to address the importance of individual choices and personal goals, even though such information is valuable in practice (Bickenbach, 2014). For example, people with cognitive disabilities may need to rely on shared decision-making and could be vulnerable to coercion, so a model that incorporates the element of respect for autonomy would be useful. Similarly, although the ICF's environmental factors incorporate socioeconomic status, it does not explicitly address how resources influence the lived experience of disability (Mitra, 2014). For example, as noted by Mitra (2014), the ICF would not capture whether or not a person with a mobility limitation has access to the type of wheelchair required. Mitra (2014) suggests the ICF could be improved by "becoming open-ended, with an explicit caveat that not all dimensions of life may be specified and classified, and thus the classification does not, and cannot be expected to provide an exhaustive account of the lived experience of health problems" or disabilities (p. 29).

## Other Models

Other disability models have received far less attention in psychology and rehabilitation research but have gained traction in disability studies and bioethics literature, addressing economic, social, and ethical questions (Clark, 2006).

### *Welfarist Approach*

The welfarist, or well-being, approach is a framework for understanding disability positioned between the medical and social models (Savulescu & Kahane, 2011). In response to what they consider an irreconcilable debate between those who believe impairment is intrinsically negative and deserves correction and social model advocates who view disability as a mere difference with all problems stemming from social prejudice, welfarist proponents offer a more pragmatic approach. From this perspective, disabilities reduce well-being and intrinsically cause harm (Savulescu & Kahane, 2011). However, the welfarist approach acknowledges that adverse effects of disability are due to both the effects of impairment and the impact of prejudice. Proponents agree that disabilities reduce well-being only in a given context, but they postulate the context need not "always be social, or that when it is social, it must always reflect prejudice or injustice" (Savulescu & Kahane, 2011, p. 46). As a result, welfarism places equal emphasis on reducing harm by changing circumstances and treating disabling conditions. A major criticism of the welfarist approach is the lack of consensus about what constitutes well-being and how the model offers added value beyond a purely phenomenological or individualized understanding of disability.

## *Capability Approach*

The capability approach (CA) views disability as "a deprivation in terms of functionings (achievements) or capabilities (practical opportunities)" (Mitra, 2013, p. 24). Disability status is dependent on the restriction of functioning or capabilities, similar to the ICF. CA, however, has an element of social justice that encompasses freedom and choice. Bickenbach (2014) described CA as "the distinction between functionings as the 'beings and doings' a person achieves, and the set of individual capabilities each of which, if the individual so chose, would become achieved functionings" (p. 12). CA proponents argue that because of these additions, their conceptualization offers a richer understanding of disability than does the ICF.

## Influence of Disability Models

The ways in which disability is conceived shape the behaviors of disabled people, family members, and health care providers. Each model described in this chapter has strengths and limitations. The moral model, for example, has been used in destructive ways toward people with disabilities, including exclusion and the promotion of shame and stigma. At the same time, the moral model has provided many disabled people with comfort and a means to make sense out of a difficult or painful experience such as a serious injury (e.g., "God will only give me what I can handle; there is a purpose behind why this happened to me"). Culturally competent disability professionals recognize the models that have defined disability over time and can identify how these models influence people with disabilities, families, and clinicians including when use of a model is detrimental to the individual's well-being or is contributing to psychological distress (e.g., "I deserved this because I am a terrible person").

With deliberate attention to timing and circumstances, it is possible to carefully present different perspectives toward disability. It is crucial to consider the entire context of the individual's experience. For example, a person in an acute rehabilitation unit following a severe injury resulting in permanent physical disability is unlikely to be interested in or open to the social model of disability, which suggests that the problem of disability relates to the environment and societal attitudes instead of limitations inherent to impairment. The disabled person is probably not ready to begin challenging beliefs about disability when he or she has not even likely yet identified his or her attitudes about a life-altering experience. Conversely, a person with a long-standing disability or someone trying to make sense of his or her experience may be very receptive to learning about disability activism efforts and the political movements of disabled peers inherent in the social and diversity models. Introducing people with disabilities to elements of disability history and culture may elicit fruitful dialogue about responses to disability in oneself and others. People with acquired disabilities and their families may have been exclusively exposed to the moral or medical model of disability. Unless provided with alternatives, people will tend to default toward societal perceptions of disability, which largely revolve around stereotypes and negative depictions of disabled people.

Disability models affect the ways in which health care providers and disability professionals approach disability. Most clinicians are primarily, if not exclusively, trained in the tradition of the medical and rehabilitation models. Clinicians following the medical model will consider disability itself problematic and focus on curing underlying impairments and medical conditions or ameliorating symptoms. In medical model contexts, disabled people are often referred to as "patients" and may even be described by their disability (e.g., "the tetraplegic in room 101"). Similarly, rehabilitation model phrases often relate to compensatory and adaptive strategies and may reflect concepts of adaptation and coping (D. S. Dunn & Andrews, 2015).

Alternatively, professionals influenced by the diversity model may elicit dialogue with their clients about experiences of discrimination or attitudinal barriers encountered throughout the lifespan. The concepts of disability culture and disability-related social justice are probably the least likely known to disability professionals unless a deliberate attempt is made to educate oneself and gain exposure to such issues. Culturally competent professionals are informed by the history and nuances of each of these models and are thus capable of educating others on the merits of a contemporary biopsychosocial perspective. The WHO ICF model can be used in interdisciplinary teams or in interprofessional settings to provide a common language that is free from the pathologizing approach inherent in the medical model. By considering the full context of disability, clinicians can offer more holistic and comprehensive assessment and management of health (WHO, 2013). This information enables professionals to partner with disabled people through a full understanding of the complex medical, social, and environmental contexts that affect disability. The ICF model acts as a foundation for person-centered care, an innovative health care system delivery philosophy that is an "approach to plan, deliver, and evaluate healthcare that is grounded in mutually beneficial partnerships among healthcare providers, patients, and families" (Joint Commission, 2010, p.1). Person-centered care can ensure that the contextual backgrounds of individuals are considered in interactions with clinicians; this is thought to be especially important in multicultural contexts and when important ethical issues are at play (WHO, 2013). Clinicians may be more prepared to engage in advocacy—for example, pointing out social or environmental barriers that affect care and reducing reliance on negative stereotypes or biases. Similarly, personal factors such as personality styles or other diversity variables such as age or sexual orientation may be less likely to be overlooked in a person-centered approach.

## Conclusion

The role of context in disability cannot be overstated. Dating back to Lewin's field theory, social and behavioral psychologists have emphasized the importance of the interaction between personal and situational factors and the environment in predicting human behavior (D. S. Dunn, 2015). Humans are predisposed to attribute the behaviors of others to individual and personal characteristics rather than the effects of the environment, called the *fundamental attribution error*. However, when considering their own behavior, people will tend to emphasize the context of the situation—a phenomenon known as the *actor/observer bias* (E. E. Jones & Nisbett, 1971). Both the fundamental attribution error and the actor/observer bias are accentuated when applied to negative or undesirable behaviors. D. S. Dunn (2015) applied these concepts to outsiders when he explained that nondisabled people are likely to ascribe difficulties or problems to the personal and individual features of people with disabilities while minimizing the impact of external factors. The ICF can serve as a cue for clinicians to thoroughly consider all relevant aspects of the individual and not over- or underfocus on impairment.

As with other identities, the concept of disability has evolved and will continue to mature as the social, political, and environmental contexts in which people with disabilities live constantly change. Each iteration has added new perspectives and built upon those before it.

No amount of smiling at a flight of stairs has ever made it turn into a ramp.
—STELLA YOUNG

# 3 Attitudes and Ableism

## Attitudes as a Primary Barrier

Disability scholars have long asserted that societal attitudes toward disability are the major barrier to full inclusion and participation for disabled people, and contemporary disability research provides empirical support for this hypothesis (Rao, 2004; Shakespeare, 2013; Voh, 1993). Attitudes reflect the beliefs and feelings that motivate behavior (Brostrand, 2006). Research indicates that negative attitudes and biases toward disability persist, despite gains in legislation, improvements in opportunities, and better environmental accessibility (Antonak & Livneh, 2000; Brostrand, 2006; Molloy, Knight, & Woodfield, 2003; White, Jackson, & Gordon, 2006).

A. Shapiro (2003) described how negative attitudes toward disability become pervasive myths and stereotypes resulting in ingrained prejudices that can impede the participation of people with disabilities in social, educational, and employment pursuits (Brostrand, 2006; Offergeld, 2012; Rao, 2004). Because negative attitudes are associated with social rejection and distancing from people with disabilities (Olkin, 1999; Wright, 1983), full equality and acceptance of disabled people are contingent upon an attitudinal paradigm shift (Antonak & Livneh, 2000).

*Ableism* refers to prejudicial attitudes and discriminatory behavior toward disabled people (Mackelprang & Salsgiver, 2016). It resembles other "-isms" such as racism and sexism (Wolbring, 2008). Others use the term *disablism*, defined by P. Miller, Parker, and Gillinson (2004) as a noun meaning "discriminatory, oppressive or abusive behaviour arising from the belief that disabled people are inferior to others" (p. 9). Those who are knowledgeable about multiculturalism are likely familiar with the term, whereas others may have never heard it, believe it is a joke, or scoff at yet another "politically correct" phrase. People have difficulty believing ableism exists, especially when it does not seem hate driven, as is often the case in other "-isms." In fact, not all forms of ableism are clearly anti-disability. In this chapter, I will discuss prevailing attitudes toward disability and the ways in which these beliefs and prejudices affect the lives of disabled people.

Some people have particular difficulty accepting disability as an identity analogous to race, religion, gender identity, or sexual orientation. This is likely the result of the persistent medicalization of disability (see Chapter 2). When people understand disability only as a medical problem, they fail to account for the important social and environmental determinants of disability and resulting discrimination (Wright, 1983). The insider/outsider distinction, which refers to the differing perspectives of disabled people in comparison to nondisabled people, is critical as it applies to attitudes toward disability (Dembo, 1982).

Family members of people with disabilities are in a unique role, typically having been lifelong outsiders and yet finding themselves close to a disabled person and gaining familiarity with the intricacies of disabled life. Are nondisabled family members insiders or outsiders? Outsiders tend to overfocus on disability, whereas insiders view disability as just one part of their lives (D. S. Dunn, 2015). Disability outsiders or observers tend to make the fundamental attribution error in response to disability. Due to the actor observer bias, witnessed difficulties are attributed to the individual with a disability instead of to the environment or other contextual issues. As a result, outsiders perceive characteristics or differences as a direct result of disability, in contrast to a Lewinian approach, which would account for situational contributions (D. S. Dunn, 2015). Familt members may have a more nuanced perspective, blending the perspectives of insider and outsider.


## Stigma

Goffman (1963) defined stigma as an "attribute that is deeply discrediting" that diminishes one "from a whole and usual person to a tainted, discounted one" (p. 3). Disability is considered a stigma, as it is generally perceived by outsiders to be wholly negative (Goffman, 1963). D. S. Dunn (2015) describes disability as a quality that is stigmatized, a social marker that "others," or defines disabled people as intrinsically different or alien. Stigma lies in the interactive relationship between those whose identities are "othered" and those who negatively appraise that attribute (Green, Davis, Karshmer, Marsh, & Straight, 2005). In 1988, Michelle Fine and Adrienne

Asch, two prolific feminist disability scholars, published an important article about the concept of stigma and the significance of the ways in which stigma is defined and applied to people with disabilities. They reflected on how social psychological scholarship has largely minimized the impact of environmental and social factors on people with disabilities, although these influences were well established by Wright (1983), and did not account enough for the role of prejudice and discrimination. Many of these concerns persist today in the ways in which we conceptualize disabled lives.

Link and Phelan (2001) developed a model of five features of stigma in relational interactions. First, the foundation of the stigma process is applying labels to undesirable characteristics. Disabilities are physical and mental differences from the norm and have traditionally been viewed unfavorably (Green et al., 2005). Research demonstrates that the more that a stigmatized identity is perceived to be within the individual's control, the worse the extent of the stigma (Corrigan & Miller, 2004). For example, mental health and learning disabilities are often believed to be controllable to some degree. Courtesy stigma, or stigma by association, varies based on the role and relationship to the person with a disability (Corrigan & Miller, 2004). Different disabilities have various labels, and terms that indicate disability have historically been used as insults to disparage people (i.e., moron, "r-word").

Link and Phelan (2001) postulate that second, stereotyping occurs, which is the pairing of negative attributes to socially salient differences. It is during this stage that disability stereotypes develop: for example, the belief that people with disabilities are useless or are a drain on society. Alternatively, a stereotype may develop that people with disabilities are inspirational and courageous for living with a disability.

Third, social distancing from the labeled or stigmatized group occurs. People with disabilities are "othered" by being segregated and avoided (Green et al., 2005). This takes place across contexts. For example, disability-accessible seating is typically segregated from the general audience at group events. Nondisabled students may avoid interacting with people with disabilities, who may use a different entrance, take different classes, and ride a different bus.

Link and Phelan (2001) argue that the fourth defining feature of stigma is that the social status of the labeled group is diminished. People with disabilities are often ostracized and excluded in this way. Finally, the fifth feature must be a power differential between the stigmatized group and others that enables discrimination to occur (Link & Phelan, 2001). Because people with disabilities do not have the power or influence to remedy an inaccessible business and may be dependent on the business for goods or services, for example, they are in a "power-down relationship" with the business owners, making it possible for the business to discriminate against disabled people. This multifaceted model of stigma represents the complexities of the process and its location within relational dynamics, not individuals. The framework also provides consideration of broader cultural and institutional factors that contribute to oppression and how other intersecting marginalized identities, including race, class, gender, and sexual identity, can affect the disability experience (Frederick, 2015).

## Measuring Attitudes

There are some assessment tools designed to measure attitudes toward people with disabilities, most of which are direct self-report surveys and are therefore susceptible to social desirability bias (see Antonak & Livneh, 2000, for a full discussion). Instruments widely used to examine attitudes toward persons with disabilities as a group include the Attitudes Toward Disabled Persons Scale (ATDP) developed by Yuker, Block, and Campbell (1960) and the Scale of Attitudes Toward Disabled Persons (SADP) developed by Antonak (1982).

Deal (2006) found that a subtle prejudice subscale to measure attitudes toward disability produced more negative attitudes than detected via direct methods that are vulnerable to capturing only socially appropriate responses. The Romantic Attraction Scale (RAS), a five-item Likert-style scale that queries attraction and desirability, was paired with pictures and vignettes of people with and without disabilities. Rojahn, Komelasky, and Man (2008) replicated a previous finding that disability did not negatively affect perceived romantic attractiveness. This time, researchers paired the RAS with the Implicit Association Test (IAT), developed to detect the implicit attitudes of respondents toward particular out-groups. The IAT assesses unconscious (implicit) bias toward a given group. Results with undergraduates indicated that although respondents with a disabled family member rated people with disabilities as more attractive than the nondisabled photos and vignettes on the RAS, they actually showed an overall preference for the nondisabled when measured by the IAT. Researchers concluded that the explicit attitudes (RAS) may have resulted from participants feeling pressure to respond in a socially acceptable way. Thus, to appear accepting, individuals may overstate their positive attitudes. This study provides evidence that the explicit and implicit attitudes held toward people with disabilities can differ significantly.

## Types of Attitudes

Outsiders may struggle to acknowledge that negative attitudes about people with disabilities exist because many harmful attitudes are expressed either indirectly, subtly, or

BOX 3.1.
PREVALENT MYTHS ABOUT DISABILITY

Disability is a tragedy
People need cures
Disabled people want special privileges
Disability access harms businesses financially
Integration of disabled children reduces resources for other children
Disabled people should get their needs met through charity

ironically, presented in the form of a compliment. This is not to say that openly hostile and hateful behavior toward disabled people does not occur; it most certainly does. However, there is low social acceptance of such open hostility, because disabled people are stereotypically viewed as vulnerable and weak. As with children and the elderly, people who are explicitly aggressive toward disability are often labeled as cruel or unfair.

Many common myths and stereotypes in contemporary culture and media portrayals reflect societal attitudes toward disability (see Box 3.1). People with disabilities are usually either excluded or reduced to stereotypes (Mackelprang & Salsgiver, 2016). An important stereotype coined by Wright (1983) is the *spread effect*, wherein a disabled person's impairments are perceived to affect the individual in a global fashion. For example, outsiders may talk slowly or loudly to a person in a wheelchair even though the disabled person's comprehension and hearing are unaffected. These and other patronizing behaviors are received as offensive to disabled people (Mackelprang & Salsgiver, 2016). D. S. Dunn (2015) noted that attitudinal responses to disability frequently involve feelings of sadness about disability or an overblown impression of the disabled person as a hero or elevated on a pedestal. One hypothesis is that these negative attitudes may actually stem from fear (Mackelprang & Salsgiver, 2016). Although some outsiders are afraid of disabled people, more often people experience fear or discomfort about the idea of becoming disabled themselves. Historically, there has been fear of contagion, that disease or disability could spread, or that association with disabled people will make nondisabled people vulnerable to such stigma (Mackelprang & Salsgiver, 2016). Indeed, disability reminds some people of their own mortality, and the resulting angst is projected onto disabled people. Finally, unfamiliarity breeds anxiety, and some nondisabled people will become so worried about offending a disabled person that they inevitably behave inauthentically and communicate unnaturally.

I developed the catastrophize–sensationalize continuum on which attitudes toward disability can be plotted (Figure 3.1). Catastrophic themes related to

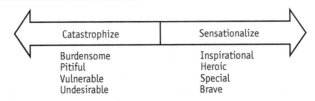

FIGURE 3.1. Andrews' catastrophize–sensationalize continuum.

disability include pity; people are socialized to feel sorry for disabled people, casting them as unfortunate (A. Shapiro, 2003). Related assumptions are that disability equates to suffering, disabled people are particularly vulnerable, disability is a burden, and being disabled is inherently undesirable. Morris (2005) noted that when disabled people are framed as helpless and always in need of care, the ability of outsiders to see people with disabilities as autonomous is undermined. Disabled people are generally portrayed or typecast as inferior and undesirable (Mackelprang & Salsgiver, 2016). Disability may be characterized as a burden for the individual and on their family. Illustrating this concept, disabled people, as members of a low-status group, are patronized and even liked so long as they fill the role the dominant culture desires—in one case, warmth (Fiske, Xu, Cuddy, & Glick, 1999). Because persons with disabilities are viewed as warm but incompetent, they elicit pity; subordination is exchanged for infantilizing positivity (Fiske, Cuddy, & Glick, 2007). In other words, disabled people are allowed to be objects of sympathy so long as they stay in their place.

On the sensationalized end of the continuum are pseudo-positive stances such as characterizing disabled people as heroes to be admired. This includes viewing disabled people as brave, special, or unique, or referring to people with disabilities as inspirational for managing basic tasks, even those not directly affected by disability. As an example of the sensationalizing attitude, disabled people may be described as "overcoming" disability to participate in a sport or another endeavor. I once saw a segment on a dance competition television show that featured a young woman with spinal thoracic dysplasia. Following her performance, the judges gushed at how brave and inspirational she was to come on the show. One judge said that all of the people at home sitting on the couch should be moved by her performance, which elicited a standing ovation from the crowd. Finally, another judge mentioned how all the other able-bodied contestants will dance better for having seen the disabled woman's inspirational performance. The young woman's performance became all about making able-bodied viewers feel relief that they are "normal," essentially that they didn't get her lot in life. This illustrates a related problem created by sensationalized reactions: How does one trust feedback to be accurate when one is constantly called a hero for getting out of bed in the morning? How does one recognize achieving superior work if the praise received is based on pity and erroneous assumptions about disability and quality of life?

This continuum of extremes reflects societal expectations for disabled people. Outsiders do not expect people with disabilities to be successful. There exists a set of prescribed standards for functioning, independence, ability, and social reciprocity. Naturally, disabled people will fall short in some of these restrictive ideals, so they are assumed to be inferior (Mackelprang & Salsgiver, 2016). As a result, it is not expected that someone with a significant impairment will hold a job, play a sport, marry, or parent children. Thus, when disabled people defy these stereotypes, outsiders presume they are either exceptions or distinct subtypes (D. S. Dunn, 2015). Outsiders who view successful disabled people as exceptions will tend to sensationalize them; this is why disabled people who engage in ordinary activities or employment often face attitudes of surprise, amazement, and admiration. A subtype assumption occurs when an outsider attributes certain characteristics to a particular subgroup; for example, an outsider may see a wheelchair basketball game and conclude that people in manual wheelchairs can be athletic, but the supposition does not extend to other members of the larger group such as those who use power wheelchairs or people with developmental disabilities.

Expectations are also confirmed by the exclusion of people with disabilities from many facets of life, so outsiders have little exposure to challenge stereotypes. For example, a business owner might object to having to build a ramp; after all, people in wheelchairs never come there. Of course, the expectation creates the reality. A prominent example involves employment settings where the idea of a disabled employee is often novel, leaving employers to base impressions on common disability stereotypes. Employers are likely to be concerned about their productivity, use of sick leave, disruption in the workplace, or whether their presence might discourage patronage from customers. As a result, those with nonobvious disabilities are less likely to disclose their disabilities, which may come at a high personal cost. The apparent absence of disabled people from professional employment and positions of leadership can only foster low aspirations and expectations of success for young disabled adults and those who acquire disabilities.

## Inspiration Porn

An emerging term in disability culture is that of *inspiration porn* (Grue, 2016), a bold phrase that can be confounding. Widely attributed to the late Australian disability activist Stella Young, whose TED talk on YouTube went viral, inspiration porn is a label that insiders have given to portrayals that objectify disabled people at the "sensationalize" end of the continuum (Young, 2012). It is easy to find examples of inspiration porn in any media type, but it is especially plentiful on social media platforms. Often these are images of disabled people, frequently children, with sentimental or motivational statements attached that "have the dual function of making the nondisabled feel better about themselves while simultaneously holding the average disabled person to an impossibly high standard" (Serlin, 2015, p. 43). Young (2012) noted that inspirational porn images typically depict a completely ordinary activity such as playing, running, competing in a sport, or drawing a picture. The accompanying text says things such as "Your excuse is invalid," "The only disability in life is a bad attitude," or "Before you quit, try."

The intent of inspiration porn is in the name: to inspire nondisabled people. These images are meant to elicit reactions of pity toward disabled people and gratitude for the privilege of being nondisabled—they represent a pernicious form of ableism. Young (2012) concluded that the unnamed disabled people in these images are used as objects of inspiration for the benefit of nondisabled people. She noted that when disabled people object to these portrayals, they risk a shift to the other end of the continuum where people with disabilities are "bitter" and "ungrateful."

Even though it is clear that inspiration porn is neither for nor about disabled people, it sends strong messages about living with a disability. Inspiration porn sets the expectation that people with disabilities are happy and smiling, overcoming all obstacles, and in total control of their own destinies, and most of all, living lives that make those around us feel good (Young, 2012). This shames disabled people who do not live up to these standards, insinuating that they are not trying hard enough to have a positive attitude and "overcome" disability.

## Microaggressions

As with other diverse groups such as racial minorities, negative attitudes exhibited toward disabled people can have a cumulative effect (Sue et al., 2007). People with disabilities encounter microaggressions, or social experiences that either indirectly or subtly insult the recipient (Keller & Galgay, 2010). Microaggressions tend to be covert, and those committing them may have little or no awareness of their impact on the recipient. As a result, confrontation of offenders may lead to denial and defensiveness, and recipients may be left doubting the accuracy of their perceptions (Keller & Galgay, 2010). In one of the only research studies to examine microaggressions, Keller and Galgay (2010) conducted focus groups of people with disabilities and qualitatively analyzed reported patterns of microaggression, leading to identification of eight distinct themes. *Denial of personal identity* occurs when outsiders overfocus on disability to the exclusion of all other personal identities. A common microaggressive theme is expressions of surprise upon learning about a disabled person's accomplishments or abilities. Again, the implication is that "people like you aren't expected to achieve such things"—such as education, employment, or personal statuses such as getting married or becoming a parent. The mirror image of this microaggression is denial of disabled identity as encapsulated in the statement "You don't look/seem disabled." If we were to substitute virtually any other identity, it is easy to see how that statement is offensive. Imagine an acquaintance saying, "You don't act like a man" or "You don't look Jewish." The underlying message is that disability is a bad thing, and you don't fit the negative stereotypes held by the observer.

*Denial of experience* is the minimization of disability or invalidation that disabled people encounter ableism. This is a particularly salient issue for people with nonapparent disabilities. Conversely, nondisabled people may attempt to connect with a disabled person by stating, "We all have a disability of some kind." This dismissive attitude suggests that disability is some type of weakness or imperfection. It also minimizes the realities faced by disabled people; it is unlikely that being a lousy cook has a similar impact as the inability to walk. *Denial of privacy* is socially sanctioned intrusion into intimate details of disabled people's lives without regard to social courtesy afforded nondisabled people. Keller and Galgay (2010) note that these interactions often derive from a nondisabled person's discomfort and may even be well intentioned but instead are received as insensitive and disruptive.

*Helplessness* refers to the expectation that people with disabilities are in constant need of help across all domains of life. This can result in unwanted offers of assistance, wherein nondisabled people become insistent that they be allowed to help, regardless of the preferences and actual need of the disabled person. *Secondary gain* refers to the idea that nondisabled people may benefit from assisting people with disabilities by attaining praise or recognition, or alternatively expressing pity toward a disabled person as a means to feeling better about oneself. In another approach stemming from the medical model, disability is often portrayed as a tragedy and an emphasis is placed on finding cures. Wright (1983) explained that outsiders tend to project personal anxieties related to deeply held assumptions or stereotypes about disability. Outsiders may make comparisons about how they believe they would respond if they were to acquire a disability or have a disabled child. A pity approach is often used for fundraising, usually for charity organizations. Although less frequent now than in past decades, telethons exemplify the use of pity to elicit charitable giving. Disability activists argue that these approaches generate profit from the fears of nondisabled people.

Described by Wright (1983), spread effect is when outsiders assume that difference or disability in one area of functioning also impacts others (physical/mental).

*Patronization* is the experience of being treated as a child, or infantilized, as a person with a disability. Often this takes the form of a nondisabled person addressing a companion instead of directly communicating with a disabled person. For disabled people, comments along the lines of "you are such an inspiration" are not usually received with gratitude, as may be expected or intended. Rather, disabled people rarely desire to be labeled in this way; it implies that the person has outperformed others in their in-group, revealing that the expectations held for disabled people are extremely low. *Second-class citizen* refers to the treatment of disabled people in ways that presume a lesser right to equal access and opportunity. Keller and Galgay (2010) noted three ways in which this plays out: lack of acknowledgment or avoidance of the disabled person; the attitude that accommodating a disabled person is an undue burden; and environmental and structural norms of separate and unequal access. The eighth microaggressive theme identified by Keller and Galgay (2010), *desexualization* and the secondary pattern of hypersexualization, is an important and pervasive theme that will be discussed in depth later in this chapter. The final auxiliary finding from their analysis was the concept of *spiritual intervention*, wherein outsiders approach disabled people with religiosity, perhaps by promising to pray for or even attempting to pray over a disabled individual. This experience can be intrusive and was described by participants as depersonalizing (Keller & Galgay, 2010). These situations likely emerge from the moral model of disability, which portrays disability as a "cross to bear" and promotes healing and cure through prayer and repentance (see Chapter 2).

The problem with disability stereotypes, both positive and negative, is that they diminish the person's individuality and reduce disabled people to caricatures. This has the effect of dehumanizing disabled people, leaving them no "middle ground" or opportunity to be or feel ordinary or normal, and to be viewed as such by the nondisabled population.

## Health Promotion Campaigns

For the past 7 years, the U.S. Centers for Disease Control and Prevention (CDC) has promoted their *Tips From Former Smokers* campaign. The CDC describes these ads as delivering "compelling messages designed to inspire smokers to quit." This is clearly a worthy goal; however, the ads released as part of this campaign are filled with harmful attitudes toward people with disabilities. The premise is to discourage people from smoking by depicting someone who has experienced significant health effects related to tobacco use. For example, one woman featured is described as having had treatment for oral cancer caused by smoking; she is shown in photographs before and after her treatment, with captions that explain how skin from her arm and muscle from her shoulder, chest, and neck were used to reconstruct her jaw and stating, "Now, at age 55, Christine has no teeth and only half of her jaw" (CDC, 2018). The "after" picture shows her pulling down her shirt over her shoulder, revealing gaps of tissues from her left clavicle area up through the left side of her face. In another ad, a young man is pictured sitting on a bed putting on liners for his prosthetic legs, which are placed nearby. The caption reads, "A tip from a former smoker: allow extra time to put on your legs." The text explains that he had Buerger's disease from smoking, leading to bilateral lower extremity amputation. Numerous other individuals are featured in this campaign, and in each one the message is clear: You do not want to end up like this person.

Copywriter Cal McAllister created a campaign for the organization Mothers Against Drunk Driving featuring a gloomy photo of a disabled parking space (Sartor, 2000). In the same style of the white-stenciled International Symbol of Access (ISA) icon and the customary grid next to the space, a sentence reads, "Every 48 seconds, a drunk driver makes another person eligible to park here." The campaign sought to highlight that the harmful effects of drunk driving extend beyond fatalities and can cause injuries and permanent disabilities as well (Sartor, 2000).

So what is the problem? Smoking is harmful to health and people should know what could happen to them so they will quit, right? Drunk driving is extremely dangerous and harms people—why shouldn't people be made to think about how they could hurt or kill themselves or others? There are two related issues with these campaigns. First, the effectiveness of fear-eliciting approaches to promoting healthy behavior and disease and injury prevention has received mixed support in the research literature on behavior change; some studies have raised the possibility of unintended consequences (Stibe & Cugelman, 2016). Behavior change is influenced by numerous cognitive, emotional, and social factors (Kelly & Barker, 2016). Tannenbaum and colleagues (2015) concluded from a meta-analysis that appeals to fear are effective, particularly when they elicit significant fear, target one-time-only behaviors, and are directed primarily toward women. Ruiter, Kessels, Peters, and Kok (2014), however, summarized the findings of six meta-analytic studies on the effectiveness of fear appeals, concluding that fear arousal can result in defensive reactions and reduce the likelihood of behavior change. For some individuals, eliciting fear may increase secrecy about the behavior and discourage them from seeking medical assistance. Both research groups agreed that mediating factors, particularly self-efficacy (the degree to which behavioral change is considered feasible by an individual), have important effects on outcomes of fear appeal approaches. More robust studies are warranted considering multiple factors in addition to average population-level health aggregates, with special attention to the stratification of health inequities, to ascertain their impact on the most marginalized peoples (Tengland, 2012).

Second, fear appeals reinforce negative stereotypes about people with disabilities and chronic illness. There is often an underlying assumption that people with an acquired disability are responsible for what happened to them, harkening to the moral model of disability. Indeed, disabilities like spinal cord injury and brain injury are sometimes caused by reckless behavior. However, these stereotypes can be extended to the entire group, which is why when you learn that someone has lung cancer, your first question is, "Did he smoke?" In addition, these tactics strengthen the myth that disability is inherently negative and a personal tragedy. The potential harm of victim blaming and stigmatization raises questions about the ethical implications of these strategies (Tengland, 2012). Beyond fear, exposure to images that depict illness, disease, death, and disfigurement also elicits shame, humiliation, and even disgust (Lupton, 2014). Besides the detrimental effects of shame and humiliation experienced by people actually affected by these health conditions, disgust in particular has been associated with "othering" of already marginalized persons (Nussbaum, 2009). Essentially, public health campaigns based on inducing fear leverage the very mechanisms that drive ableism—projection of existential anxiety, objectification, and dehumanization. There is little to no consideration of the ethical concern that these tactics threaten the worth, equality, and dignity of disabled and chronically ill people in the literature. Only a few scholars have recognized this quandary and proposed alternative solutions of empowerment and humanity for all (Tengland, 2012).

## Social Proximity and Relationships

Attitudes toward disability have been shown to be affected by the nature and context of the relationship: in other words, the social proximity to the disabled person. See Figure 3.2 for an illustration of how attitudes toward disability are stratified by social proximity, what I refer to as the continuum of social proximity. Research has yielded inconsistent results about differences in attitudes toward people with disabilities among nondisabled respondents who report that they have a family member with a disability. For example, Shannon, Tansey, and Schoen (2009) found that undergraduate students who reported having a family member with a disability were no more likely to have positive attitudes toward people with disabilities than students without disabled family members.

B. Hunt and Hunt (2000) found that undergraduate college students who had a professor with a disability have significantly more positive attitudes toward people

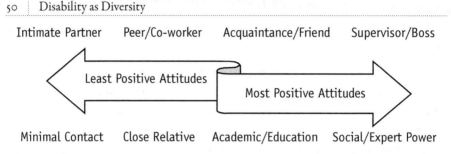

FIGURE 3.2. Andrews' continuum of social proximity.

with disabilities on the ATDP than students without exposure to a disabled profes-sor. This finding suggests that attitudes toward disability improve when a disabled person possesses social power or is in the role of expert such as a college profes-sor. In addition, repeated experience with a disabled faculty member also leads to familiarity—in short, the disability becomes less salient as the professor comes to be seen as a person rather than a "condition."

E. Miller, Chen, Glover-Graf, and Kranz (2009) created the Relationships and Disability Survey (RAD) to explore the willingness of nondisabled people to engage in personal relationships with disabled peers. Administration of the RAD to a college sample produced variable results in participants' stated willingness to enter relationships with people with disabilities. The authors found that severity of impairment was inversely correlated to relational willingness. Nondisabled people in their sample were most open to relationships with people with various types of impairment in the following order: sensory impairments, physical impairments and health conditions, cognitive limitations, and lastly, mental health disabilities (E. Miller et al., 2009). Nondisabled participants expressed a slightly greater degree of willingness to engage in friendship or develop an acquaintance with someone with sensory, health, or physical impairments when compared to peers with cognitive or psychological disabilities. Participants were most willing to engage in platonic relationships with disabled people such as friendships and close acquaintanceships. Scores were less positive toward entering marriage/partnerships or dating someone with a disability (E. Miller et al., 2009). In other words, willingness decreased as social proximity became closer and romantically focused; hesitancy was greatest when considering dating, partnership, or marriage (E. Miller et al., 2009).

Hergenrather and Rhodes (2007) adapted the Disability Social Relationship Scale to measure undergraduate students' attitudes toward people with disabilities in the relational areas of work, dating, and marriage. They found that hypotheti-cal work relationships elicited more positive attitudes toward disabled people than did marriage or dating. Women in their study expressed more positive attitudes toward people with disabilities than did males. This study was limited by collapsing impairment groups into a broad disability classification and by the likelihood of eliciting socially desirable responding patterns. In a cross-cultural study of attitudes among college students toward dating people with disabilities, Chen, Brodwin, Cardoso, and Chan (2002) found that attitudes were more negative toward dating people with disabilities in two Asian cultures compared to American respondents. There was a significant difference in terms of gender only among Americans; females had more favorable attitudes toward romantic partnership with people with disabilities than men. This is consistent with previous findings that females hold more favorable attitudes toward disabled people than do men (Livneh, 1982).

One hypothesis for the hesitancy to form relationships close in social proximity is that the spread effect results in an overfocus on disability by nondisabled people during interactions with people with disabilities. The salience of disability paired with a lack of social scripts may elicit discomfort and awkwardness in these social exchanges (D. S. Dunn, 2015; Green et al., 2005; Shakespeare, Gillespie-Sells, & Davies, 1996). Nevertheless, disabled people often develop elaborate strategies to dispel stereotypes and manage the perceptions of others, which can require significant effort (Frederick, 2015).

## Within-Group Attitudes

Extant literature suggests that attitudes among disabled people toward one another are highly variable. Deal (2003) explored attitudes toward disabled people among those with and without disabilities and found the groups generally held similar attitudes. As might be expected, he found that disabled people who intentionally sought to spend time with other people with disabilities had the most positive attitudes toward disability of any group; intergroup attitudes ranged from avoidance of others with disabilities to strong preference in favor of the company of other disabled people.

People with disabilities do not necessarily want to associate with other people with disabilities, either with similar or with vastly different impairments (Deal, 2003). Among disabled people, "internalized" prejudices and stereotypes can affect one's attitude toward oneself and others with disabilities (Di Giulio, 2003). Some people with disabilities avoid association and reject romantic or sexual partnership with other disabled people, either within their own disability group or with those who have other types of disabilities. Because of the prevalence of spread effect, some physically disabled people, for example, may shun those with intellectual disabilities out of concern that they themselves will be mislabeled. This is congruent with the concept of a within-disability hierarchy, wherein those with physical disabilities are the least stigmatized and those with intellectual or mental health disabilities are the most stigmatized (Deal, 2003; Chen et al., 2002). Deal (2003) found evidence for a hierarchy of impairment among people with disabilities that suggests that sensory and physical disabilities are viewed more favorably within the disability group, whereas people with cognitive and mental health disabilities are perceived the least favorably; this was very similar to the rankings produced by respondents without disabilities.

## Attitude Change

Attitudes are influenced by a number of factors including social learning, learning through association, personal experience, and positive or negative reinforcement (Wright, 1988). While considering the impact of attitudes toward disability, it is important to discuss the variables that affect such attitudes. The role of direct experience may be particularly important in attitude formation. Perhaps most well known in psychology is the *contact hypothesis*, first explored by the social psychologist Gordon Allport (1954), wherein prejudice was reduced by bringing diverse groups together for face-to-face contact. In general, research has provided strong support for the *contact hypothesis* among diverse groups, although it is important to note that attitude change toward people with disabilities has had lower effect sizes when compared to other out-groups (Pettigrew & Tropp, 2000). One important variable appears to be the length of time involved in the contact; in studies with only brief contact between disabled and nondisabled people, prejudice was only reinforced. Hewstone (2003) noted that when contact involves a negative interaction of induced fear, prejudices can actually increase; this emphasizes the importance of interactions that challenge stereotypes rather than strengthen them (Pettigrew & Tropp, 2000). Yuker (1994) found that although contact is indeed important, information and the characteristics of the disabled person (e.g., social skills) were highly influential. It appears that the attitudinal consequences of contact with disabled people are mediated by the attributes of both parties as well as the nature and context of the encounter between the two (Yuker, 1994). A consistent finding in this body of research is that the mechanism of attitude change is highly affective, or driven by emotion (Hewstone, 2003; Pettigrew, 1998). This is particularly salient, as research has shown that disability often elicits fear and discomfort in outsiders (Livneh, 1982; Wright, 1988).

Au and Man (2006) compared the attitudes of health care discipline students and four groups of health professionals toward people with disabilities using the ATDP instrument. They found that better quality of contact was associated with higher (more favorable) attitude scores. General scores among participants in Hong Kong were significantly lower than scores obtained by samples in other countries; the participants' area, level of education, and age affected their attitudes toward disabled people. These results suggest that the effects of contact may be culturally, generationally, and educationally mediated.

Deal (2006) found that the contact hypothesis was not supported in his research on attitudes of people with disabilities toward others with diverse functional impairments. He suggested that whether the contact between people with disabilities is voluntary or involuntary may be a significant variable. Unsurprisingly, people who voluntarily chose to associate with other disabled people demonstrated more positive attitudes, but the impact of involuntary or assigned contact is unclear (Deal, 2006). Hewstone (2003) found that five factors best facilitate a decrease in intergroup prejudice: conditions of equal status; situations where stereotypes are likely to be disconfirmed; when intergroup cooperation is required; where participants are adequately acquainted; and situations with social norms of equality. Put differently, contact in certain social contexts can decrease anxiety and improve attitudes toward persons with disabilities (B. Hunt & Hunt, 2000; Yuker, 1994). Interactions with persons from similar backgrounds and experiences may create more comfortable situations and promote positive attitudes (B. Hunt & Hunt, 2000). However, different social contexts can have the opposite effect. Novel experiences and encounters with others who represent significant contrast from oneself can elicit anxiety and discomfort (Wong, Chan, Da Silva Cardoso, Lam, & Miller, 2004). In these contexts, the interaction between persons with disabilities and those without may actually worsen negative attitudes toward disability.

In essence, the quality of the interaction—not just the quantity of contact—affects attitudes toward disabled persons. Ishige and Hayashi (2005) found that social interactions with someone with a mental illness experiencing obvious impairment (e.g., psychosis, mania) can reinforce negative attitudes toward persons with psychiatric disabilities, whereas interactions that highlight the positive attributes or personal strengths of the disabled person encourage more positive attitudes. E. Miller et al. (2009) found that particular attributes affected openness among nondisabled people toward relationships with disabled people, including the characteristics of intelligence, kindness, and humor. The perceived presence of these attributes appears to mitigate the stigma associated with disability. Disabled people are largely aware of this concept and often have honed a well-developed ability to put nondisabled people at ease. Although socially useful, it is important to understand that doing so consumes significant effort on the part of disabled persons, reduces their degree of authenticity, and creates undue pressure to present oneself as "less disabled."

Attention has been paid to mechanisms by which attitudes toward people with disabilities could be improved, but the results of these efforts have been mixed (Shannon et al., 2009; A. Shapiro, 2003). These approaches often include facilitated positive contact between disabled and nondisabled people, dissemination of accurate information about disabilities intended to reduce bias, legal or policy advocacy meant to reduce exclusion, modeling of positive attitudes by leaders and influential people, and disability simulations.

## Disability Simulations

There are pitfalls to some common approaches to enhance disability awareness such as disability simulations. In educational and rehabilitation settings, professionals have conducted experiential role-playing experiences—called disability simulations—to attempt to elicit empathy and increase awareness among other professionals, students, and the general public. These activities are often employed during disability awareness education occasions in schools or workplaces (Brew-Parrish, 2004).

Disability simulations consist of exercises wherein nondisabled people role-play by simulating impairments. There are many approaches to disability simulations; typically, participants are instructed to adopt particular impairments by utilizing medical equipment or other supplies. For example, students may sit in wheelchairs and try to navigate a campus, place earplugs in their ears and attempt to communicate with others, or wear a blindfold and explore their surroundings.

Proponents believe that these role-plays allow nondisabled people to better understand the perspective of someone who has the lived experience of disability by temporarily taking the perspective of a disabled person (Herbert, 2000); these activities are reportedly popular among participants (Nario-Redmond, Gospodinov, & Cobb, 2017). However, the impact of disability simulations is rarely measured objectively, and only recently has it been empirically examined (Flower, Burns, & Bottsford-Miller, 2007).

Activists in the disability community have long objected to the use of disability simulations (Brew-Parrish, 2004; Lalvani & Broderick, 2013), arguing that nondisabled people usually emerge from disability simulations with stereotypes reinforced, such as believing life is a tragedy for persons with disabilities (catastrophizing), feeling grateful they are not personally disabled, or being amazed at the incredible things that disabled people can do (sensationalizing). Research over the past several decades has confirmed many of these reservations: that these activities do not improve attitudes toward disability, but instead increase distress and evoke pity (Nario-Redmond et al., 2017). In a meta-analysis of disability simulation experiments, Flower et al. (2007) found that simulations were ineffective in modifying attitudes or behavior. Beyond simple ineffectiveness, evidence further suggests that these simulations may actually do harm (Lalvani & Broderick, 2013; Nario-Redmond et al., 2017).

Nario-Redmond et al. (2017) conducted two experiments that demonstrated that simulating disability increased negative emotions and disability stereotypes among participants, even as their self-reported feelings toward disabled people warmed. Although the researchers label this dimension of warmth a measure of empathetic concern, it seems possible that this rating could instead reflect the construct of sympathy, even pity, and as such, a face-valid query could be especially susceptible to social desirability bias. Following the simulation exercises, nondisabled participants in both of the studies by Nario-Redmond et al. (2017) reported greater levels of confusion, anxiety, embarrassment, helplessness, and vulnerability to becoming disabled. Not surprisingly, the simulations did not improve nondisabled attitudes toward interaction with people with disabilities; these attitudes worsened, and nondisabled people were not more willing to interview disabled students for a campus accessibility project. Replicating previous psychiatric simulation studies (Ando, Clement, Barley, & Thornicroft, 2011), and in line with meta-analyses (Flower et al., 2007), the utility of disability simulations was not supported—they led to more harm, undermining the goal of improved understanding. In a similar fashion, Silverman, Gwinn, and Van Boven (2015) found that blindness simulations actually reduce the perceived capabilities of disabled people in employment and independent living, illustrating how simulations can backfire.

Despite these contradictory findings and the long-standing objections of disability activists, disability simulations persist. Critics remain concerned that by emphasizing the salience of impairment and neglecting the contextual factors, the lived experience of disability is perceived in a skewed manner by simulation participants. Consequently, they fear that disability simulation only furthers oppression (Lalvani & Broderick, 2013). Some advocates suggest that simulation exercises be utilized judiciously, restricted to demonstrating the adverse impact of environmental barriers, and the participants thoroughly debriefed and afforded the opportunity to process their reactions. Others in the disability community object entirely to the use of disability simulations, comparing them to such culturally offensive actions as wearing blackface or the cultural appropriation of dressing in indigenous costumes. Because the activities are interactive and may be interpreted as humorous (e.g., watching someone blindfolded walk into a wall or a nondisabled colleague do a "wheelie"), disability simulation can feel quite trivializing to the complex physical, social, and emotional aspects of the lived experience of disability.

It is important to fully understand the cultural implications and to measure the outcomes of any disability awareness trainings or activities. These exercises are at best culturally insensitive, and disability simulations can even be considered cultural appropriation, where "the lived experiences of different and marginalized others are made the object of undue curiosity or scrutiny by socially privileged others for the material and intellectual gratification of the latter" (Mpofu, Chronister, Johnson, & Denham, 2012, p. 547). It can no longer be assumed that simulations are harmless, and professionals need to be aware of and responsible for the possibility of adverse consequences, however unintended.

## Conclusion

In sum, insiders often identify others' attitudes as the most difficult aspect of living with a disability (Rao, 2004; Shakespeare, 2013; Voh, 1993). Culturally competent health care providers must have a solid grasp of the pervasive attitudes toward persons with disabilities and be willing to reflect on their own biases. Harmful attitudes toward people with disabilities are perhaps most challenging because they are so insidious; it is difficult for disabled people to identify whether or not discrimination has occurred or if there has been a microaggression. It takes tremendous courage to challenge sensationalized attitudes when the social expectation is to accept compliments and when the intent may not have been to offend. Therein lies the challenge: to increase awareness of the harmful effects of attitudes on both ends of the continuum so that nondisabled people can make an impact that matches their intent.

Disability culture is not how we are treated, but what we have created.

—S. BROWN (2002, p. 48)

# 4   Disability Culture

IN THIS CHAPTER, I discuss the characteristics, functions, and beliefs associated with disability culture. Although some claim that disability culture does not possess adequate characteristics to constitute a culture, my perspective is that the debate is over. People with disabilities have rich traditions in history, language, aesthetics, and sociopolitical stances that make up a distinct cultural experience.

## What Is Disability Culture?

Disability culture is the recognition of disability as a cultural experience—a unique and meaningful connection to others who share a disabled identity (S. E. Brown, 1996; Gill, 1995). Although disability culture has been developing for decades, it is often ignored or unknown because of its incongruence with the medical model and pathological definitions of disability, which are deficit based and focused on impairment (Gill, 1995; see also Chapter 2). Because the pervasive societal view of disability is one of misfortune and undesirability, outsiders may have particular difficulty grasping how a characteristic associated with so much negativity could be valued or even embraced (Andrews et al., 2013). In response to these historically negative perceptions, people with disabilities began to explore positive attributes and commonalities among themselves, the first evidence to support the existence of a distinct disability culture (Mackelprang & Salsgiver, 2016). As the academic field of disability studies emerged, increasing attention has been paid to the concept and content of disability culture (S. E. Brown, 1996).

Carol Gill, a professor at the University of Illinois at Chicago, is one of the foremost scholars of disability culture; she began describing its tenets in the 1980s and subsequently published important descriptions of the elements that comprise disability culture (1987). According to Gill (1995), disability culture promotes connection, camaraderie, and shared purpose among the diverse range of people with various disabilities. Instead of accepting negativistic views of disability, those who identify with disability culture experience pride in being associated with the largest minority group in the United States (Andrews et al., 2013). Disability culture has also been described as an assertion of independence of a people motivated to positively and constructively address their own social, civil, political, and economic needs (Gill, 1995, 2001).

Another important scholar of disability culture is Steven E. Brown, a cofounder of the Institute on Disability Culture, who published an enduring definition of disability culture in 1996:

> People with disabilities have forged a group identity. We share a common history of oppression and a common bond of resilience. We generate art, music, literature, and other expressions of our lives and our culture, infused from our experience of disability. Most importantly, we are proud of ourselves as people with disabilities. We claim our disabilities with pride as part of our identity. We are who we are: we are people with disabilities. (S. E. Brown, 1996, pp. 80–81)

Brown's definition captures Gill's (1995) contention that disability culture is not exclusively based on experiences of shared oppression, although mutual instances of discrimination and persistent prejudices are indeed one part of disability culture. Rather, Brown (1996) explains that disability culture is "not primarily how we are treated, but what we have created." Indeed, there are many other important facets of disability culture including art, political stances, values, and traditions, all of which are claimed by disabled people as an expression of our collective experience (Brown, 1995). At its core, disability culture is inclusive; S. E. Brown (2001) posits that a more accurate term may be "cross-disability culture," referring to the broad range of disabilities and cultures encompassed in disability culture. This is important, because responses to the marginalization of disability in broader society typically involves distancing oneself from one's disability and from other disabled people, particularly from more harshly stigmatized disability types such as intellectual and mental health disabilities. Instead of carefully distinguishing the needs of, say, physically disabled people from those of cognitively disabled people, disability culture proponents work to dismantle traditional disability hierarchies by promoting unity and the philosophy of shared destiny. In other words, what is good for some people with disabilities should be good for all disabled people.

The preeminent disability scholar Paul Longmore noted how the American disability rights movement shifted from a focus on equal rights to a quest for collective identity, or what he refers to as the "second wave." Longmore (1995) was a proponent of marrying activism with academia; he encouraged disability studies to grow as a discipline by explicitly examining the culture of disability (including disability arts) as a means to discover disabled values, explore the social and cultural construction of disability, and challenge dominant nondisabled perspectives. Longmore (2003) captured the essence of disability culture:

> Beyond proclamations of pride, deaf and disabled people have been uncovering or formulating sets of alternative values derived from within [their own] experiences. . . . They involve not so much the statement of personal philosophies of life, as the assertion of group perspectives and values. . . . Those values are markedly different from, and even opposed to, non-disabled majority values. They declare that they prize not self-sufficiency but self-determination, not independence but interdependence, not functional separateness but personal connection, not physical autonomy but human community. This values formation takes disability as the starting point. It uses the disability experience as the source of values and norms. (p. 222)

Literature suggests that definitions of disability culture share the following characteristics. Disability culture (a) is intentionally created and developed by the disability community; (b) includes a diverse and full range of disabilities; (c) affirms disability identity; (d) includes shared values; (e) rejects dominant cultural narratives and assumptions that disability needs to be cured, endured, or overcome; and (f) cultivates pride in the unique perspectives and experiences of disabled people (S. E. Brown, 1996; Gill, 1995; Mackelprang & Salsgiver, 2016).

## Unique Aspects of Disability Culture

There are certainly similarities between disability culture and other cultural groups including racial, ethnic, sexual orientation, and gender identity minorities, and some disability issues parallel the struggles of other oppressed groups. However, there are several unique aspects to the concept of disability as diversity that produce a divergence between disability culture and those of other identity groups. Most notably, there are numerous ways in which disability can be acquired. Essentially, every member of society could ostensibly join the group at any given time. Some people were born disabled, some have lived with disabilities for decades, and still others have only recently become disabled. For some people, disability onset is the result of an injury or the outcome of a disease process, which may or may not be perceived as a traumatic life event. In other instances, disability is unassociated with the individual's health. Disability is sometimes obvious to outsiders from the way an individual appears, sounds, or behaves, but disability is frequently not apparent (sometimes called "invisible"). Because dominant societal views of disability have historically focused on negative aspects of impairments, the celebration and reappropriation of a disability identity can seem counterintuitive. Indeed, there are inherent facets of some disabilities that are objectively undesirable such as progressive muscle weakening, chronic pain, or difficulty breathing. Many of these problems can elicit fear and discomfort.

Disability culture does not necessarily attempt to minimize aspects of disability that may be painful or unpleasant. Rather, disability culture claims ownership of those experiences along with many others that are the hallmarks of living as disabled (Mackelprang & Salsgiver, 2016). A 1998 online edition of the disability magazine *Ragged Edge* quotes activist Nadina LaSpina discussing the way in which pain is part of her disability and yet does not detract from her experience of pride as a disabled person:

"It's like being Italian," she goes on. "I'm proud of being Italian. There are things I'm ashamed of, like the existence of the Mafia - but these things do not stop me from embracing my Italian-ness. I love being a woman, but I hate going through menopause. But I wouldn't want a sex-change operation just because of menopause. Certainly the pain and physical limitations of disability are not wonderful, yet that identity is who I am. And I am proud of it." (Johnson, 1998, para. 15)

Those who identify themselves as a member of disability culture can experience pressure to embrace disability all the time. Even though many disabled people lead productive and satisfying lives despite expectations of misery and dysfunction (Albrecht & Devlieger, 1999), stereotypical assumptions persist. Thus, disabled people often feel compelled to exhibit disability pride and positivity, to embody their allegiance to disability culture, and to reinforce their beliefs that disability is a form of diversity, an identity of which they are proud. In fact, many disability advocates who express pride and cultural identification reject the notion of either wanting or accepting a disability cure (Hahn & Belt, 2004). People who are proud of disability and embrace the culture still find certain aspects of disability undesirable and sometimes feel shame when they find themselves feeling dissatisfied or resentful about an aspect of disability that is negative. The suppression of such feelings, which can lead to isolation within the community, is not inherently part of the disability cultural narrative, but disabled people often experience such pressure nonetheless.

## Functions of Disability Culture

Gill (1995) describes four primary functions of disability culture: fortification, unification, communication, and recruitment. Fortification is the sense of energy, strengthening, and endurance that can occur only in the context of a shared disability community, something that Gill postulates as necessary to fight oppression and advocate effectively for equal rights. From a practical perspective, this theory makes good sense. Instead of several different and smaller constituencies promoting universal design or defending the Americans With Disabilities Act (ADA), joining forces increases power, particularly given that approximately one out of every five Americans has one or more disabilities (Brault, 2012). Imagine the strength with which disability issues could be championed with even a fraction of that membership harnessed. Disability culture promotes alliances among different disability groups and champions the reduction of intradisability hierarchies.

Gill (1995) proposes that unification is another purpose of disability culture. Traditionally, there has been a great deal of splintering among disability groups within the broader disability community, largely as a result of external oppression (Mackelprang & Salsgiver, 2016). As described in Chapter 3, one of the most common stereotypes about disability is that of spread effect; that is, disability is presumed to affect all aspects of one's functioning (D. S. Dunn, 2015; Wright, 1983). For example, a physically disabled person may be presumed to have low intelligence, and in a response to dispel this assumption, the physically disabled person may adopt attitudes and behaviors to specifically differentiate and distance him- or herself from people with intellectual disabilities or become an academic overachiever. Without the hierarchical stigma attached to different types of disabilities, it becomes easier to see the ways in which people with disabilities have a shared heritage and that participation in cultural activities can unite people of all disabilities toward common goals, promote communal support, and emphasize shared philosophies (Gill, 1995). Part of disability culture is an expression of belongingness and mutual destiny.

Communication is an important reason for disability culture (Gill, 1995). Because disabled people typically have little exposure to others who identify as disabled, it is easy to become isolated from others with whom one might forge a shared disability identity. Without exposure to disability culture, many disabled individuals remain unaware of the world of disability arts, language, symbols, and rituals "that help us articulate to the world and signal to each other who we are as a distinct people" (Gill, 1995, p. 17).

Finally, Gill postulates that recruitment is an essential rationale for the development of disability culture. As a result of the isolation and separation often experienced by people with disabilities, both attitudinal and physical, there are few organically occurring disability communities (Deaf culture is an exception). Instead, organizations or groups have been created around particular disabilities or issues. Often, these endeavors are initiated and controlled by nondisabled people or focused on medical aspects of disability (such as charity for cure research) or serve primarily as support and networking for family members of disabled people, frequently parents of children with disabilities. In contrast, disability culture is created and controlled by disabled people who wish to change the disability narrative. As Gill (1995, p. 17) put it, "the expression of our culture is a positive and defiant conversion of our social marginalization into a celebration of our distinctness." Instead of distancing, disability culture invites those with disabilities to boldly embrace and take pride in their own bodies and minds and to feel part of something bigger than themselves. To ensure succession, disabled persons who have long identified with disability culture serve to initiate younger and newly disabled people into the community.

## Characteristics of Disability Culture

There are specific artifacts, traditions, and phrases associated with disability culture (Brown, 1995). I will cover the major themes here and offer examples of disability culture in real life; however, this discussion is by no means exhaustive, and as time goes on, disability culture will unquestioningly continue to evolve.

In Gill's (1987, 1995) initial writings, she theorized that there are several core values within disability culture. One prominent concept is that of disability humor. Indeed, people with disabilities have long used humor as a healthy coping skill, a way to relate to one another, and even a means to put nondisabled people at greater ease. Disabled people who subscribe to disability culture are likely to joke around about their impairments or limitations; often, these jokes are directly aimed at topics that outsiders may consider taboo such as incontinence or personal grooming. Gill (1995) notes that disability humor is the ability "to laugh at the oppressor or situation, however dire" (p. 17).

The spokesperson for disability humor was undoubtedly John Callahan, who struggled with alcoholism and became tetraplegic following a spinal cord injury as a young man (Haller & Ralph, 2003). Callahan was a writer, cartoonist, and television creator who challenged the traditional narrative of pity with his witty, sharp, and provocative work. Rather than historical jokes made at the expense of disabled people (e.g., Helen Keller jokes), Callahan skillfully poked fun at the disability experience, including ableist attitudes, in a way that only an insider could. He did not shy away from incendiary topics and earned both criticism for his occasional offensiveness and praise for his authenticity in depicting disability (Haller & Ralph, 2003).

Another of Gill's (1995) core values is an appreciation of human diversity. Proponents of disability culture view personal differences as assets rather than liabilities. In general, those who identify with disability culture express acceptance of a wide range of people and may feel particular affinity toward groups of people with whom they perceive as having commonalities with disability struggles. For example, compared to a person with a disability who rejects the notion of disability culture, a culturally identified disabled person may be more likely to identify racism as a serious problem or support gay rights. Of course, this is not universally true, and the disability rights movement has long and accurately been criticized for its lack of racial and ethnic diversity, among exclusion of other intersecting identities (Bell, 2010). S. Brown (2002) explicitly recognized that disability culture is not the only culture most disabled people belong to and that many people have intersecting membership identities such as racial and ethnic minorities, nationalities, religions, and so on. For multiply marginalized people, disability culture may not be their primary or even secondary identity. Within disability culture, oppression exists related to other diverse identities, and, like other human rights movements, privilege has historically been associated with being White, male, cisgender, heterosexual, Christian, minimally disabled, and exclusively physically disabled. The substantial contributions of disabled genderqueer persons of color, for example, have been too often overlooked, or even ignored (Clare, 2015).

Gill (1995) submits that champions of disability culture hold a value of "acceptance of human vulnerability and interdependence as a natural part of life." In contrast to dominant Western values of independence, disability culture espouses that total independence is neither realistic nor desirable. Disabled people often encounter the nondisabled perspective that requiring physical assistance for tasks of daily living, including bathing, dressing, and toileting, is somehow "undignified." The culturally disabled believe that the need for assistance is a natural part of life, and so long as such assistance is affordable and available, and within their range of comfort and privacy, it is not in the least degrading. In fact, being able to select and employ a personal care assistant (PCA) can be extremely empowering to a disabled individual who has previously relied only on family for help with daily life tasks. A tolerance for lack of resolution and unpredictability and the ability to accept ambiguity or less-than-desired outcomes may be viewed as character strengthening.

Many disabled people develop extraordinary skill in problem solving and multi-tasking, which is why Gill (1995) includes this as a core value of disability culture along with taking a "flexible, adaptive, or non-traditional approach to tasks" (p. 16). Often without intervention, guidance, or assistance, disabled people develop innovative ways to do things. Gill (1995) calls these "strategies for surviving and thriving" (p. 16) We may use objects or tools in unconventional ways; a friend of mine with limited ability to bend her arms and reach above her head uses a long-handled pasta spoon to lather shampoo into her hair. Ironically, it is these simple but unexpected solutions that elicit the most surprise and amazement from outsiders, and yet the ability to solve these problems is a fundamental feature of disability culture.

I have observed that people with disabilities can become exceptionally skilled at reducing outsiders' discomfort around disability, sometimes to a fault. People who have lived disabled for all or most of their lives can automatically "break the ice" with charismatic fluency, immediately relieving nondisabled persons' unease. I believe that disabled people learn these strategies to alleviate uneasiness in awkward situations in part because the expected role of people with disabilities in society is to be deferential, polite, and cooperative. Additionally, disabled people may find themselves at the mercy of nondisabled people for assistance to access goods or services. If one wants to get into an inaccessible restaurant for a family dinner, for example, behaving in a forgiving, harmonious manner may be the only way to salvage participation in a planned social event. Disabled people are put in a "power down" situation, sometimes dependent on the perpetrator of discrimination; the problem is that people with disabilities are not empowered to advocate and typically are assigned ownership (by themselves as well as others) of problematic encounters, making it is unlikely that ableist behaviors or structures will change. A serious concern is that disabled people can exhaust themselves emotionally if the onus is continually on them to placate nondisabled people.

## Language in Disability Culture

Many terms and phrases have developed from disability culture. Shared language and terminology represent intentional attempts by disabled people to "take back" ownership of an insult or put a new spin on derogatory words. The most common example is the use of the word *crip*, insider disability slang for *cripple*, a word that was previously associated with pity and cruelty. Culturally disabled people might affectionately refer to themselves as *crips*, or sometimes *[g]imps*. Stemming from this is the concept of the quintessential overachiever in the disability world—the *super-crip*. A common image on display in rehabilitation settings is that of a young athletic person with a spinal cord injury literally climbing a mountain from a wheelchair.

Outsiders likely believe that image would inspire others with disabilities to believe that there are no limits to what they can achieve. A culturally disabled person would probably roll his or her eyes; in disability culture, we reject the notion that we have to overcome our disabilities or prove anything to anyone to establish our worth. Disabled people can be found reminding one another that it is not necessary to be a supercrip. Another twist is the use of *crip-* as a prefix; for example, when culturally disabled people refer to crip-time, we mean the norm of tasks taking longer, integrating disability humor about how challenging it can be to function according to a nondisabled clock. Others prefer the term crip-culture instead of disability culture (Snyder & Mitchell, 1996). Another intersection of humor and disability solidarity is the term *TAB*, which stands for temporarily able-bodied. Disabled people often refer to the nondisabled as *able-bodied* or *ABs*. The use of TAB is a reminder that although outsiders may not be disabled currently, they could join our ranks at any time.

## Disability Art and Symbolism

Disability art is an area that has grown over the past several decades but continues to receive little attention in broader society (Brown, 1995). Disabled art includes creations such as painting and poetry as well as performing arts and dance (Kuppers, 2007; Sins Invalid, 2016; Whatley, 2010).

Rather than simply art created by disabled people, the disabled arts reflect an expression of the disability experience; the primary intended audience is other disabled people (Solvang, 2012). Essentially, such art is disability culture embodied. Instead of traditional approaches to assimilate into nondisabled art (Sins Invalid, 2016), the disability arts do not make any attempt to conform to nondisabled norms, and the goal is not to alter the perceptions of nondisabled persons (Conroy, 2012). The aim is simply artistic expression by and for the culturally disabled (Brown, 1995). Effects on nondisabled consumers are incidental by-products of the art form (Conroy, 2012).

Performing arts have traditionally excluded disabled people from anything but marginal or stereotypical roles (Solvang, 2012), but increasingly there are more integrated companies and studios where disabled and nondisabled performers work together (Conroy, 2012). There are also exclusively disabled dance troupes that celebrate the experience of disability through art. Congruent with disability culture's rejection of conventional norms, disabled art can often be provocative and intentionally elicit discomfort (Conroy, 2012). A prominent example is the performance group Sins Invalid, whose work creatively integrates the experiences of marginalized people at the intersections of disability, race, ethnicity, sexual orientation, and

FIGURE 4.1. The International Symbol of Access.

gender identity (Sins Invalid, 2016). The artistic work of Sins Invalid makes a clear political statement against the medicalization of disabled bodies.

As in other cultures, symbols play a role in disability culture. The International Symbol of Access (ISA), also known as the Wheelchair Symbol, is a blue square depicting an image of a person in a wheelchair, illustrated in Figure 4.1. It is considered the international standard to represent accessibility, and it is most commonly seen to identify disabled parking spaces. The ISA can be used to direct disabled individuals to alternate or segregated entrances and points of access. However, it is important to understand that such symbols do not always guarantee full access. For example, it is not uncommon to notice an ISA sticker on the front door of a business even though the door does not open automatically or have any other disability features.

Evolving symbols have gained traction in the last decade. In 2011, two designers in Boston, Sara Hendren and Brian Glenney, began a street art campaign by altering public signs featuring the ISA. They transposed a diaphanous sticker over the ISA, one depicting a more active image of the wheelchair user leaning forward with an arm propelling the wheelchair, shown in Figure 4.2. Hendren and Glenney describe themselves as disability allies and maintain that disabled people are on their design

FIGURE 4.2. The Accessible Icon.

team. According to Hendren (n.d.), "the arm pushing a chair is symbolic—as all icons are symbols, not literal representations. Our symbol speaks to the general primacy of personhood, and to the notion that the person first decides how and why s/he will navigate the world, in the broadest literal and metaphorical terms." The new symbol, called the Accessible Icon, is considered to be more progressive, and it has gained significant media coverage, replacing the ISA in some places since it is in the public domain.

Annie and Stevie Hopkins, disabled siblings from Illinois, debuted a symbol in 2007 at the Chicago Disability Pride Parade. The symbol, designed by Annie, is similar to the ISA except that the circular line portraying the wheel is illustrated as a heart, as depicted in Figure 4.3. The image appeared to quickly gain traction among disabled advocates who wore clothing and adorned adaptive equipment with stickers of the International Symbol of Acceptance, also known as the "wheelchair heart." Annie passed away in 2009, but her brother has continued offering merchandise featuring their trademarked symbol thorough his 3E Love company, whose mission is to "embrace diversity, educate society, and empower each other to love life" (Hopkins, n.d.).

One of the most appealing aspects of the wheelchair heart initially was that it clearly emanated disability pride; the Hopkins siblings described it as a "symbol of society accepting people with disabilities as equals and a symbol that people with disabilities accept their challenges and even embrace them" (Hopkins, n.d.). I have sported a wheelchair heart on the back of my own chair since 2010. Once I saw another woman in a wheelchair with the sticker on it, and I knew immediately that she identified with disability culture and was an advocate. Never before had I been so certain that another disabled person would want to connect based on our shared identity.

In recent years, the marketing efforts of 3E Love have expanded. First, the "Proud" series was marketed, where allies, including family members, could display solidarity with the disability community; my husband has a "Proud Husband" T-shirt with the "o" replaced by the International Symbol of Acceptance. Undoubtedly popular with parents of disabled children, 3E Love further moved into an "occupational" line that

FIGURE 4.3. International Symbol of Acceptance.
*Credit:* 3E Love.

features apparel for nondisabled people who work in disability service professions such as "Bus Aide," "Occupational Therapy," or "Special Education." This, coupled with the use of the symbol as a fundraising tool, suggests that 3E Love may have shifted from its original role in developing pride symbols created by and worn by disabled activists to an expression of general support for or even benevolence toward the disability community. This evolution may risk the symbol being associated too closely with pity-based movements of the past and becoming alienated from the very culture in which it developed. Nonetheless, Hopkins clearly states on his website that the symbol was never intended to represent pity or solicit charity (Hopkins, n.d.).

### Sociopolitical Views

Disability culture encompasses certain sociopolitical philosophies; although there is variance in the stances of individuals and activist groups, several core issues have been strongholds for disability pride and culture. First, the independent living movement profoundly shaped disability culture. Culturally, it is unacceptable for disabled people to lose control over their own lives or to be placed residentially in opposition to their preferences. Thus, a primary political focus has been emancipation from nursing homes and funding for suitable in-home personal care attendants, which allows disabled persons to stay in their communities, as they often prefer and is actually more cost effective (Kaye, Harrington, & LaPlante, 2010).

Similarly, disability culture advocates for equal, unsegregated access to affordable housing and transportation. The national activist group ADAPT engages in nonviolent direct action, including civil disobedience, to assure the civil and human rights of people with disabilities to live in freedom. ADAPT is one of the most important policy activism groups working from a disability culture perspective (Putnam, 2005).

Disability culture promotes particular standpoints on controversial issues in contemporary American society. First, many disability advocates raise strong objections against what is referred to as eugenic abortion—abortion based exclusively on the identification of disability. Disability culture does not fundamentally oppose abortion but does view selective abortion based on the presence of disability to be objectionable, comparable to gender-based selective abortions. In related fashion, disability culture advocates have expressed significant criticisms of the practice of genetic prenatal testing, contending that decisions about the desirability or quality of life of children with disabilities are unduly influenced by the inaccurate and stereotypically negative societal perceptions of disability (Parens & Asch, 2000).

Another contentious issue of importance to disability culture is that of assisted suicide. Disability rights advocates have been outspoken opponents of legislation to legalize physician-assisted suicide (PAS), primarily out of concern that the prejudicial and stigmatizing attitudes toward disability create an environment in which individuals actually have very limited choices and may feel subtle and not-so-subtle pressure to proceed (Golden & Zoanni, 2010). Both Gill (2010) and Paul Longmore have written full and extensive descriptions of disability culture opposition to PAS. Although PAS is often framed as a merciful act and a means to increase individual autonomy, disability activists contend that given the attitudinal, financial, and psychological barriers faced by people with disabilities, terminally ill people cannot make a decision uninfluenced by the underlying context of disability in society (Golden & Zoanni, 2010). Opponents assert that ethically, PAS holds inherent risks for the socially marginalized and vulnerable, resources consumed should never be a measure of humanity and worth, and meaningful choice should not be the exclusive right of the privileged (Gill, 2010).

However, Lennard Davis, another well-respected disability scholar, has spoken out in favor of legislation that would allow PAS:

> Disability studies in activism is all about empowerment and control. So when terminally ill people want to control their own death, they aren't doing anything radically different from what people with disabilities want to do. In fact, there is a commonality of purpose between people with disabilities and people who seek physician-assisted suicide. What disability activists seek the most is control over their own lives. Why would they want to deny that to someone who is terminally ill? (Davis, 2005, para. 7)

Disability rights advocates find themselves at odds with progressive agendas in unexpected ways. For example, environmentalists have moved to reduce U.S. consumption of plastics; one way this agenda has advanced has been through plastic straw bans in some cities (i.e., pending legislation in Seattle and New York City, among others) and corporate decisions not to offer plastic straws in restaurants (e.g., Starbucks). The disability community has been very outspoken, especially on social media, about the negative impact that straw bans can have on some disabled people. Although straws may seem like a small and perhaps insignificant issue to nondisabled people, the issue illuminated that the needs of the disability community are rarely considered in corporate and governmental decision making. Advocates have pointed out that non-plasic straws lack the same strength, flexibility, and safety and note the pitfalls of available alternatives: paper straws that become moist and disintegrate (potential choking hazard), biodegradable straws that cannot withstand hot temperatures, and inflexible and sharp glass and steel straws that can impede safety. The concern is that such actions negatively affect the disability community disproportionately, and straws themselves play only a small role in overall plastic waste

(Jambeck et al., 2015). Straws have become both a symbol of the unnecessary waste of single-use plastics and a representation of the exclusion and disregard felt by the disability community.

The place of those insiders who dissent from the dominant disability cultural view on polarizing topics is unclear. Not Dead Yet, a national organization that advocates against assisted suicide, is a powerful and well-respected group in the disability community. Most prominent disability advocates agree with their position. Harriet McBryde Johnson (2003) was a well-known activist who argued against assisted suicide, selective abortion, and infanticide very publicly with philosopher Peter Singer.

These are not simple issues, and not everyone with a disability shares the same viewpoints. It is crucial to realize, however, that in disability culture, these arguments are more than merely philosophical, and in fact deeply personal.

### Identification With Disability Culture

The degree to which individual disabled people identify with disability culture varies immensely and may be related to a person's disability identity development, or lack thereof. One's attitude about one's own disability may range from feelings of shame and embarrassment to experiences of disability pride (Andrews et al., 2013). Those with disabilities are not immune from the same biases toward disability stigma as nondisabled people, so there is potential for internalized oppression. It has been hypothesized that disabled people young enough to have been influenced by the disability rights movement, or who have lived most or all of their lives under the protection of the ADA, may be more likely to view disability as an aspect of diversity (Gill, 2001).

## Disability Justice

Historically, disability rights work and disability culture scholarship have been dominated by White voices; people of color and members of other marginalized groups have been forced to make choices between involvement in disability activism or joining other efforts to promote equality such as lesbian, gay, bisexual, transgender-plus (LGBT+) rights and combating racism (Andrews et al., 2019). Disability is off the radar of most other social justice efforts, and the disability rights movement has largely ignored intersectional identities. It is not that disabled people of color and disabled people who identify as LGBT+ did not play an important role in the disability rights movement—they most certainly did, but these efforts were largely ignored and minimized compared to the actions of White activists (Bell, 2010).

Those in the disability community with multiple and intersecting diverse identities lead the contemporary development of disability culture and advocacy. A small group of disabled persons of color and LGBT+ people coined the term *disability justice*, which is the "second wave" of disability rights activism (Sins Invalid, 2016, p. 12). Disability justice is a movement that explicitly links ableism to other forms of systemic oppression including racism, sexism, classism, and heterosexism by emphasizing how these systems all subjugate and "other" those who do not meet rigid definitions of normality or supposed superiority. Disability justice activists argue that traditional disability rights efforts have overfocused on legislation and litigation, which they contend address the "symptoms of inequity but not the root" (Sins Invalid, 2016, p. 11). Instead, disability justice is a grassroots, popular movement driven by those who have historically been marginalized within disability rights movements and excluded from disability culture—such as disabled people of color, gender nonconforming and trans disabled persons, and disabled immigrants.

According to the Disability Justice Primer, published by Sins Invalid (2016), there are 10 principles of this emerging framework. The first and core tenet is appreciation for the intersectionality of multiple identities. The second principle is the importance of leadership by those who are most affected by and experienced with resisting oppressive systems. Third, disability justice is anticapitalist, identifying the Western focus on productivity as harmful to disabled people and recognizing the wealth inequity in the United States. The fourth principle of disability justice is cross-movement solidarity, or unification with other social justice movements. Fifth, disability justice promotes recognition of wholeness or the inherent worth of all individuals. The sixth disability justice principle is long-term self-sustainability and self-care. Seventh, disability justice emphasizes cross-disability solidarity, breaking down hierarchical division with the disability community in favor of collective advocacy (Mingus, 2011). The eighth principle of disability justice is the disability culture characteristic of interdependence, which is linked to the traditional customs of many cultures that have been subjugated in the United States such as indigenous communities. Ninth, disability justice promotes collective access or using the creativity and resourcefulness that have defined disability culture to assume collective responsibility for universal access. Finally, the 10th principle of disability justice is collective liberation, described as a commitment to working together across lines of disability, race, gender, class, and sexual orientation. Disability justice may be best summarized in the words of disability rights activist Mia Mingus: "We don't want to simply join the ranks of the privileged; we want to dismantle those ranks and the systems that maintain them" (Mingus, 2011, para. 5).

## Significance of Disability Culture

Increasingly, identification and celebration of cultural differences are occurring in the United States. Instead of the obsolete "melting pot" description of American society, a "mosaic" of cultures and identities appears more accurate. In contemporary society, many groups maintain their cultures and unique identities and may experience dual or multiple cultural identities. Rather than being marginalized, separated, or assimilated, integrated individuals hold positive attitudes toward involvement with both their diverse culture and the dominant culture (Naumann, Benet-Martínez, & Espinoza, 2017).

It is important for individuals to be aware of their cultural backgrounds to effectively relate to one another. Disability has primarily and detrimentally been left out of that dialogue. Many people with disabilities experience pain or fatigue. Disabled people have important and varied needs to function effectively in society—access to Braille, TTY service, and wheelchair access, to name only a few. Yet very few people outside disability culture are aware of these needs or the tools required to ensure full access. For example, most residential homes in the community are not wheelchair accessible, making it difficult for those with mobility impairments to socialize at friends' residences. Nondisabled people may avoid the subject or withhold an invitation out of concern or embarrassment. Instead of hiding our bodies and minds away as personal medical problems, disability culture encourages explicit ownership and openness around disability. Disability culture instills confidence to bring up accessibility issues and not apologize for being "an inconvenience." For disabled people to fully participate in society, we need to cultivate an awareness of who we are. The aim of the moral model was to hide, and the goal of the medical and rehabilitation models is to assimilate. Indeed, Longmore called the medical model "the institutionalized expression of societal anxieties about people who look different or function differently" (1995, para. 10). The social and diversity models suggests that society instead may need to flex in order to gain the full benefit of the participation of disabled people. S. E. Brown (2001) stated:

> It is absolutely not our job to fit into mainstream society. Rather it is our destiny to demonstrate to mainstream society that it is to their benefit to figure out that we come attached to our wheelchairs; our ventilators; our canes; our hearing aids; etc. and to receive the benefit of our knowledge and experience. Mainstream society needs to figure not how we fit in, but how we can be of benefit exactly the way we are. (para. 5)

## Conclusion

S. E. Brown (2015) reflected on disability culture 20 years after his initial scholarship on the topic. He reminisced that when he and others began discourse on the subject, the notion of disability culture was controversial and not widely accepted. Disability studies has been a legitimate area of study for decades. Contemporary advocates are younger; S. E. Brown (2015) refers to them as "Generation ADA." Widespread Internet access opened up the lines of intra- and interdisability communication, as disabled people are no longer too constrained by ambulation or transportation issues to connect with other disabled people or join a disability group. Social media in particular defines Generation ADA. There are many disabled voices sharing online; this has given subcultures tremendous traction, such as the neurodivergent community. These advocates on the autistic spectrum have used social media extensively to voice criticism of disability groups that are purportedly run for—but not by—disabled people, such as the organization Autism Speaks (Saunders, 2018). Social media has enabled instant activism and public social consequences for discrimination. These media have also allowed for a greater degree of political action and more efficient recruitment. Activism in the present is focused on issues that may have seemed unlikely in the 1980s—topics like the right to parenthood, inspiration porn, and universal access. Finally, disability culture today has moved toward fuller intersectionality, and the diverse voices among us are strong and will be heard. Disability justice is emerging as a popular movement. Although there remains much work to be done, the dialogue is open, and the crips control the conversation.

It is thus within language and discourse that the potential
to unshackle the disabled identity lies.

—ROSE GALVIN

# 5   Disability Language

IN PSYCHOLOGY, LANGUAGE is considered a powerful tool, a means to convey thoughts and feelings in ways that affect both the communicator and the recipient. Consistent with this perspective, scholarship in diversity and multiculturalism has explored ways in which language shapes psychological phenomena such as stereotyping, prejudice, and discrimination. The idea that language affects the ways in which people perceive and think stems from the Sapir–Whorf hypothesis (D. S. Dunn & Elliott, 2005), which, in its purest form, constitutes linguistic relativity— that is, language determines cognition. That hypothesis is extreme and is not widely accepted scientifically, but a milder version has received considerable support (E. Hunt & Agnoli, 1991). To be acceptable, the hypothesis must also be bidirectional, recognizing that language is also influenced by cognition (Chandler, 1994). Also, the hypothesis refers primarily to the social context of language, not solely the lexical and semantic details (Chandler, 1994; E. Hunt & Agnoli, 1991).

Certainly, then, language affects the way that disabled people are perceived. The language used to refer to groups of people is meaningful, and it is incumbent upon disability and rehabilitation health care providers to be thoughtful and consider the potential impact of the terminology they employ (D. S. Dunn & Elliott, 2005). The potentially harmful effects of labeling and use of pathologizing vocabulary to describe people with disabilities has been well established (Caplan, 1995; Caplan & Shechter, 1993; Gouvier & Coon, 2002).

There are many perspectives on diversity and language. Scholars and researchers seek definitions and conceptual clarification to accurately measure and study the experiences of various groups and cultures (Cox, 1994). Indeed, precise definitions and classification enable researchers to adhere to the highest scientific rigor. However, language is constantly evolving, and the expressed terminological preferences of diverse groups and cultures have thus changed over time. Members of diverse groups may prefer that outsiders use certain terms, and members of the particular group may use selected terms only within the group. These complexities can be frustrating at times to people who do not keep up with current diversity scholarship, and terms selected for academic use do not always reflect everyday terminology use within and outside of diverse groups.

Many groups, including racial and ethnic minorities and lesbian, gay, bisexual, transgender-plus (LGBT+) people, have seen the words used to refer to them change in recent decades. For example, the difference between the terms *Hispanic* and *Latino* has become increasingly nuanced in relation to geographic and sociopolitical differences (Taylor, Lopez, Martínez, & Velasco, 2012; Valdeón, 2013). The recently popularized term *Latinx* is used to capture the intersectionality of gender identity and ethnicity by eliminating the dominance of the masculine suffix, thereby creating space for nonbinary individuals (Scharrón-del Río & Aja, 2015). *Latinx* is hardly accepted universally and has received considerable criticism (Alamo, 2015; Guerra & Orbea, 2015); nonetheless, *Latinx* seems to have taken hold in social media, advocacy groups, and academia. This term did not even exist when Comas-Diaz (2001) wrote a seminal work on identity, and as she accurately foretold, "names that are appropriate today may be obsolete or even offensive tomorrow" (p. 116).

Beyond preferences about group labels, many terms are considered derogatory and offensive. Certain terms associated with LGBT+ identities such as *gay* have been adopted as putdowns. Croom (2015) makes the distinction that slurs have different meanings based on the context in which they are used and the identity of the user. Some terms that are considered racial slurs or insults, however, may be used by in-group members to refer to one another, such as use of the n-word among Blacks. The term *queer* was once used negatively and it now is used with pride by many of those to whom it applies. The acronym LGBT+ has gained popularity in recent years for its inclusivity but has also garnered criticism for how quickly it has evolved, with some groups frustrated by exclusion and others exasperated by the length and confusion. Regardless, *LGBT+* is an umbrella term that brings together people whose identities are related yet different, but with whom solidarity is beneficial.

## Slurs and Insults

Just as certain slurs may insult other diverse groups, some terms can offend people with disabilities or are used to insult nondisabled persons by suggesting they are disabled. The terms *cripple* and *midget*, for example, are considered to be offensive and insulting. The term *handicapped* is mostly seen as outdated but not necessarily insulting. People with disabilities themselves may use outdated words and phrases out of habit (e.g., "handicapped parking spaces").

Derogatory terms for intellectual disability such as *idiot* and *moron* are frequently used as an affront. One of the most stigmatized and commonly used insults in the past several decades is the r-word, a slang term derived from the medical classification of mental retardation (Albert, Jacobs, & Siperstein, 2016). The r-word has been used casually as a slur to describe not just people but virtually anything negative, and its pejorative use remains high among American youth (Albert et al., 2016). Intellectual disability advocates have spoken out against the use of the r-word. Recent governmental efforts have attempted to reduce the use of the term. In 2010, President Barack Obama signed Rosa's Law, which changed federal legislation references from "mental retardation" (outdated and considered disparaging) to "intellectual disability" (Friedman, 2016). In 2009, the Special Olympics Committee campaigned to "Spread the Word to End the Word" (Lyle & Simplican, 2015). Lyle and Simplican (2015) measured participant use of the r-word before and after exposure to campaigns intended to discourage its use and found that it only exacerbated negative attitudes or had no effect on the use of the term. Unfortunately, these initial data indicate that such efforts have done little either to shift public attitudes toward people with intellectual disabilities or to reduce the derogatory use of the r-word (Lyle & Simplican, 2015).

## Media Language

The use of language in the media and among outsiders is characterized less by blatant insults and more by dehumanizing attitudes. Recall the catastrophize–sensationalize continuum from Chapter 3; many contemporary descriptors used to reference disabled people fall on each end. For example, language may victimize an individual by overfocusing on weakness and vulnerability; this affects how the person with a disability is perceived. Common phrases include *confined to a wheelchair* and *suffering from* or *afflicted with*. These phrases inherently paint the disability as distressing, even when content is positive or references strengths. To cast disabled people as victims is to strip them of self-determination (Fine & Asch, 1988).

On the other end of the spectrum, media often cover stories about disabled people's achievements such as in sports. In these instances, the person with a disability may be described as "inspirational" or "courageous." News headlines read that individuals have "overcome" disability or achieved "despite disability." Language that is biased or emotionally charged in this way only strengthens problematic public perceptions about disability. Unfortunately, this limited and slanted media coverage may be the only exposure some people have to disability.

## Euphemisms

A number of terms have emerged over time that are meant to be less offensive alternatives to the term *disability*. Likely in an attempt to emphasize the strengths of persons with disabilities, terms such as *differently abled, physically challenged*, and *handicapable* emerged (Hojati, 2012; Marks, 1999). The disability community has largely rejected these euphemisms for several reasons (Longmore, 1985). First, they have principally been developed by nondisabled people (e.g., parents of children with disabilities) and as result do not represent the chosen identities of disabled adults (Galvan, 2003). First, despite a label that is positive, these terms are often viewed as superficial and ineffective at advocating for real change (Marks, 1999). Second, some disability activists have expressed concern that euphemisms actually cover up the reality of the social oppression faced by disabled people; it is as if using a "nice word" levels the playing field, when in reality that is not the case (Linton, 1998). It is not possible for replacement labels, no matter how positive sounding, to combat long-standing prejudice and discrimination (Galvan, 2003).

Third, the disability community is wary of infantilization; the history of pity-based charity campaigns and other societal attempts to address disability have led to caution when it comes to the motives of nondisabled people and many disability organizations (Linton, 1998). Finally, some disabled activists believe that euphemisms strip the disability community of language essential to the social justice goal (Gilson, Tusler, & Gill, 1997). There is an emerging consensus among disabled people that these terms are considered patronizing and should be avoided regardless of good intentions.

In school settings, educators often use the term *special needs*, which is also frequently used by nondisabled parents of children with disabilities. Ostensibly, the label is meant to reduce stigma and normalize that children with disabilities are stills kids—that they are not disabled but just have "special needs." Disability advocates, on the other hand, view the term as trivializing—"a need isn't special if it's something everyone else takes for granted" (Carter-Long, 2017).

## Disability Erasure

Disabled activists have promoted the use of the word *disability* through social media, culminating in the #SayTheWord campaign, a viral hashtag meant to embrace the term and discourage the nondisabled from avoiding the word *disability* as an identity. Similarly, the #ThisIsWhatDisabilityLooksLike movement motivated disabled people to post photos of themselves online with the hashtag to demonstrate the diversity of the disability community and dispel stereotypical expectations about disability. Replacing the term *disability* can be experienced from a disability culture perspective as "identity erasure" (Andrews et al., 2019).

Disability activists have been motivated by other social justice efforts such as Black Lives Matter, whose members challenge the belief that race is irrelevant by publicizing the disproportionate number of Black people killed by police violence. This has become especially salient because in many of these instances, those killed are disabled people of color, illustrating how multiple levels of marginalization can have real and even deadly consequences.

Efforts to avoid the term *disability* may reduce the visibility of disability in the broader social justice movements and risks losing ground in terms of hard-earned disability rights (Andrews et al., 2019). It is difficult to advocate for equal access to rights and services for a group that is not clearly defined. For the culturally disabled, the sociopolitical context is important—while the term *disability* is being avoided, many services and programs central to the lives of people with disabilities are facing legislative threats such as weakened access to equal education and attempts to overturn the medical care protections of the Affordable Care Act (Kennedy, Wood, & Frieden, 2017; Lindner, Rowland, Spurlock, Dorn, & Davis, 2018). For these reasons, *disability* as an umbrella term could serve as a unifying force that has never been fully harnessed; even though people with disabilities are the largest minority group in the United States, there is no real coalesced disabled voting bloc (Belt, 2016).

## Taking Terms Back

Disability culture has reclaimed some terms that were used disparagingly in the past. These terms have become a disability lexicon of sorts, supporting a linguistic claim to culture. Sometimes the use of these words can provoke surprise and discomfort among outsiders. Probably the most prominent example of this trend is the word *cripple*. Insiders in the disability community have taken back the term to a large extent, adopting *crip* as an insider term conveying solidarity. Disability advocates often refer to themselves and one another as *crips*. Phrases like *crip justice* and *crip culture* have started to infiltrate the field of multiculturalism and diversity. Much like the emergence of the term *Latinx, crip theory* is exploration at the intersection of disability, sexual orientation, and gender identity (McRuer, 2006).

Disability activists use several insider labels that help to build a communal disability identity and incorporate the disability culture value of disability humor. Other examples are the terms *gimps, quads*, and *paras*. As with the reclaiming of slurs by other diverse groups, disability outsiders should not use such terms to refer to disabled people, but rather they should be aware of and respect the context and history behind their use (M. Johnson, 2006).

## Ableist Language

Ableist language is common in regular conversation. For example, terms in everyday language demonstrate the diminished status and value of people with disabilities; it is not a compliment to be called stupid, crazy, or lame. We use the term *blind* as a synonym for ignorant, and *deaf* to connote cluelessness. There are countless casually accepted terms and phrases that constitute disability microaggressions. These common sayings subtly insult disabled people. One instance is the metaphor *the blind leading the blind*, which uses blindness to illustrate uninformed and incompetent people leading others who are similarly incapable. The phrases *turn a blind eye* and *turn a deaf ear* needlessly conjure impairments to suggest willful ignorance and stubborn refusal. Terms for sensory disabilities are frequently used as insults or expressions of exasperation—for example, "Are you deaf?" An often overlooked term is the word *lame*, which in recent years has come to be used to describe something boring, disappointing, or underwhelming. It is commonplace to hear the word *lame*, which refers to gait impairment or inability to walk, as a description for something or someone pathetic or inept.

Even the term *rehabilitation*, a cousin of the medical model, is focused on the modification of the individual rather than on ameliorating the contributions of society that hamper the function of disabled individuals (Mackelprang & Salsgiver, 2016). Rehabilitation puts the onus on disabled people to change, cope, or adapt to the nondisabled world (Galvan, 2003) while the societal context within which disability exists is ignored. In some places the term *rehabilitation* has been replaced with the phrase *functional restoration*, but the meaning continues to reflect the change process of an individual, as if it is in a vacuum from the broader social and physical environment that more wholly determines outcomes.

## Person-First and Identity-First Language

One of the most controversial issues in disability is the debate between person-first or identity- or disability-first language, although there is no consensus that the language dispute is truly nconseqential. In a discussion of models of disability, Shakespeare (2013) asserted that "while terminology is important, it is not [so] important as underlying values. . . . [Q]uibbling over 'disabled people' versus 'people with disabilities' is a diversion from making common cause to promote the inclusion and rights of disabled people" (p. 19). It is in that spirit, and under the assumptions of the mild version of the Sapir–Whorf hypothesis, that the merits and limitations of each of these approaches are explored.

### Person-First Language

Social psychologist Beatrice A. Wright, one of the foremost founders of rehabilitation psychology (D. S. Dunn, 2015; McCarthy, 2011), was among the first to adopt the social model of disability, stemming from her study of the interaction between people with disabilities and their environments. Wright promoted the use of person-first language in response to medical model terms that dehumanized people with disabilities by referring to them as objects, ignoring individual characteristics or features (McCarthy, 2011; Wright, 1991). In her seminal volume on psychology and disability, she encouraged professionals to never equate a person with his or her impairment (Wright, 1983). By emphasizing that the person always be placed before the disability, Wright (1983) believed that people with disabilities would be less medicalized and more humanized. Indeed, language stemming from the medical model can be quite depersonalizing (e.g., "the cerebral palsied"). In an approach to normalize disability and reduce stereotyping, Wright (1983) used person-first language to counteract the spread effect, where the identity of disability overshadows one's entire personhood (McCarthy, 2011). Whenever individuals are considered solely in reference to one identity (in this case disability), other qualities and characteristics may be unjustly ignored or overlooked (D. S. Dunn, 2015).

As a means to eliminate prejudicial language, person-first language was intended to reduce the focus on labels, diagnoses, and categorization. Person-first language involves replacing terms like *epileptic* or *autistic* with *person with epilepsy* and *person with autism* so that the disability becomes secondary to the individual (D. S. Dunn & Andrews, 2015). Consistent with the Americans With Disabilities Act (ADA, 1990) and general disability rights progress, person-first language was endorsed to counteract the medicalization of disability and the reduction of persons to diagnoses. Further, the avoidance of phrases such as *disabled person* tries to convey that the entire individual is not disabled; in other words, only part of the person is affected by disability (Peers, Spencer-Cavaliere, & Eales, 2014). The deliberate use of person-first language is meant to offset negative attitudes and stigma around disability.

The American Psychological Association (APA, 2010) publication manual requires the use of person-first language, and this has encouraged its widespread use in academia and journalism (Peers et al., 2014). The APA argued for the use of person-first language to demonstrate respect for research participants and disabled subjects of study: "It is essential for psychologists to understand how stereotypical and stigmatizing language, attitudes, and behaviors can demean and devalue people with disabilities and have an adverse impact on self-concept, self-esteem, self-efficacy, and relationships with others" (APA, 2008, p. 1). Consistent with the publication manual, the APA Guidelines for Assessment of and Intervention With Persons With Disabilities (APA, 2012) recommends the use of person-first language, although it concedes that not all organizations and people with disabilities universally accept it.

Other organizations have also prescribed the use of person-first language including the Associated Press, the American Medical Association, the American Speech-Language Hearing Association, and the American Psychiatric Association (Gernsbacher, 2017). Many disability organizations have adopted person-first language, and it is commonly taught as the "correct" way to talk about disability (Blaska, 1993). Indeed, various resources on "disability etiquette" promote the exclusive use of person-first language (National Disability Rights Network, n.d.; United Spinal Association, 2011), and some government agencies have also endorsed its use (CDC, n.d.).

Despite the positive intention of person-first language and its worthy goal of correcting historical wrongs, it has shortcomings. In recent years, disabled people and the field of disability studies have challenged the premise behind the exclusive use of person-first language (D. S. Dunn & Andrews, 2015). Notwithstanding the dominance of person-first language, it has been re-examined in recent years and has received criticism, particularly from disability activists (D. S. Dunn & Andrews, 2015). First, person-first language can be grammatically awkward (e.g., "I am a person with amputations"). Adjectives in English are typically placed before nouns, so putting *disability* after *person* defies standard grammatical structure (L. Brown, 2012).

Second, person-first language increases length, thwarting attempts to be concise. In scholarly and academic writing, where page and word limits are common, the language often ends up abbreviated anyway for the sake of space (e.g., people with disabilities abbreviated as PWD). It is hard to believe that PWD has a particularly meaningful effect on readers' perception of disabled people (D. S. Dunn & Andrews, 2015).

Third, it is not clear empirically whether or not the use of person-first language confirms the Sapir–Whorf hypothesis; in other words, it is not established that using person-first language is actually effectual as intended (Collier, 2012). Lynch, Thuli, and Groombridge (1994) studied the use of person-first language and found that its use in a vignette about a job applicant with a disability yielded no difference in the attitudes of respondents compared with the use of disability-focused terminology. Schmidt (2018) explored the use of person-first language to describe people with cancer and HIV/AIDS and found that it had no effect on measures of stigma, empathy, and feelings of closeness toward these individuals. Similarly, Gernsbacher (2017) found no differences in attitude toward disability between groups exposed to person-first language and disability-first language on measures of stigma and dehumanization.

Finally, and most important, the very premise of person-first language has been challenged. Although the goal is to convey respect and humanize people with disabilities to reduce stigma, many disability scholars and activists contend that putting the person first does just the opposite (Gernsbacher, 2017). They argue that person-first language signals something inherently negative about disability, and by dissociating the disability from the person, it endorses the very stigma it was intended to combat (D. S. Dunn & Andrews, 2015; Gernsbacher, 2017). Interestingly, Gernsbacher (2017) found in a review of the scientific literature that person-first language is used more often to describe children with disabilities than disabled adults and that person-first language is used most frequently to refer to children with the most stigmatized disabilities such as developmental disabilities like intellectual disability and autism. This finding suggests that stigma itself may affect choices to use person-first disability language.

Some activists argue against the use of person-first language, contending that it is too medicalized and entirely inconsistent with disability identity and culture, choosing to communicate disability as something one has rather than who one is (J. Johnson, 2013). Disability is clearly viewed as undesirable if it must be separated from the person (Duffy & Dorner, 2011; Jaarsma & Welin, 2012), contributing to the fragmented sense of identity experienced by many disabled people (considered in more detail in the next chapter). Deliberately de-emphasizing disability by separating the person from the disability may inadvertently impede formation of a positive disability identity (D. S. Dunn & Andrews, 2015).

D. S. Dunn and Andrews (2015) point out that it is not commonplace to encounter person-first language about other diverse groups. For example, *people who are female* or *people with Latin heritage* are unlikely terms when it is far clearer just to say *women* and *Latinos*. The phrase *people of color* is the only widespread term that approximates person-first language. People of color are non-White individuals who share to some extent a history of racism, discrimination, and oppression in the United States (Aspinall, 2002). It is not without its critics (see Yuen, 1997), but the term appears to serve a unifying purpose rather than a distancing one (D. S. Dunn & Andrews, 2015). Ultimately, person-first language was a crucial development that served to discourage the use of offensive terminology but may have become an over-correction by unintentionally reinforcing disability stigma.

## Identity-First Language

Critics of person-first language usually prefer and espouse identity-first language, wherein disability is chosen as a central facet of identity. Sometimes called "disability-first language," this approach is grounded in the diversity (or minority) model of disability and is considered an expression of disability pride. For example, the person-first phrase *person with autism* is replaced by *autistic person* or simply *autistic* (D. S. Dunn & Andrews, 2015). In this way, disabled people affirm a disability identity without shame, taking it back from the institutionalization and medicalization that has for so long governed the lives of people with disabilities. Brueggemann (2013) contends that this empowers disabled people and increases self-determination.

Deaf culture has always claimed identity-first language. Deaf people are a cultural, linguistic minority who reject the notion of pathology and refer to themselves as (capitalized "D" for) Deaf, which shows pride in their cultural identity (Whyte, Aubrecht, McCullough, Lewis, & Thompson-Ochoa, 2013). It is commonplace to use a capital "D" to demarcate being culturally Deaf and identify as a member of the Deaf community. When referring to the physical difference of being without hearing, many use the lowercase "d" for "deaf." In a complete rejection of person-first nomenclature, Deaf people take offense to being referred to as "hearing impaired"; Deaf people do not identify as having impairments, but rather identify as a unique cultural and linguistic minority (Sheppard & Badger, 2010; Whyte et al., 2013). Although some Deaf people consider themselves to be disabled, many others reject the disability label and view themselves insularly (Branson & Miller, 2002). Deaf disabled advocates (those who both are Deaf and have at least one other disability) contend that the differentiation between Deaf and disabled is fundamentally ableist, by using social construction to distance themselves from a more stigmatized group (Ruiz-Williams, Burke, Chong, & Chainarong, 2015).

The National Federation of the Blind (NFB) endorses identity-first language, eschewing person-first language as a euphemism that promotes shame instead of equality (D. S. Dunn & Andrews, 2015). Individuals associated with the neurodiversity movement—a self-advocacy effort by autistic people to reject the medical model of autism as a deficit and to object to the societal focus on etiology and cure—believe that autism is a defining feature of who they are; they call themselves "autistic" with pride (Collier, 2012; Kapp, Gillespie-Lynch, Sherman, & Hutman, 2012). Identity-first language aims to challenge the societal belief that disability is inherently negative. By owning and claiming disability, disabled people reject the notion of being defective, undesirable, or broken (Brueggemann, 2013; D. S. Dunn & Andrews, 2015). Disabled people use identity-first language to show their allegiance to disability culture and their pride in a collective disability identity (Brueggemann, 2013).

Identity-first language has been criticized for neglecting other aspects of identity besides disability and allowing a diagnosis or impairment to describe an individual. Although disability may be an important part of identity, it is certainly not the only aspect of a person's sense of self.

*Preferences*

The data are unclear and incomplete regarding the preferred terminology of disabled people. McCoy and DeCecco (2011) found that only 23% of undergraduate student human service majors sampled used person-first terms in common language. A study of blind individuals found that regardless of age or gender, many participants had no preference for identity-first language or person-first language; among those who did have a preference, identity-first language was selected by three quarters of respondents (Bickford, 2004). Lynch et al. (1994) reported that 60% of participants in their study of person-first language use among disabled government employees favored "person with a disability" over "disabled person," although 26% considered the two phases to be equivalent. In a large and diverse sample of people with disabilities in the United States, Rottenstein (2014) found that most respondents selected "person with a disability" as the label that most accurately described them.

Feldman, Gordon, White, and Weber (2002) studied the use of person-first language among counselors and found that 38% reported using it in every instance, 64% reported they used it more than half the time, and 20% did not use it at all. St. Louis (1999) administered a questionnaire to people with disabilities, human service delivery students, and the general public and found that person-first language was preferred in only two instances (i.e., when compared to "psychotic" and "Leper"). Otherwise, he found no significant preference for person-first language to describe a wide range of disabilities.

Granello and Gibbs (2016) surveyed groups of people with differing language (i.e., "the mentally ill" or "people with mental illness") and found that participants in the group exposed to person-first language perceived those with mental health diagnoses as less dangerous, inferior, childlike, and repulsive. These results suggest that the use of person-first language may positively affect attitudes toward mental health disabilities.

*What to Do?*

How should clinicians know what they should do? What language should you use? What is correct? What will not offend? There are no easy answers to those questions, and there likely never will be. We know that language evolves along with society, and it is clear that there is no universal agreement on terminology. It makes good sense to ask individuals their preference for language, and yet doing so could feel "other-ing" (i.e., "What do you want to be called?"). If a language preference is expressed, it should be honored. It is also worth considering if disability is even relevant to the topic at hand. In many instances, disability is not salient and should not become the focus of attention. Indeed, disabled people seek care for many reasons, as will be discussed in Chapters 8 and 9.

Person-first language is "safe," because it is so widely accepted and prescribed. Use of both identity-first language and person-first language interchangeably has gained some traction in recent years (D. S. Dunn & Andrews, 2015). This approach is not an attempt to establish what is correct or to please everyone, but rather an effort to be maximally inclusive while representing the current state of the evolution of disability language (D. S. Dunn & Andrews, 2015). Gill (1995) favors the use of Disabled with a capital "D," parallel to the D/deaf approach, to refer to those who identify with disability culture.

## Conclusion

Ultimately, attitudes and language are inextricably linked. Attitudes influence the ways that people write and speak about disability, and the terminology that is chosen can affect the perception of disabled people. Clinicians possess both power and knowledge. Galvan (2003) notes the invisibility experienced by many people with disabilities; indeed, disability has been called the "invisible" minority (Fine & Asch, 1988). To be disabled risks erasure, "being patronised, ignored, devalued, and rejected, and of not being heard no matter how hard one tries to be understood" (Galvan, 2003, p. 159). Psychology and rehabilitation health care providers must not fall into the trap of providing a voice for disabled people. Instead, listen and resonate the voices of those who have been suppressed and silenced.

How can one develop a sense of identity with an attribute
that one has been taught to overcome?

—HAHN (1988, p. 310)

# 6    Disability Identity Development

DISABILITY IDENTITY DEVELOPMENT has received scant attention in the
fields of psychology and rehabilitation; instead, the concept has primarily advanced
within the field of disability studies. The term *disability identity* refers to the extent to
which disability is adopted as part of one's identity. Although there is some overlap,
psychological adjustment to disability and disability identity development are distinct concepts. Psychological adjustment to acquired disability is a well-developed
area of scientific inquiry that has been studied for decades (e.g., Heinemann, 1995;
Li & Moore, 1998; Shontz, 1977). Extant research covers the impact of stress, loss
and grief, self-concept, body image, and quality of life of individuals who sustain
disabling injury, illness, or chronic disease (Heinemann, 1995; Livneh & Antonak,
2005). As with other areas of disability, the primary focus has been on negative psychological responses (Kendall & Buys, 1998), and understanding and addressing
maladaptive reactions to disability certainly has important implications for rehabilitation outcomes, physical and mental health, and the economics of care (Livneh,
Lott, & Antonak, 2004).

Some researchers have also explored favorable reactions to acquired disability
such as resilience and posttraumatic growth, primarily under the rubric of positive
psychology (e.g., Ehde, 2010; Elliott, Kurylo, & Rivera, 2002; McMillen & Cook,
2003). Psychological adjustment to disability is a personal concept, addressing the
ways in which individuals build their own lives in relation to disability. In contrast,
disability identity formation is a communal concept that "connects the social and
the personal and involves the individual putting themselves in a collective context"

(Shakespeare, 1996, p. 99). Even so, it can be difficult to parse out the differences between the concepts of adjustment to disability and disability identity development (Forber-Pratt, Mueller, & Andrews, 2018).

Disability identity development lacks a precise and agreed-upon definition (Putnam, 2005). In this chapter, I will use disability identity development and formation interchangeably, and refer to this process as a form of identity politics wherein a marginalized group membership becomes an internalized, integrated, and important aspect of oneself, much like racial, gender, or sexual identities (Darling, 2013; Putman, 2005). Whereas psychological adjustment primarily refers to how one thinks and feels about disability and behaves in response to it, disability identity development is the degree to which one integrates disability as a core aspect of one's sense of self (Forber-Pratt, Mueller, & Andrews, 2018). In other words, the extent to which one adapts (or "adjusts") to an acquired disability is related to, but not the same as, the degree to which one integrates disability as part of one's identity. A person who sustained a spinal cord injury, for example, could be very well adjusted to his disability and function exceptionally well: He may have a successful career, raise a family, and play an active role in his church. However, this does not tell us much about his disability identity. Perhaps he minimizes the extent to which disability affects his life, strives to pass as nondisabled when possible, surrounds himself with nondisabled people, and considers disability irrelevant to his personal identity. On the other hand, he could be involved in disability advocacy, intentionally seek out relationships with other disabled people, and consider disability as one of the most important aspects of his life. These are the types of factors that contribute to disability identity formation.

Forber-Pratt, Lyew, Mueller, and Samples (2017) describe disability identity as "a unique phenomenon that shapes individuals' ways of seeing themselves, their bodies, and interactions with the world" (p. 198). Like other identity research on gender and race, disability identity development is "both a question of social categorization and meaning-making as well as fundamentally physical and biological" (Forber-Pratt, Lyew, Mueller, & Samples, 2017, p. 204). Individuals with disabilities vary widely in terms of disability identity development, as it is affected by personal, cultural, and disability factors (Darling, 2013). Attitudes toward disability identity among disabled people can range from feelings of shame and embarrassment to experiences of disability pride (Olkin, 1999). Although considering oneself to be disabled and formulating a disability identity are not the same thing (Forber-Pratt, Mueller, & Andrews, 2018), self-identification is an aspect of disability identity and possibly even a prerequisite for the formation of a positive disability identity (Darling & Heckert, 2010). Many factors contribute to the development (or lack thereof) of one's identification of oneself as disabled including disability severity and perception of stigma (Bogart, Rottenstein, Lund, & Bouchard, 2017). Nario-Redmond, Noel, and Fern (2013) reported that between 7% and 18% of disabled research participants identified as abled-bodied or nondisabled, even though they reported the presence of impairment. Several other studies have shown that despite objective impairments, functional limitations, and difficulties with activities of daily living, some people still \do not identify themselves as disabled (Iezzoni, McCarthy, Davis, & Siebens, 2000; Kelley-Moore, Schumacher, Kahana, & Kahana, 2006; Langlois et al., 1996).

The field of psychology tends to focus on individual and personal factors that affect identity development, but societal and systemic factors may be equally important (Forber-Pratt, Mueller, & Andrews, 2018). In this chapter, I will present several models of disability identity development, discuss ways of measuring this concept, and explore how disability identity development is important for cultural competence.

## Concept of Identity Formation

As theories of multiculturalism and diversity have developed, a number of socially constructed identities have received empirical attention. Most prominently, researchers have explored racial identity (W. E. Cross, 1995; Helms, 1990), ethnic identity (Phinney, 1990), sexual orientation (McCarn & Fassinger, 1996), and gender identity (O'Neil, Egan, Owen, & Murry, 1993). Disability identity formation shares some similarities with identity development models of other marginalized groups, including decisions about how much assimilation into the dominant (i.e., nondisabled) culture is desirable, the concept of "passing," and the inherent risks in celebrating differences that society devalues. There are also stark contrasts to the processes described by other diverse groups; disability, unlike most other identities, can be and often is acquired, and many disabled people have impairments that may be unpleasant in their own right (i.e., pain).

### Identity Status Theory

The dominant approach to studying identity development is that of identity status theory research, based on Erikson's (1950, 1968) identity development theory. Erikson (1950, 1968) considered identity development an essential task for healthy psychological growth. He proposed three distinct identity levels. Ego identity involves developing consistency in one's internal knowledge of oneself, whereas personal identity is focused on developing stable beliefs, values, and goals. Social identity, then, is the process of solidifying connections with groups to which one belongs. Incorporation of these three identities leads to identity synthesis resulting in a secure and holistic sense of self (Erikson, 1950, 1968). For example, a person's ego identity could include personal characteristics such as an outgoing demeanor or being adopted, whereas ego identity might involve the belief that education is important, leading one to value continued learning. Examples of social identity are religious affiliation, sexual orientation, and regional background.

Contemporary scholars believe that identity development occurs throughout the lifespan, although the work of Erikson (1950, 1968) and Marcia (1966) was focused on the transition from adolescence to early adulthood (McLean & Syed, 2014). Marcia (1966) applied Erikson's psychosocial stage of *identity versus role confusion* in research settings to more specifically elucidate the subprocesses occurring. His identity status theory was plotted on two axes: crisis and commitment. Individuals find themselves in one of four identity statuses: diffusion, foreclosure, moratorium, or identity achievement (Marcia, 1966). Identity moratorium is a period of crisis marked by a struggle to declare allegiances. Conversely, during the identity foreclosure status, the individual expresses commitment to the ideology of others (e.g., parents) but has yet to experience an identity crisis of his or her own. Identity diffusion occurs when the individual is unattached to any particular ideology or prospects. Finally, identity achievement represents a person who has weathered an identity crisis and emerged committed to a firm sense of self-identity.

### Narrative Identity

In a different Eriksonian tradition, McAdams (2001) and others have explored the concept of narrative identity. This approach to identity formation is based on one's personal life story of making meaning, which develops and changes throughout the lifespan (McAdams & McLean, 2013). The individual is the narrator, and the story is framed by the cultural and social realities of his or her life (McAdams, 2001). This life story approach to self-understanding has implications for disability identity because disability onset, etiology, and trajectory are likely to be what McAdams (2001) considers self-defining memories—those that are selected to play a crucial role in the reconstructed self-narrative.

Both identity status and narrative identity approaches have been applied to disability identity formation. Common themes across disability identity development models include stages of reframing disability; awareness of disability identity politics; thinking collectively or with a critical consciousness; constructing personal identity while moving toward a more open identification with the devalued group; and expressing the need to be valued and accepted as a whole, integrated human being. A tradition of oral personal narratives about the experience of disability in American culture has informed the exploration of disability identity formation (Charmaz, 1994, 1995; Frank, 1993; Phillips, 1985, 1990).

*Social Identity Theory*

In contrast to the individualized Eriksonian theories, social identity theory has been less often applied to disability identity development, although it is highly relevant (Bogart, 2014). Social identity theory is focused on the development of identity as part of a social category or group (Hogg & Abrams, 1988). Whereas the Eriksonian approaches focus more on subjective aspects of identity, social identity theory emphasizes the process of self-categorization to form a social group-based identity and the ways in which group identities are activated when they become salient (Stets & Burke, 2000). During self-categorization, individuals accentuate perceived similarities with the socially constructed in-group by making positive social comparisons that enhance both the collective and self-concept (Hogg & Abrams, 1988; Stets & Burke, 2000). Once aligned with the group, members tend to identify as increasingly alike in their perceptions and express commitment to the group without desire to leave it, even if the group has diminished social status such as disability (Hogg & Abrams, 1988; Stets & Burke, 2000).

Bogart (2014) applied social identity theory to disability, proposing that when disabled people move toward disability identity, they are responding to the stigmatized status of the group by affirming their identity and rejecting the stigma placed upon the group by society in favor of disability pride. Alternatively, Bogart (2014) points out that the opposite response—rejection of disability identity or development of negative disability identity—occurs when disabled people opt to minimize disability, assimilate into the nondisabled majority, and distance themselves from other people with disabilities. These individuals may internalize stigma toward disabled people and experience feelings of shame regarding disability (Bogart, 2014). Development of a positive disability identity can be a protective factor fostering well-being for those who are significantly disabled or have an obvious impairment (Bogart, 2014).

Contemporary disability identity "scholarship is more speculative than either theoretical or empirical" (Dunn & Burcaw, 2013, p. 154), but it is worth exploring specific models in greater detail, moving from early qualitative work to contemporary empirical approaches.

## Theories of Disability Identity Development

*Livneh's Model of Adaptation to Disability*

Livneh (1986) made one of the first coherent attempts to model a process of disability identity formation, although it overlaps considerably with the psychological adjustment literature and is geared specifically toward acquired disabilities. From his meta-analysis of rehabilitation research, Livneh (1986) conceptualized a five-stage model of adaptation to disability. It bears striking similarities to the well-known model of the stages of emotional acceptance of death (Kubler-Ross, 1968), which is one reason it is viewed rather negatively from a disability culture perspective. Livneh's (1986) first stage was the initial impact characterized by the shock of onset or diagnosis of conditions producing impairment. He identified defense mobilization, marked by the classic psychodynamic defenses of bargaining and denial, as the second stage (Livneh, 1986). The third stage was the initial realization of disability, accompanied by mourning, and the fourth stage was retaliation with externalized anger. Livneh's (1986) fifth and final stage was reintegration, culminating in adjustment and acceptance of disability. The linear nature of his completely individualized model, which has a clear endpoint with disability having been "overcome," is consistent with the ways in which disability has historically been conceptualized in the rehabilitation literature, that is, as a personal tragedy (Livneh, 1986). Later, disabled scholars developed models with more nuance and complexity.

## Charmaz's Studies of Disabled Men

Charmaz (1994, 1995) conducted some of the earliest qualitative work on identity in disability and chronic illness, although her findings were more focused on adjustment to disability than disability identity development. Charmaz (1994) explored identity issues in men with chronic illnesses that caused significant functional limitations. Participants were interviewed and shared their experiences of identity dilemmas wherein loss of ability threatened their sense of self and caused uncertainty about the future. Identities were reconstructed through a process of reappraisal and reprioritization (Charmaz, 1994). Attitudes toward their own disabilities ranged from negative to positive depending on the context and circumstances; many participants came to find value in the experience of disability while also striving to maintain previous aspects of their identities (Charmaz, 1994).

Charmaz (1995) also explored the role of the body in identity issues with the same sample, theorizing several stages of adaptation that involve changes in identity. Qualitative findings indicated that many disabled participants altered their identity goals in response to physical, social, and emotional reactions to disability. They experienced identity conflicts when they perceived that their disabilities interfered with other goals, and then substituted aspects of identity by giving up a valued aspect of identity to adopt new ones, choices that in turn were strengthened by validation from others in their social environments. Charmaz (1995) referred to the last phase in her model as a surrender wherein disabled men stopped trying to push their bodies beyond their physical limitations and were able to integrate their disability identity into a greater sense of self. The work of Charmaz (1995), although representative of some positive identity development, was largely influenced by medical model conceptualizations of disability and the idea of disability as an individual and personal struggle. For example, Charmaz (1995) never explored the role of connection to the broader disability community in the development of identity among her disabled participants.

### Gill's Stage-Based Model

The most well-known model of disability identity development was described by Carol Gill, a disabled psychologist. Gill (1997) noted that disability identity formation is impeded by oppressive barriers such as isolation, inaccessibility, segregation, stigma, and poverty. Most disabled people are the only ones with a disability in their family of origin, which means there are no models of disability identity in the home, and it is easy to feel distant from the disability community (Gill, 1997). Gill's model is stage based (although she calls the stages "types") and linear, and is considered an identity status model. Her theory includes four types of integration of disability identity for those with both congenital and acquired disabilities that can occur at any point during the lifespan.

Gill's first type of integration is *coming to feel we belong* (integrating into society) and is the adoption of the belief that disabled persons deserve inclusion, while rejecting the notion that segregation and exclusion are acceptable. Gill (1997) reflects that for many disabled people, it was a drastic societal transition to affirm that people with disabilities are entitled to the same civil rights as others and worthy of accommodations and accessibility as mandated by the Americans With Disabilities Act (ADA) and other legislation. This type of integration may vary with age; Gill's generation grew up in a country largely without civil rights for disabled people, whereas young adults today were born after the ADA and never knew the United States without some protections based on disability and federally mandated accessibility legislation.

Gill (1997) calls her second type of integration *coming home* (integrating with the disability community), wherein the individual begins associating with other people with disabilities. Many people with disabilities deliberately avoid contact with other disabled people for reasons such as recollections of distressing childhood separation from nondisabled peers, resistance to segregation, rejection of disabled persons' worth, and hesitation related to stigma (Gill, 1997). Other people with disabilities who are raised by disabled parents or have siblings with disabilities become exposed to the disability community from an early age. Many disabled people do ultimately come together, some opting to connect more fully with disabled peers for support and companionship. Gill (1997) pointed out that for disabled people who have been isolated from peers, the fulfillment of connecting with other disabled people is often pleasantly surprising. It is this type of collective integration into the disability community from which disability culture developed.

During the third type of integration, which Gill (1997) called *coming together* (internally integrating our sameness and differentness), disabled people's attitudes toward their own disability evolve toward self-acceptance. Outsiders tend to focus on helping young or newly disabled people compensate for disability and develop skills and abilities unaffected by disability (Gill, 1997). For example, a bright young woman with cerebral palsy who cannot walk may be encouraged to focus her efforts on academic pursuits and be discouraged from playing sports. As Gill (1997) put it, "all people with disabilities are socially pressured to cover their differences and emphasize their normality" (p. 45). This approach insists on rejection of disabled parts of the self and celebration of nondisabled parts leading to internal division that "results in a sense of self in conflict or a self-image riddled with significant gaps (Gill, 1997, p. 43). Thus, the task of disability integration is valuing disability as a part of one's whole self and claiming disability as a portion of one's identity, while rejecting the mainstream culture that has so strongly denigrated disability (Gill, 1997).

The final type of Gill's (1997) disability identity integration is *coming out* (integrating the internal experience with presentation to the larger community). She described this process as an integration of the private and public selves, wherein people allow themselves to show their authentic disabled self without trying to pass as nondisabled and to cease deliberately minimizing their differences in an attempt to accentuate normalcy. Gills stated, "such persons have forsaken 'normality' in quiet, healthy defiance" (Gill, 1997, p. 45). Overall, Gill's (1997) identity formation process follows a path from emerging from isolation, connecting with disabled peers, rejecting mainstream cultural values, and finally returning to society with a newly integrated sense of self (Gill, 1997).

## Weeber's Positional Model

Under the tutelage of Carol Gill and in the tradition of the social model of disability, Weeber (2004) developed a model of disability identity integration that consists of six positions. Her research was largely phenomenological and qualitative, as she gathered oral narratives via interview from leaders of the disability community about their own disability identity development processes. Like Gill (1997), Weeber uses a stage-based framework labeled with "positions." The first position is marked by rejection of disability; people in this position try to pass as nondisabled or minimize disability-related characteristics or tendencies. It is important at this point to portray oneself as completely normal to blend with mainstream society. Disabled people experience feelings of shame and inferiority regarding their disability, and they avoid contact with other disabled people in this position.

Weeber's (2004) second position involves realization that disabled people are treated unfairly and not afforded the same opportunities as nondisabled peers as a result of disability. In this position, disabled people are likely to feel angry and disillusioned with society and perhaps even resentful toward nondisabled individuals. In Weeber's (2004) third position, disabled people begin to form connections with people whose disabilities are similar to their own. Weeber (2004) suggests that disabled people in this phase are likely to subscribe to a hierarchy of disabilities and are prone to avoid associating with people whose disabilities differ from their own. For example, a person with a physical disability in this position would not consider him- or herself to have much in common with someone with a cognitive or developmental disability and may actively avoid interactions with people with other types of disabilities. This may be done partly to counteract the impact of spread effect wherein disabled people are assumed by others to be globally impaired because of the presence of a disability (Wright, 1983).

In Weeber's (2004) fourth position, disabled persons expand their range of interactions with the broader disability community and experience increased comfort in associating with those with a wide range of disabilities. Commonalities and collective goals among the disability community are recognized. During Weeber's (2004) fifth position, individuals experience a reduced desire to conceal obvious manifestations of disability, and they elect not to "pass" as nondisabled even when possible. In this position, disabled people experience increased self-assurance and draw confidence from belonging to the disability community. The sixth and final position developed by Weeber (2004) addresses generativity (in the Eriksonian sense), as the person invests resources to benefit future generations of disabled people by activism in the disability movement and by providing mentorship to other people with disabilities, indoctrinating them into disability culture.

## Disability Identity and Attitudes Among Activists

The first quantitative exploration of disability identity development was conducted by sampling the membership of the disability activism organization ADAPT (Hahn & Beaulaurier, 2001; Hahn & Belt, 2004). The authors found, unsurprisingly, that affirmation of disability was associated with rejection of a hypothetical disability cure (Hahn & Beaulaurier, 2001). Hahn and Belt (2004) found that value for communal affiliation was stronger among those who integrated disability into their lives as opposed to those isolated from the disability community who were less likely to experience affirmative private beliefs and sentiments toward disability.

Hahn and Belt (2004) also found a significant inverse correlation between refusal of a cure and the belief that people with disabilities "should be considered courageous for having overcome their disabilities" (p. 460), indicating that disabled activists with a strong sense of disability identity reject the notion of overcoming disability as an inspirational trope. Hahn and Belt (2004) found that personal affirmation of disability was greater among those with early-onset disability than among those with adult-onset conditions. Among those with disability onset prior to adulthood, there was a stronger sense of personal disability identity and a higher value placed on communal affiliation compared to those with later-onset disability (Hahn & Belt, 2004). These results suggest that those who are disabled by adolescence and early adulthood may be more likely to develop a strong sense of disability identity.

## Political Disability Identity

Putnam (2005) explicitly explored the political realm of disability identity development, noting that those with well-developed and positive disability identities share a view of the importance of connection to the broader disability community. The philosophy of "the personal as political" is characteristic of the academic discipline of disability studies. Putnam (2005) observed that the disability community is largely built around disability rights activism and commitment to common goals. She developed six domains of political disability identity, each with subdomains. These domains contain many of the same elements as the models of Gill (1997) and Weeber (2004) including establishment of self-worth as a disabled person, developing disability pride, recognizing the effects of discrimination and oppression, and coalescing around common causes for social justice that are cross-disability (Putnam, 2005). Like Hahn and Belt, (2004), Putnam (2005) emphasizes the understanding that the environment is often more disabling than the individual's impairment and that social structure and policy can alter that reality. The final domain of her model, then, is political constituency and social action toward change. Putnam makes explicit what other models imply: that integrating a strong sense of disability identity is inextricably linked to a commitment to social justice.

## Gibson's Disability Identity Model

Gibson (2006) proposed a straightforward stage model of disability that is tailored more so than other models to the experiences of those with congenital disabilities. Gibson's (2006) first stage is a passive awareness prominent during childhood. At this point, disabled people lack role models of disability, and medical care is prioritized over social aspects of disability. Disabled people in this stage often feel pressure to be compliant and acquiescent and are likely to avoid others with disabilities (Gibson, 2006).

The second stage of Gibson's (2006) model is realization, which may be salient in adolescence and early adulthood. In this stage, the disabled person starts to integrate disability into his or her self-concept (Gibson, 2006). However, this stage may be marked by self-hatred or internalized oppression in conjunction with anger and self-pity; these individuals are overly concerned with the perceptions of others and may be preoccupied with appearance (Gibson, 2006). Gibson (2006) postulates that it is in this stage that the "Superman/woman" complex may emerge; this phenomenon, known as "super crip" in disability culture, refers to someone with a disability feeling the need to overcompensate for limitations by excelling in some area such as adaptive sports, an entrepreneurial career, or academics.

Gibson's (2006) third stage is acceptance, which she postulated is associated with adulthood. During this stage, disabled people's perspective may move from self-deprecation to embracing oneself (Gibson, 2006). People with disabilities are likely at this point to view the self as important, although no more so than other people, and start to integrate other people with disabilities into their lives (Gibson, 2006). It is at this stage that disabled individuals become involved in disability advocacy and activism and still feel comfortable in a mainstream society that is dominated by nondisabled people (Gibson, 2006). Gibson (2006) emphasized that identity formulation is dynamic and that disabled people may progress or regress through the stages at various points in the lifecycle.

## Orientation Toward Disability

Darling (2013) developed a concept called *orientation toward disability* that consists of disability identity, adherence to a particular model of disability, and extent of disability rights activism. Darling and Heckert (2010) define self-identity as cognitive and evaluative appraisals with some behavioral outcomes. They contend that orientation toward disability is similar but more encompassing than the concept of disability identity as addressed by other scholars. Darling's (2003) Questionnaire on Disability Identity and Opportunity (QDIO) is a psychometric measure meant to determine the prevalence of specific disability orientations to inform appropriate intervention strategies. Darling and Heckert (2010) conceptualized disability orientation through the measurement of three dimensions on a continuum: one's disability identity, belief in the social or medical model of disability, and level of involvement in disability activism.

The disability identity dimension of the QDIO is an assessment of a person's degree of disability pride versus disability shame. High scorers on disability identity were those who claimed disability as an important part of themselves and expressed pride, whereas low scorers denied disability as an identity and endorsed efforts to hide or minimize disability-related characteristics (Darling & Heckert, 2010). The disability model dimension was stratified between subscription to either the social model or medical model of disability. Those oriented toward the social model responded that attitude and other external barriers are predominant problems, whereas those with a medical model orientation indicated deference toward health care clinicians and considered the problem of disability to reside within the person (Darling & Heckert, 2010). Activism, the third element of disability orientation, measured behavioral correlates such as political participation and civil rights advocacy in contrast to passive acceptance marked by inaction (Darling & Heckert, 2010).

Evaluating a sample of 388 persons with varying disabilities, Darling (2003) used cluster analysis and cross-tabulation to propose several typologies. The four factors identified were disability pride, exclusion and dissatisfaction, social model, and personal/medical model (Darling, 2003). Darling's (2003, 2013) five proposed orientation typologies included resignation, normative typicality, personal activism, affirmative activism, and affirmative typicality.

Those in the *resignation* typology were the least socially active and most unlikely to engage in disability activism; they predominantly subscribed to the medical model and reported feelings of disability shame (Darling, 2003). These were typically the oldest participants who had the lowest income, were the least educated, and tended to acquire disability later in life (Darling, 2003). They also required the most assistance with daily activities and felt excluded from society (Darling, 2003).

Persons who fell into Darling's (2003) *normative typicality* typology did not fully endorse either the medical or social model; disability pride and activism were absent. These participants felt more involved in society and required little to no assistance with daily activities; they were younger participants and were the most likely to have an acquired disability. Respondents in the *personal activism* typology reported congenital disabilities and feelings of exclusion from society. They were more likely to be unemployed and less socially active, although they did indicate that they engaged in disability activism; they also reported that they believed in the social model and had some degree of disability pride.

Participants who reported the strongest feelings of disability pride and were highly engaged in social activism fell into Darling's (2003) *affirmative activism* typology. These individuals favored the social model and reported being socially active; they tended to be young and college educated, and most often had congenital disabilities (Darling, 2003). Persons in Darling's (2003) *affirmative typicality* typology were among her youngest participants and were likely to have higher levels of education and earnings. They reported having congenital disabilities and required little to no assistance with daily activities (Darling, 2003). These individuals reject disability as a part of their identities; although they are socially active within mainstream society, they are not highly involved with the disability community (Darling, 2003). This group was neutral on Darling's (2003) social versus medical model continuum and responded neutrally toward the concept of disability pride.

It is worth mentioning that almost a quarter of respondents did not fit into any of the five clusters (Darling, 2003). Although there is evidence that the QDIO has good validity and reliability as a tool to assess disability identity development among a heterogeneous disability population (Darling, 2003), it has not undergone rigorous psychometric evaluation in different samples. Like Weeber's (2004) position model, Darling and Heckert's (2010) orientation model allows for a full spectrum of perspectives on disability identity, and it offers a means by which to measure rejection of disability identity, an important concept that has been overlooked in models more concerned with development of a positive disability identity.

### Caldwell's Disability Identity Themes

Rather than a linear model, Caldwell (2011) qualitatively identified themes related to disability identity formation. Like Weeber (2004), he studied a small sample of leaders and advocates in the disability community. The first of Caldwell's (2011) themes is resistance: As disabled people identify their differences from idealized social norms, they may respond with feelings of shame, and thus attempt to hide or minimize their disability to the extent possible. This theme evolves into expressing worth as a person, questioning the oppression of social structures, and finding one's voice.

Caldwell's (2011) theme of connection with the disability community involves association with other people with disabilities and identification of shared and collective experiences. Reclaiming disability and personal transition, according to Caldwell (2011), involves recognition of the positive and enriching aspects of disability. Individuals in this state are able to suppress internal oppressive thoughts and feelings and experience increased acceptance of limitations and embrace interdependence. Caldwell (2011) postulates that this sets the stage for the formation of disability pride.

The theme of interconnections with the broader disability movement involves examination of one's own biases and acknowledging that a hierarchy exists within the disability community. At this point, Caldwell (2011) posits that the individual must work actively to challenge stereotypes and reach out to people whose disabilities are different than his or her own. Caldwell's (2011) final theme is bonding with social justice and interdependency. In this theme, the disabled person most clearly identified as a member of a marginalized group and, as such, formed a bond with other oppressed communities, recognizing the common struggles among disenfranchised peoples.

## Narrative Disability Identity Themes

The narrative approach is focused on making meaning of life experiences and on the development of the self-identity (McAdams & McLean, 2013). Ellis-Hill, Payne, and Ward (2008) contend that social reality is made up of one's past, present, and future life story. They defined the self-narrative, or the life thread, as "the re-creation of events and actions in a symbolic structured way so that the motives of the actors and the morality of the situation can be understood by self and others" (Ellis-Hill et al., 2008, p. 155). In this way, individuals develop a plot that defines their identity, emphasizing certain circumstances while discounting others. Taken together, the narrative plot serves to convey moral stances and personal values to others. Importantly, narrative theory postulates that actual events are value-free and that the lens through which the individual interprets the event determines the tone and valence of the event (McAdams & McLean, 2013). Cultural considerations and historical context affect these narratives so that social and cultural structures and norms are strengthened through retelling (Ellis-Hill et al., 2008).

The life thread model is an adaptation of narrative identity theory that provides a framework for understanding identity changes following an acquired disability (Ellis-Hill et al., 2008; McAdams, 2001). The life thread provides continuity and a holistic self-concept; one's psychological health is promoted through an integrated personal identity that anchors one across varying circumstances throughout the lifespan. This process provides a basis for assurance about the future (Ellis-Hill et al., 2008). Present identity is the result of creating a life story and is essential in giving one's life a sense of meaning and direction (McAdams & McLean, 2013). Some life threads continue over much of the lifespan, whereas others are more important during some life stages than others. For example, a woman's role as a sister is likely to have continuity, but her identity as high school valedictorian probably will have less salience in her later life. In this way, identity and self-concept are malleable and may be repeatedly recreated throughout the lifetime.

So how does the life thread theory apply to the experience of disability? Medical sociologists and other scholars have explored how individuals negotiate self-identity within health care; they believe that the moral and social aspects of the self-narrative are important to the understanding of disability and chronic illness (Ellis-Hill et al.,

2008). Because the narrative consists of both memories and plans, one's sense of stability and consistency can be disrupted by the onset of disability (Ellis-Hill et al., 2008). In an unfamiliar place, newly disabled people must grapple with significant psychological and existential identity questions. One way this has been described in the literature is that an acquired disability acts as a disruption of biography, an unexpected event requiring narrative reconstruction (Ellis-Hill et al., 2008). The metaphor of life threads represents the narrative strands that are created and recreated throughout life (Ellis-Hill et al., 2008).

The work of Ellis-Hill et al. (2008) with stroke survivors indicated that many experience a separation from their sense of self. They found that participants learned to make sense of their altered experiences by redefining themselves through weaving the story of disability into their life thread, recreating their story as one of successful adjustment and overcoming adversity. In this way, the narrative changes from sufferer to skilled survivor, demoting the medicosocial story of inadequacy or deficit. Ellis-Hill et al. (2008) argue that health care providers are inherently a part of the disability narrative and have the power to affect the re-creation of disability stories and identity reformulation.

D. S. Dunn and Burcaw (2013) used a narrative approach to qualitatively investigate themes of disability identity by examining the writings of disabled authors. They compare disability identity to a compass that directs values, goals, and actions in disability-salient situations. Based on a review of the work of Gill (1997) and that of Hahn and Belt (2004), D. S. Dunn and Burcaw (2013) asserted that disability identity entails both affiliation with the disability community and positive affirmation of disability, suggesting that it may develop as a means to cope with discrimination, prejudice, and social ostracism. They further hypothesized that a well-developed disability identity could help to externalize rather than internalize disability-related problems (e.g., inaccessibility). In narrative identity research, the content of narratives reveals the inner beliefs and understandings of the individual (Ellis-Hill et al., 2008); the veracity of events is not nearly as relevant. The six identity themes identified by D. S. Dunn and Burcaw (2013) were communal attachment, affirmation of disability, self-worth, pride, discrimination, and personal meaning.

Like Ellis-Hill et al. (2008), and more so than status-based models, D. S. Dunn and Burcaw (2013) hone in on the process of making personal meaning an important aspect of disability identity. This process can include finding significance or trying to make sense out of one's situation, and even realizing benefits or positive aspects of disability. As Wright (1983) emphasized, positive adjustment outcomes are linked with realization of existing strengths as well as shifting, widening, or reprioritizing one's values. In this way, adjustment to disability may set the stage for the formation of a positive disability identity (D. S. Dunn & Burcaw, 2013).

*ADA Generation Model*

Most recently, Forber-Pratt and Zape (2017) conducted qualitative research with college students—the "ADA Generation"—who have only known American life with those protections in place. Based on interviews, their findings informed a model of psychosocial identity development for people with disabilities, an identity status model in the tradition of Erikson (1950, 1968) and Marcia (1966). They identified four developmental statuses: acceptance, relationship, adoption, and engagement (Forber-Pratt & Zape, 2017). The first status, acceptance, is congruent with the concept of adjustment to disability; in essence, the participants described their process of coming to terms with their disability. Relationship status is the second phase, which involves connecting to other people with disabilities and allegiance to the disability community, particularly around social justice issues such as accessibility. During the third phase, called adoption status, individuals learn the nuances of disability culture, determine which of the core values to make their own, and more fully engage with the disability community. Finally, in the engagement status, disabled people focus on role-modeling for junior members of the culture and engaging in activism.

## Differences Between People With Congenital and Acquired Disabilities

There is much interest but little data regarding differences in disability identity development between those with acquired and congenital disability. Using a modification of the Acceptance of Disability Scale (Linkowski, 1971), Li and Moore (1998) found that people with congenital disabilities reported greater acceptance of disability than those with acquired disabilities. Though not a direct measure of disability identity, Li and Moore (1998) captured participants' attitudes toward disability and the ways in which disability impacted their lives. Bogart (2014) compared positive versus negative disability identity in people with congenital and acquired disabilities using the Personal Identity Scale (Hahn & Belt, 2004). She found that congenitally disabled people produced higher scores on positive disability identity and satisfaction with life compared to participants with acquired disabilities, consistent with previous findings of more positive disability identities among people with earlier onset disabilities (Hahn & Belt, 2004). Darling and Heckert (2010) found that congenital disability was the best predictor of positive disability identity; these individuals reported greater disability pride, whereas persons with disabilities acquired later in life reported greater disability shame. Time since disability onset was also positively associated with disability pride (Darling & Heckert, 2010).

People with congenital disabilities may be more likely to embrace a disability identity because they have no other personal reference point, in contrast to people with acquired disabilities who have been confronted with a change in their body and/or functioning (Bogart, 2014). Similarly, those with congenital disabilities are historically familiar with their disability and functional abilities and are fully acclimated to moving within the world from a disabled perspective; in fact, they know no other existence. Bogart et al. (2017) contend that people with acquired disabilities, in contrast, lose abilities and access and as a result experience uncertainty in adapting to their new reality. Some scholars have posited that people with acquired disabilities struggle to adopt an identity to which they have been socialized negatively (Bogart, 2014), but there is no empirical evidence that those with congenital disabilities do not internalize that same stigma toward disability.

Another common hypothesis is that, congruent with Erikson's theory, those whose disability is present at the time of adolescence are more able to integrate disability into their identity formation. Children and adolescents with either congenital or acquired disabilities may be more malleable in their self-concept and more readily adopt new skills or ways of doing things (Bogart et al., 2017). An alternate explanation is that those with congenital disabilities simply have had more time to adapt and integrate disability into their identities. However, older people with disabilities have actually been found less likely to express disability pride and adhere to the social model of disability (Darling & Heckert, 2010). It is unclear the extent to which generational, social, and cultural influences play a role versus challenges associated with acquiring disability later in life. Future research should focus on clarifying the impact of disability on identity when acquired during various developmental stages, particularly adolescence and older adulthood. Research must also parcel out the significance of time since disability onset for those with acquired disabilities. Finally, the identity development of people with congenital disabilities warrants further exploration to determine the importance of familiarity with impairment versus the social influence of disability stigma.

## Measuring Disability Identity Development

The measurement of disability identity development remains in its infancy, even though the initial work was conducted decades ago. Many of the authors discussed previously developed measures congruent with their theories of disability identity development, but all of those instruments have significant limitations in terms of reliability and validity. In this section, a few of those measures of disability identity development will be discussed. For a comprehensive review of the literature on approaches to measurement of disability identity development, see Forber-Pratt, Lyew, Mueller, and Samples (2017).

As mentioned previously, Hahn and Belt (2004) developed the Personal Identity Scale, which is probably the most commonly utilized measure of disability identity and has been adapted for use by other researchers. This is an 8-item measure of disability integration into personal identity, extent of positive disability identity, and sense of belongingness within the disability community. This measure was developed using a poorly described mixed mobility disability sample that was homogeneously White (Bogart, 2014, 2015; Zhang & Haller, 2013). In addition to Hahn and Belt's original finding that elevated disability identity scores were correlated with decreased desire for a cure among people with mobility disabilities, Bogart (2014, 2015) found that higher scores also were correlated with decreased scores on measures of anxiety and depression.

Darling and Heckert's (2010) QDIO was designed to measure their theory of disability orientation mentioned previously. It captures three dimensions: identity, role, and preference for model of disability. The instrument is a 30-item scale that was administered to a large cross-disability sample and analyzed through factor analysis, making it the most scientifically robust of the published measures to date. Darling and Heckert (2010) identified four factors including disability pride, which were described in detail previously.

A promising development in the field of disability identity development is the creation of a new instrument by Forber-Pratt, Lyew, Samples, and Mueller (2017). Their scale is in development following a pilot administration to a large cross-disability sample. The initial construction utilized exploratory factor analysis, which yielded several distinct factors. Forber-Pratt plans to validate these factors utilizing confirmatory factor analysis (personal communication). The proposed Disability Identity Development Scale is undergoing subject matter expert review for content validity. This work, when complete, will be the first psychometrically sound and robust measure of disability identity (Forber-Pratt, Zape, & Merrin, 2018).

## Does Identity Development Matter?

Bogart et al. (2017) posit that positive disability identity predicts several favorable outcomes such as higher levels of well-being and satisfaction with life, and may lower psychological distress (Bogart, 2014). Nario-Redmond and colleagues (2013) found that positive disability identity is correlated with higher scores on a measure of self-esteem. As discussed earlier, a robust disability identity may allow disabled people to externally attribute the negative aspects of disability rather than internalizing them (Bogart et al., 2017), leading to a more positive self-concept.

Interestingly, Li and Moore (1998) found that higher levels of perceived discrimination were correlated with lower scores on a measure of disability acceptance. This finding has implications for disability identity development because recognition of discrimination is often proposed to be an important part of the process of disability identity development. Acknowledgment of discrimination is associated with both externalizing disability-related problems in the tradition of the social model and encouraging identity alignment with the marginalized group (Bogart et al., 2017). In addition, Nario-Redmond and Oleson (2016) found that discriminatory experiences encourage political advocacy. However, Li and Moore's (1998) results suggest that higher perception of discrimination may be related to internalized oppression. In other words, disabled people appear to respond differently to an increased awareness of disability discrimination; for some people it reinforces negative self-beliefs, and for others it increases their in-group pride. Clearly, the area merits further research.

## Clinical Recommendations

Culturally competent health care providers should understand the difference between adjustment to disability and disability identity formation. Clinicians can use models of identity development to help conceptualize where their clients are in their journey of disability identity formation (Forber-Pratt, Mueller, & Andrews, 2018). Recognizing, inviting, and honoring disability narratives can validate patients' experiences and help them to solidify their disability identity over time (D. S. Dunn & Burcaw, 2013). D. S. Dunn and Burcaw (2013) suggest thoughtful elicitation of disability narratives from disabled clients, using tools such as journaling or blogging. In addition, some disabled people find it empowering to read the work of other disabled people; for some, this is their first exposure to the thoughts, feelings, and ideas of other people with disabilities. Attending closely to what clients share as their lived experience of disability can help clinicians understand where they are and what types of experiences for which they may be ready (Forber-Pratt, Mueller, & Andrews, 2018). To illustrate, if a patient is exhibiting signs of disability shame and rejection of a disability identity, sharing the merits of peer support and participation in disability groups or activities is unlikely to be productive. Conversely, a client beginning to show interest in other people with disabilities or experiencing some anger related to perceived disability discrimination may be quite well-prepared and receptive to such suggestions. To be effective, it is important to assess the outcome of these interventions and to always carefully consider disability identity formation in timing and approach to avoid adverse outcomes (Forber-Pratt, Mueller, & Andrews, 2018).

## Conclusion

Disability identity formation is an important yet underdeveloped area in rehabilitation and psychology. The most well-developed models are not linear, have no endpoint, are developmental in scope, and emphasize that disabled people exhibit different responses in different areas of their lives in different contexts. Limitations in measurement and an excessive focus on personal adjustment have stifled the forward movement in the field of disability identity development. Despite some progress in disability rights and mildly increased inclusion of disability as a type of diversity, the proportion of people with disabilities who fully embrace disability identity remains very low (D. S. Dunn & Burcaw, 2013). Unfortunately, the idea of proud identification as disabled remains unknown to the vast majority of people with disabilities (Hahn & Belt, 2004). Perhaps with new energy and developments from the ADA Generation in this area, such a concept will no longer be so unfamiliar.

We must not confuse our ignorance of life with a physical difference for an account of that life; nor should we forget that the particulars of our own ignorance are likely a more crucial determinant of the disabilities manifest in some lives than any differences in the physical makeup of the people.

—MCDERMOTT AND VARENNE (1995, p. 329)

# 7 Cultural Competence

THE U.S. SUBSTANCE Abuse and Mental Health Services Administration (SAMHSA, 2014) defines cultural competence as "an ongoing process of organizational and individual development that includes learning more about our own and other cultures; altering our thinking about culture on the basis of what we learn; and changing the ways in which we interact with others to reflect an awareness and sensitivity to diverse cultures" (p. 12). Cultural competence in the field of psychology gained significant traction in the late 1990s with the work of psychologists Stanley Sue and Derald Wing Sue, who promoted the importance of cultural considerations of race and ethnicity in psychotherapy (S. Sue, 1998; D. W. Sue, 2001). Generally culture is defined as a pattern of shared beliefs, customs, and values. D. W. Sue (2001) asserts that race and ethnicity are the most salient characteristics, as they elicit "greater discomfort" (p. 792) than do other factors. In light of significant disparities in health across racial and ethnic groups that are unexplained by other factors, as well as evidence of clinician bias and discrimination (Betancourt, Green, Carrillo, & IIa, 2003; A. Nelson, 2002), the concept of cultural competence across all health care professions became increasingly significant. Sociocultural factors have received considerable attention as the root of such disparities, but the definition and practical meaning of cultural competence among health care providers vary considerably (Betancourt et al., 2003).

The term *cultural competence* has been criticized. Fisher-Borne, Cain, and Martin (2015) expressed concern that *competence* connotes broad knowledge about diverse culture identities that may be mistaken for understanding the cultural experiences of a particular individual. Some scholars prefer the term *cultural humility*, which more distinctly describes a lifelong process that requires humbleness (Tervalon & Murray-Garcia, 1998). The word competence can imply mastery, but it is crucial to acknowledge that cultural effectiveness by nature can never be fully mastered (Isaacson, 2014). According to Fisher-Borne et al. (2015), cultural humility is not a sense of mastery, but rather one of accountability, and an active, responsible, and continuing commitment to self-reflection. In this chapter, the terms *cultural competence* and *cultural humility* will be used interchangeably, the premise being that cultural competence is not a simple set of technical skills or a communication style (Fisher-Borne et al., 2015). Cultural competence cannot be acquired quickly or easily (Kleinman & Benson, 2006). Instead, it is an endless, recursive process of shifting power differentials that "requires a fundamental change in the way people think about, understand, and interact with the world around them" (A. M. Dunn, 2002, p. 107).

The goal of increasing cultural humility is for health care providers to improve their effectiveness with a wide range of families, couples, and individuals with varying characteristics through decision making and treatment planning that take account of these factors (Campinha-Bacote, 2002). In a review of the literature, Beach and colleagues (2005) found strong evidence that cultural competence training affects outcomes including health professionals' knowledge, attitudes, and skills, and improved patient satisfaction. Cultural humility affects relationships positively by fostering communication that is respectful of and responsive to the beliefs, practices, and cultural and linguistic needs of diverse individuals and communities (Chipps, Simpson, & Brysiewicz, 2008). However, there is not yet empirical substantiation that cultural competence interventions directly affect patient adherence or patient health outcomes (Beach et al., 2005).

Some diversity factors are readily apparent such as race and observable disability, whereas others may be hidden until disclosed or exposed (Balcazar, Suarez-Balcazar, & Taylor-Ritzler, 2009). People with disabilities often find that health care providers have very little, if any, training and experience working with disabled patients. Given their training in the medical field, many health care providers conceptualize disability through the medical model and tend to overfocus on amelioration of symptoms (Marks, 2007). Lack of knowledge and cultural responsiveness can cause clinicians to overlook crucial health promotion and disease prevention issues, which may or may not be related to disability. Consequently, disabled people may become wary of utilizing health care services (Marks, 2007).

In this chapter, I discuss the fundamental assumptions that underlie the concept of cultural humility and explore specifically how to apply them to people with disabilities. Cultural competence can expand clinicians' awareness and skills, fostering their ability to provide more sensitive, more culturally relevant, and, as a result, more effective disability and rehabilitation services (Bau, 1999).

## Assumptions of Cultural Competence

For the purposes of this chapter, cultural competence is construed as the deliberate development of an evolving set of attitudes, behaviors, and skills to appreciate, understand, and effectively interact with others who have diverse cultural and linguistic experiences, identities, and beliefs. The foundation for building cultural competency is appreciation for diversity. It is crucial to be able to accept and respect differences between ourselves and others to provide care to people with diverse backgrounds and experiences as well as shape services to best fit individual needs (Center for Community Health and Development, 2017). The ultimate goal is to deliver fair and effective health care to all people, irrespective of cultural identity (Betancourt et al., 2003).

There tend to be greater differences within cultural groups than across groups (Campinha-Bacote, 2002; Phinney, 1996). Cultural humility includes awareness that groups vary in the extent to which they share historical, geographical, physical, or language characteristics. In the same way, cultural assumptions about disability can be erroneous. Factors other than disability such as gender, race, ethnicity, age, sexual orientation, or socioeconomic status are sometimes much more significant (Center for Community Health and Development, 2017). Thus, it is essential to consider the intersecting identities of people with disabilities to better understand the complexity of diversity. For example, a gay man who uses a wheelchair may face exclusion in the gay community related to limited accessibility at gatherings; he may also experience discrimination from some disability factions because of his sexual orientation. Cultural factors can both hinder and help people with disabilities to adapt, function, and progress in rehabilitation; attending to cultural issues and working to align values are essential to achieving rehabilitation goals (Stodden, Stodden, Kim-Rupnow, Thai, & Galloway, 2003).

Intersectionality (the ways in which multiple identities interact) is important for clinicians to consider when working with disabled clients. Different cultural groups have distinct cultural beliefs, practices, and values about disability. Individuals vary in terms of their identification with cultural traditions, but it is helpful for clinicians to understand how the interaction of multiple identities may be salient. For example, in some Asian and indigenous cultures, disability may be attributed to supernatural forces (Stodden et al., 2003), and exploring culturally mediated beliefs and customs can be advantageous. The goal is not to alter the cultural conception of disability but to help clients and their families explore these issues and identify cultural factors that can be used as strengths. This is illustrated by the role of faith healers, spiritual masters, and folk modalities; instead of assuming that the Western perspective of medicalization is superior, clinicians can exhibit cultural humility and learn from traditional interventions (Mackelprang & Salsgiver, 2016). In many cases, they complement the medical and psychological resources provided. This is particularly relevant when it comes to treatment planning. In Western rehabilitation and medicine, the focus is almost always on helping clients to achieve independence. In many non-Western cultures, it is expected that disabled persons will receive care from family members and that they will live in the home among immediate and extended family (Stodden et al., 2003). Clinicians should remember that independence and autonomy are not synonymous. The reality for many disabled people is that interdependence is the best fit; this is consistent with disability culture values, and independent living may mean different things for different people from different cultures.

## Cultural Competence Continuum

T. L. Cross, Bazron, Dennis, and Isaacs (1989) developed a cultural competence continuum tool to assess organizational or individual progress within the dynamic process of cultural competence. The continuum has both a negative and positive side. Cultural destructiveness, the most negative category, means that cultural differences are seen as problematic and as obstacles to dominant culture assimilation that is expected of everyone. We saw historical examples of this in Chapter 1 in the rise of eugenics and involuntary procedures and experimentation on disabled people. More contemporary examples include removing children of disabled parents from their families because of a parental disability, and a focus on efforts to eradicate disability such as the Muscular Dystrophy Association annual telethon, which raises money primarily for curing and eliminating muscular dystrophy.

Cultural incapacity, or the lack of ability to work cross-culturally, is the next stage of the model (T. L. Cross et al., 1989). People who demonstrate cultural incapacity do not necessarily or even usually have bad intentions, but they can nonetheless cause harm unintentionally. Disability examples of this behavior include infantilization of the disabled person by addressing his or her companion, and a failure to provide accommodations such as an American Sign Language (ASL) interpreter.

Cultural blindness[1] is the middle stage of the continuum and harkens to the "colorblind" philosophy that race and ethnicity are irrelevant (T. L. Cross et al., 1989).

---

[1] Use of the term *blindness* to mean unawareness is ableist and illustrates how disability has traditionally been left out of the diversity discourse.

People in this stage of unawareness deny the importance of cultural identity and profess that all people are alike; they perceive themselves as without prejudice or bias—the result is erasure of disability identity. This stage is exemplified by over-looking disability altogether—phrases often used toward disabled people include "I don't see you as disabled" and "The only disability in life is a bad attitude."

Cultural precompetence is the first stage on the opposite, positive, end of the continuum. Culturally precompetent people are aware of disparities and attempt to ameliorate them (T. L. Cross et al., 1989), but they do not have the requisite knowl-edge, skills, and abilities to do so. A disability example of this stage is being cogni-zant of the ways in which physical disability and accessibility are important, but not considering the linguistic needs of those with other disabilities such as Deaf people. Another characteristic of cultural precompetence is *tokenism*—the idea that having one disabled friend or hiring one or two persons with a disability is sufficient to demonstrate one's commitment to diversity and inclusion. A typical response from a health care provider in this stage is to express anxiety in response to realization of oversights such as an inaccessible office or ignorance about how to find an ASL interpreter.

According to T. L. Cross and colleagues (1989), cultural competence is the capac-ity for continual learning and self-reflection about one's own biases, in addition to identifying and appreciating differences. Those in this stage seek cross-cultural con-sultation and input. A culturally competent disability researcher, for example, may use methods such as participatory action research, where the views of people with disabilities are included throughout the entire research process.

Cultural proficiency involves exhibiting an exceptional commitment to and value for diversity and multiculturalism; those at this stage prioritize continuous self-growth in this area (T. L. Cross et al., 1989). Culturally proficient people are inten-tional in their words and actions as they relate to those from different backgrounds. Often, they build careers around diversity and become experts and researchers of culturally competent practice (T. L. Cross et al., 1989). Someone culturally profi-cient in disability would understand the complexities of intersecting identities, be aware of the historical context in which disability is lived, and engage in advocacy for disabled human rights.

## Clinical Cultural Competence

All the major models emphasize that cultural humility is a process, a continual jour-ney toward ever-improving knowledge, skills, and ability; cultural competence is a value and has no endpoint (Campinha-Bacote, 2002). Cultural humility requires the provider to be humble and able to acknowledge and admit the boundaries of his or her abilities (Tervalon & Murray-Garcia, 1998). Cultural humility involves taking action through behaviors and attitudes in diverse cultural situations (Center for Community Health and Development, 2017). Most models include some element of willingness, awareness, knowledge, skill, and self-examination. Several of the key models and their application to disability are discussed here.

## Desire

The Center for Community Health and Development (2017) describes cultural awareness as openness to attitudinal change. Balcazar et al. (2009) developed and validated a four-factor model of an iterative process toward cultural competence in a rehabilitation setting. Willingness to engage is considered a prerequisite for movement toward cultural humility in this model; in other words, the clinician must want to engage individuals with diverse identities. Cultural desire is described by Campinha-Bacote (2002) as the intrinsic motivation to become more culturally aware, knowledgeable, and skillful in cultural encounters. Cultural encounters occur when clinicians deliberately connect with patients from different cultural backgrounds to check their own assumptions and prevent stereotyping (Campinha-Bacote, 2002). Campinha-Bacote points out that efforts by clinicians to simply complete obligatory questions or culturally targeted interventions will likely fall flat. Patients respond more favorably when they perceive that a clinician is genuinely enthusiastic about providing culturally competent care. Disabled people attune to the authenticity of a health care provider's efforts by gauging the extent to which the clinician seems prepared and demonstrates investment in their care. Campinha-Bacote (2002) cautions that limited experience with a few members of a certain cultural group does not suffice to confer expertise.

## Self-Awareness

Cultural awareness consists of self-examination to become cognizant of one's own cultural biases and to recognize personal biases, prejudices, and assumptions about people from other groups (Bau, 1999). These attitudes are often part of the societal narrative that privileges some voices over others, and power is unequally distributed. Campinha-Bacote (2002) is among those who assert that the self-reflective process is necessary to avoid cultural imposition, or the tendency to press one's own beliefs and values on others (Balcazar et al., 2009). One aspect of what Balcazar et al. (2009) describe as the "cognitive factor" of their model is critical awareness, or ownership of cultural biases toward other cultures. Ownership must occur through examination of personal privilege and experiences of oppression. Part of this examination must be acknowledgment of the inherent power differential between patient and clinician (Fisher-Borne et al., 2015).

Self-awareness is an active process that requires intentional exploration and willingness to identify and accept that one holds biases; in other words, self-reflection must involve self-critique of our interactions with others (Isaacson, 2014). All of us hold prejudices and make assumptions about other groups, but many of us are either unaware of these implicit biases or unable to acknowledge them. Fisher-Borne et al. (2015) argue that critical self-awareness must examine and challenge the inherent power imbalance within clinical encounters. For example, a nondisabled White clinician must acknowledge that privilege has benefited her at the expense of marginalized others (Sins Invalid, 2016). She must become aware of personal values and behaviors that are unconsciously exclusionary. Isaacson (2014) found that clinicians rated themselves as culturally competent while concurrently harboring negative stereotypes about another culture, suggesting that self-report assessments of cultural humility are likely to be less accurate than objective feedback.

Because of the insidiousness of prejudices against people with disabilities (see Chapter 5), it is easy to be unaware of biases and negative assumptions. Asch and Rousso (1985) suggested that "the roots of frightened and hostile feelings are found in unconscious anxieties regarding wholeness, perfection, loss, and weakness" (p. 3) elicited by contact with disabled people. Nondisabled health care providers may especially fear vulnerability and weakness, given the emphasis of the medical model on healing and cures. Beyond that, disability is a group that nondisabled people recognize (at some level) they ostensibly could become a part of, increasing their anxiety and fear (Chalfin, 2014). In health care settings, clinicians may feel pulled to intervene or try to fix disability or disability-related issues, even if that is not the individual's purpose in seeking care.

The Center for Community Health and Development (2017) defines cultural sensitivity as appreciation for cultural differences without passing judgment. This process is not always easy. For example, contact with a family whose cultural beliefs are negativistic toward disability or who seem hesitant to expend resources caring for a disabled family member may elicit negative thoughts and feelings in the clinician. Niemeier, Burnett, and Whitaker (2003) assert that interdisciplinary rehabilitation must reduce the risk for biased clinical judgment by intentional critical thinking including accounting for inconsistencies, considering multiple hypotheses, and gathering information from multiple sources. By suspending judgment and taking a nonthreatening and inquisitive stance, clinicians are better able to understand cultural factors and provide additional education in a gentle and sensitive manner, increasing the odds of forming partnerships to improve the lives of people with disabilities (Ravindran & Myers, 2012).

Disability culture emphasizes interdependence, whereas dominant American culture holds independence in high esteem. A strong argument can be made that all humans are by nature interdependent, but the notion of independence is a prized value to many nonetheless (Eddey & Robey, 2005). It is common, for example, for a nondisabled person to assert that he or she would rather be dead than have to rely on others for basic tasks such as eating, bathing, dressing, and toileting. For outsiders, including clinicians, the concept of being dependent for those aspects of life can elicit significant fear or pity, but for long-time disabled people, requiring assistance is a perfectly normal part of life. It would be easy for a nondisabled clinician to assume that the disabled person's primary concern is his or her lack of independence, when the presenting clinical issue could be any of the range of reasons for which other (nondisabled) patients seek care.

*Knowledge*

Much education in multiculturalism has focused on increasing categorical knowledge or teaching particular customs, values, beliefs, and behaviors of different cultural groups. The Center for Community Health and Development (2017) describes cultural knowledge as having a cultural awareness of another cultural group. This approach may be overly simplistic and result in lists of "dos and don'ts" for clinicians (Betancourt et al., 2003). Rightfully, several concerns have been raised about a solely factual method for increasing cultural competence. First, it seems implausible that any one person could become familiar with the vast number and types of cultural groups and identities. Second, emphasis on learning cultural facts may promote stereotyping, which can be harmful (Bau, 1999; Betancourt et al., 2003). Niemeier et al. (2003) caution that each individual has values and cultural beliefs, and these may not be congruent with the customs and beliefs of others in the same culture due to acculturation or intersecting identity factors. Knowledge obtained from media or limited experiences with people from different cultures can perpetuate stereotypes. For example, based on mainstream portrayals of blindness, clinicians could assume that those with visual impairment are in constant need of assistance from sighted people; this is inaccurate and could adversely affect the relational alliance (Marks, 2007). Fisher-Borne et al. (2015) point out that knowledge-based approaches risk implying that learning cultural facts and history is sufficient, and they may diminish the need for social justice efforts to eliminate inequality and systemic oppression.

However, some benefits of knowledge-based competence have been identified. Primarily, acquiring information is useful when relevant to culturally based syndromes, ways in which diseases and medications may specifically manifest or affect members of particular groups, cultural and spiritual practices that could influence treatment, and contextual data about historical interactions within the health care system or pervasive experiences of certain groups (Betancourt et al., 2003). Although culture shapes behavior, it is not the sole determinant (Marks, 2007). To obtain cultural knowledge, Campinha-Bacote (2002) suggests that clinicians should learn fundamental information about culturally mediated health-related beliefs and cultural values, disease incidence and prevalence, and treatment effectiveness. This is distinguished from stereotyping, and Campinha-Bacote (2002) emphasizes the importance of completing individualized cultural assessments taking into account not only culture but also life experiences and acculturation.

The second cognitive factor noted by Balcazar et al. (2009) is appreciation and familiarization with various cultural norms and, like Campinha-Bacote (2002), is focused on specific health-related practices and attitudes and behaviors common in medical settings. For example, culturally competent care by a physician would involve knowing which medications might increase the risk of autonomic dysreflexia in patients with spinal cord injuries. It is similarly prudent for an obstetrician to be aware of the historical involuntary sterilization of disabled women before offering a tubal ligation.

It is useful to know that disability culture has a torrid history with medical systems, and many disabled people are therefore leery of health care settings. Personal and shared historical experiences of feeling disregarded, humiliated, and angry in response to a lack of understanding on the part of clinicians has evolved into a cultural belief system (Eddey & Robey, 2005). Many disabled people or family members believe they know more about their disability or health condition than health care providers; most have had numerous experiences with professionals who have little to no training or education about disability, and quite often the patient or his or her family member indeed holds more knowledge than the clinician (Eddey & Robey, 2005).

Awareness and sensitivity to cultural values can facilitate effective provision of services. Specific aspects to consider with disability and rehabilitation include traditional family structure, cultural constructions of the meaning of disability, attitudes toward authority, perspectives on interdependence, comfort-seeking resources and care, and expectations for helping (Bau, 1999). These cultural elements can affect symptom expression and response to disability (Stodden et al., 2003). Bau (1999) noted that the medical model perspective, dominant in most Western cultures, emphasizes disability as illness and normalizes intervention by medical professionals. Those from diverse cultures may be more comfortable seeking care from native health care providers or spiritual healers who may use rituals, herbs, or other alternative intervention (Bau, 1999). Some individuals and families from diverse cultures receive interventions that emphasize mind–body dualism or incorporate religious or spiritual beliefs, and unless invited to share by clinicians, they may not disclose this information (Ravindran & Myers, 2012).

Other cultural traditions may be consistent with a moral model of disability. In many cultures, disability is viewed as a form of punishment, a curse, or the result of wrongdoing by the individual or his or her family, as discussed in Chapter 2 (Groce & Zola, 1993). Some cultures blame mothers for having a disabled child, who is viewed as a repercussion of her sins (Rogers-Adkinson, Ochoa, & Delgado, 2003). In certain cultures that believe in reincarnation, it is believed that disability derives from transgressions committed in a past life (Groce & Zola, 1993). Other cultures consider disabled members to have special gifts or a specific role or destiny within the cultural community (Rogers-Adkinson et al., 2003). Western and Southern European cultures, from whom most White Americans are descendants, traditionally held folk beliefs about "bad blood," that disabilities are widely inherited and that certain conditions like intellectual disability result from incestuous intermarriage (Groce & Zola, 1993). These beliefs have strong implications for the resources that a family or community will elect to devote to a disabled member and their expectations for that individual's life (Ravindran & Myers, 2012).

The continuum of collectivism and individualism is important when determining from whom people with disabilities seek to receive assistance and social support. Those from collectivist cultures who receive considerable support from their extended families may avoid seeking care from medical providers or organizations, whereas members of individualistic cultures tend to be more reliant on formal health care structures and lack substantial familial support (Ravindran & Myers, 2012).

Clinicians should learn about the strengths and assets associated with particular cultures. Especially in instances where members are widely considered disenfranchised, health care providers may overfocus on barriers and overlook the ways in which cultural membership is adaptive (Tervalon & Murray-Garcia, 1998).

*Skill Development*

Cultural skill involves the capacity to obtain important cultural information about the cultural identities of individuals and their families to collaborate with patients to select appropriate treatments (Campinha-Bacote, 2002). Tervalon and Murray-Garcia (1998) note that patient-focused interviewing, which is marked by a less authoritative style and deference to the patient as an expert about his or her own cultural realities, is a hallmark of cultural humility. Isaacson (2014) emphasized the ability to listen attentively, openness to other cultures, and comfort with being fully present in the moment. Niemeier et al. (2003) emphasize the need to listen carefully and actively and take time get to know the family to build an effective rapport with diverse patients.

In working with people with disabilities, understanding disability identity development and the nature of intersecting identities are examples of cultural skill. It requires such skill to elicit information about cultural conceptions of disability and traditional cultural responses. Balcazar et al. (2009) consider such skills to be a clinician's ability to communicate effectively, integrate cultural values and experiences, and flexibly tailor clinical services to the needs of diverse groups. Interdisciplinary rehabilitation team members should strive to individualize the care of every patient (Niemeier et al., 2003). To apply these processes, clinicians must be able to engage in problem solving, appreciate the dynamics of power and privilege, and have a strong grasp of the contextual factors that affect people with diverse backgrounds (Balcazar et al., 2009).

Culturally competent communication requires clinicians to allow individuals to be experts about their own experience yet not require them to bear the burden of educating each clinician with whom they come into contact. Each individual person is an expert on his or her experience of a culture but should not be viewed as a representative or an expert of that cultural group (Marks, 2007). It can be exhausting and feel "othering" for disabled clients to have to constantly educate health care providers about disability issues. Culturally competent clinicians learn, listen, observe, and adapt to the particular context and situation (Bau, 1999). Eddey and Robey (2005) use the example of recommending a cosmetic prosthesis over a functional one as incongruent with disability culture and caution against health care providers promoting treatments or devices simply for the purpose of assimilation into nondisabled culture. Although this may be a form of cultural imposition, it is also important to understand that many disabled people themselves are unfamiliar with the tenets of disability culture (see Chapter 4) and their desired level of assimilation is related to their disability identity development (discussed at length in Chapter 6). In other words, clinicians should develop skills to gauge the patient's preferences when presenting options and not presume knowledge of the individual patient's goals.

Effective communication skills enable clinicians to discern membership in diverse groups that are not readily apparent such as hidden disabilities. Bau (1999) suggests the use of various modalities to communicate, including aural, tactile, and kinesthetic forms. In cultural encounters, clinicians must assess linguistic needs and avoid using untrained interpreters, friends, or family members to communicate. This is particularly important for Deaf patients fluent in ASL and disabled patients who speak languages other than English. Without an appropriately trained interpreter, harmful mistakes and miscommunication can occur (Campinha-Bacote, 2002). Using family members to interpret is not advisable, as they may alter information

BOX 7.1.

DISABILITY CULTURAL INCOMPETENCIES

Assuming that speech or physical impairment is an indication of cognitive impairment

Addressing disabled patient in condescending tones or in an "infantilizing manner"

Assuming that persons with physical disabilities are somehow more childlike

Treating disabled patients as children, both attitudinally and medically

Ignoring the individual as a potential key source of clinical information

Dismissing role as a partner in the care process, failing to fulfill basic obligations of autonomy

Addressing care attendants or family members instead of the disabled person

Overlooking secondary health condition by overfocusing on primary disability

Neglecting preventative care and health promotion

when translating, and patients may withhold information from the clinician that they wish to keep from the interpreting family member (Bau, 1999).

Eddey and Robey (2005) suggest that clinicians may need to take time getting to know nonverbal patients to learn what methods they use to communicate so as to maximize patient input and participation in care. For patients with cognitive impairment, health care providers should learn how to slightly reduce the complexity of speech so as to be better understood, and they should be sure to actively solicit patient feedback and responses (Eddey & Robey, 2005). Box 7.1 lists several common disability cultural missteps made in health care settings.

Balcazar et al. (2009) assert that cultural competence culminates in the integrative practice and application of all the aforementioned components, including desire, self-awareness, knowledge, and skill within particular clinical contexts. The authors note, however, that clinical cultural humility at the individual health care provider level is limited in what it can achieve; systemic and organizational factors are equally important in the provision of culturally competent care.

## Organizational Cultural Competence

Research on the application of cultural competence suggests that it is contingent upon organizational and systemic factors (Balcazar et al., 2009; Betancourt et al., 2003). Policies and guidelines of health care systems have important implications for the quality of care delivered to patients from diverse backgrounds. If organizational factors discourage patronage from those with certain identities or structural barriers interfere with care, no degree of cultural knowledge or skill on the part of clinicians will suffice (Balcazar et al., 2009). For example, a health care practice on the second floor of a building without an elevator or an exam room without tables that raise and lower demonstrates a lack of organizational support for culturally competent practice.

## Structural Cultural Competence

Mistakes in health care are far more likely to result from systems and process problems rather than individual clinician behavior (Donaldson, Corrigan, & Kohn, 2000; Marks, 2007). Structural cultural competence involves ensuring all patients have full access to high-quality health care (Betancourt et al., 2003). Structural problems have been identified in complex health care systems that are driven by economic and bureaucratic demands. When policies and procedures are unnecessarily complicated and service providers are underresourced, vulnerable patient populations are the most likely to suffer (Betancourt et al., 2003; Stodden et al., 2003). For example, when there is a high burden on patients to self-advocate, manage, fund, or coordinate their own care, those with the fewest internal and external resources are the least able to access needed care. Unfortunately, given what we know about health disparities, these are the individuals who likely need the care most.

Concrete structural omissions include lack of interpreter services. Despite research showing that effective interpretation is associated with better quality patient–provider relationships, improved understanding of diagnosis, adherence with prescribed medications and care instructions, greater attendance at follow-up care, and decreased utilization of emergency departments, many health care systems do not offer interpreters or fail to educate clinicians about the availability of interpreters. Instead, health care providers are left to use problematic interpreters including untrained staff or family members (Betancourt et al., 2003). Other tangible structural problems include a paucity of culturally and linguistically suitable health education materials, complicated or difficult intake processes, inflexible scheduling, and long wait times for appointments. For instance, disabled people who rely on public transportation may show up late for services or miss appointments. Having access to informational materials in Braille involves institutional investment but shows organizational sensitivity and commitment to cultural humility.

## Staff Diversity

Employing people who represent diverse cultures is one of the best ways to demonstrate a commitment to cultural competency. A diverse staff enhances the credibility and visibility of the agency among diverse groups in the community (Betancourt et al., 2003). Organizational cultural humility takes initiative to recruit leadership and build a workforce that is diverse and representative of its patient population (Betancourt et al., 2003). Racial and ethnic minorities and people with disabilities are woefully underrepresented in the health care workforce, particularly in positions of leadership (Mitchell & Lassiter, 2006; Stodden et al., 2003). A diverse staff makeup can increase access to care for diverse populations. For example, Black patients are significantly more likely to receive their care from Black health care providers; generally, clinicians who are members of diverse groups treat higher proportions of vulnerable and underserved population than their peers (Mitchell & Lassiter, 2006). Health care staff diversity may also contribute to increased patient satisfaction and facilitate better communication (Sullivan, 2004).

Recruitment and retention of a diverse health care workforce does not happen by chance; it requires intentional effort and implementation of strategies to attract people from diverse cultural identities (Chiriboga & Hernandez, 2015). Recruitment and retention techniques specific to disability have received very little empirical attention. Chan and colleagues (2010) found that organizational knowledge of the Americans With Disabilities Act (ADA) including disability-related accommodations predicted the likelihood of having disabled employees. Inclusion of disability in organizational diversity definitions and training materials was also significantly associated with organizational commitment toward employing people with disabilities (Chan et al., 2010).

Probably the best way to recruit disabled staff is for people with disabilities to be evident within the organization. When applicants are able to identify opportunities for peer mentorship, they may be more attracted to the organization. Some agencies even offer a formal mentorship or preceptor program to support career development and professional growth for employees with disabilities (Bruyère, Erickson, & VanLooy, 2004). Successful disabled employees are the ultimate proof of inclusivity and can foster a positive reputation for the organization as culturally competent. Conversely, one or two negative experiences among disabled applicants can quickly cultivate a reputation of poor inclusiveness.

Another strategy is for organizations to advertise a commitment to diversity by explicitly including disability in their definition of diversity and expressing willingness to provide reasonable accommodations (Markel & Barclay, 2009). Hiring officials should be trained to assume there may be disabled applicants in any pool and discuss reasonable accommodations in a routine and normative fashion (Bruyère et al., 2004). This way, those with nonapparent disabilities may feel more comfortable disclosing disability and requesting needed accommodations. Box 7.2 includes sample statements that organizations can use to show their dedication to equal employment access.

To retain disabled employees, organizations must set the stage for success. It is important for employers to understand that disability-related needs may shift over

BOX 7.2.
SAMPLE AFFIRMATIONS OF EQUAL EMPLOYMENT ACCESS

"We encourage people with disabilities and from other diverse backgrounds to apply."

"We do not discriminate based on disability."

"We provide reasonable accommodations as needed to people with disabilities."

"Our materials are available in alternative formats (Braille, electronic, large print, etc.) upon request."

"Our building is wheelchair accessible."

"ASL interpreters are available as needed."

"Our faculty/trainees/staff reflect a wide range of socioeconomic, cultural, and religious affiliations, including people with disabilities."

time and are not always apparent initially. Organizations should develop and communicate a clear process for requesting and considering reasonable accommodations (Bruyère et al., 2004). It can be helpful to conduct routine reassessments of all work areas to ensure reasonable accommodations have been offered and that employees know how to request them. Rather than predetermining or automatically limiting options for reasonable accommodations for individuals with disabilities based on the agency's perception of disability needs, culturally competent organizations are flexible in considering creative or nontraditional work arrangements (Bruyère et al., 2004). Employers can set the tone for an open dialogue around disability instead of putting the onus on individuals to bring it up. For example, leaders can model willingness to discuss disability topics in an open, nondefensive manner. Although it is not appropriate (and also illegal) for organizations to ask employees directly about disabilities, they can cultivate an environment that invites disclosure by providing a safe and affirmative atmosphere (Markel & Barclay, 2009).

Structural efforts to create accessible and universally designed workplaces, spaces, processes, and opportunities also send a message that disabled people are valued by the organization (Bruyère et al., 2004). It may be helpful to emphasize that these types of changes benefit all employees, not just those with disabilities. For example, the installation of automatic door openers is useful to nondisabled employees who have their hands full, just as it is to an employee who uses a walker.

*Organizational Behavior*

Similar to individual clinicians, an organization's behaviors, attitudes, policies, and structures must reflect diversity-affirmative values and principles to provide access and work effectively with members of different cultural groups (Marrone, 2012). According to the Center for Community Health and Development (2017), valuing diversity includes institutional recognition, acceptance, and respect for cultural differences. The practices of organizations who adapt well to diversity clearly reflect those values.

Organizational willingness to conduct ongoing self-assessment is crucial to sustaining culturally competent practices because culture and language evolve and change over time (Marks, 2007; Marrone, 2012). Surveys and discussion can elucidate organizational norms and identify areas for growth. Feedback from patients and clinicians can be instrumental in planning and implementing improvements. Organizational changes should be transparent and support reciprocal communication to promote learning within the organization and between the organization and those that it serves (Chiriboga & Hernandez, 2015; Marrone, 2012).

Many models of organizational cultural competence discuss the importance of institutionalizing cultural knowledge (Center for Community Health and Development, 2017). This is the process of continually obtaining cultural knowledge and integrating it into all aspects of policymaking, administration, practice, and service delivery (Marrone, 2012). Ongoing staff training is required to increase cultural knowledge and to be able to apply cultural skills. The Center for Community Health and Development (2017) suggests that organizational policies should be sensitive to cultural diversity. This could include aspects such as facility dress codes or permission for others (e.g., family members, traditional healers) to attend medical visits. Any type of literature or educational materials can promote inclusion by depicting accurate images of people from many different cultures, including those with disabilities. Institutionalizing cultural knowledge is only possible through the purposeful and ongoing involvement of people from diverse cultures who utilize and work within the system and their communities (Center for Community Health and Development, 2017).

## Community Connections

Culturally competent organizations develop and maintain close ties to diverse cultural communities whose members they serve (Chiriboga & Hernandez, 2015). By inviting community leaders from target groups to join the organization's board of directors, for example, members of the local disability community will have better representation and opportunity for input into plans for future development (Chiriboga & Hernandez, 2015). Including representatives from underserved populations (such as disabled people of color and with LGBT+ indentities) in planning and evaluation efforts will allow organizations to evolve in ways that are compatible with the values of the community and promote shared responsibility for improvements (Chiriboga & Hernandez, 2015).

Community partner involvement is key to addressing the dynamics of diversity and promoting effective cross-cultural interactions. As discussed earlier in regard to clinical cultural humility, the historical context in which diverse groups interact with health care systems can influence current perceptions. For example, people with disabilities have long been institutionalized, deprived of their freedoms, and excluded from community integration. Disabled infants were sometimes denied care and left to die or were euthanized. Whether or not those particular practices still occur or the institutions still exist, cultural mistrust remains and is passed on generationally (Center for Community Health and Development, 2017). Conversely, these contexts are unknown or minimized by the dominant culture. Organizations must heed the importance of these dynamics to be effective with diverse cultures. Memories or bad experiences can persist, and if the target community is not kept abreast of pertinent organizational changes, they are unlikely to re-engage. For example, disabled people who identify with disability culture are likely to seek out contact with other disabled people in their communities as a main source of information and advice. If a pregnant participant at a Center for Independent Living learns that a certain hospital alerted the child welfare system years ago when a blind woman gave birth, she will probably take that into consideration in choosing which facility she will use for maternal health care. Unless the organization makes active efforts to change and openly communicates their commitment to improvement, negative actions will continue to plague them. In this way, organizations benefit from anticipating and responding to cultural growth and change (Center for Community Health and Development, 2017).

## Conclusion

Cultural humility is crucial effective work with disabled people. It is clear that quality diversity training that includes information about disability culture is lacking in health care training and education (Eddey & Robey, 2005; Niemeier et al., 2003). In addition, there is a paucity of research examining the effectiveness and outcomes of cultural competence education programs (Chipps et al., 2008). From existing literature, we know that addressing self-examination, cross-cultural knowledge, and communication skills are important aspects of cultural competence education and training (Betancourt et al., 2003). Future studies should use consistent and objective measures, sound methodologies, and include disability among diverse intersectional identities.

Clinicians who wish to improve their cultural humility must strive for a posture of openness and flexibility to work toward acceptance of differences and to strengthen similarities (Campinha-Bacote, 2002). Individual growth is only one piece of the broader picture of cultural competence; organizational and institutional account-ability are required to effect meaningful change over time (Balcazar et al., 2009; Betancourt et al., 2003). The ongoing process of learning and critical self-reflection must address power imbalances that underlie inequality and oppression (Fisher-Borne et al., 2015). Instead of falling prey to simplistic solutions that only encompass awareness and understanding while ignoring systemic inequalities, health care providers are called upon to be advocates and act as agents for change.

One must never commit the cardinal sin of confusing
absence of evidence with evidence of absence.

—H. L. TEUBER (1969, p. 19)

# 8 Providing Culturally Competent Testing and Assessment

PSYCHOLOGICAL ASSESSMENT IS an integral function of psychologists. Rather than a simple process of test administration and scoring, psychological assessment is a complex, integrative, and conceptual activity (Krishnamurthy et al, 2004). In conducting a truly comprehensive psychological assessment, clinicians must attempt to answer questions from referral sources and solve complex problems by integrating multiple informants including test data; educational, occupational, military, and medical records; and information gathered from behavioral observations and interviews with the patient and family members (Vanderploeg, 2000). The American Psychological Association (APA, 2012) "Guidelines for Assessment of and Intervention With Persons With Disabilities" discusses the utility of three different approaches to psychological assessment with disabled people: quantitative, qualitative, and ecological. Quantitative assessment is considered to be the "gold standard" in psychology, with empirically derived measures that are statistically validated, standardized, and normed. Qualitative assessment focuses on clinician observations and interview, with both the individual and collateral sources of information. An ecological approach, like qualitative assessment, involves observation, but instead of an office or clinic setting, ecological assessment takes place in a natural environment such as the person's home or community. A fourth approach, very useful in rehabilitation settings, is functional assessment (Dijkers & Greenwald, 2012) that often involves collaboration with other health care disciplines such as occupational and physical therapy or speech-language pathology (Gaylord-Ross & Browder, 1991). Functional assessment focuses on real-world daily life skills that someone with a disability uses to maximize functioning (Dijkers & Greenwald, 2012; Gaylord-Ross & Browder, 1991).

The APA has implored psychologists to gain appropriate cultural knowledge, awareness, and skills and to acknowledge the limitations of conventional psychological testing to competently assess individuals from diverse populations, including persons with disabilities; this is considered a tenet of ethical practice (APA, 2002). It is imperative that in assessing people with disabilities, clinicians take care to select suitable methods that are psychometrically valid, impartial, and thorough and that are not spuriously affected by factors other than the ones the test purports to measure (APA, 2012). For example, although a person with tetraplegia may be able to manipulate the stimulus materials from the Wechsler Block Design subtest, he or she will likely do so slowly and awkwardly, thereby losing possible points for rapid execution. The *Standards for Educational and Psychological Testing*, a collaborative effort of the American Educational Research Association (AERA), American Psychological Association (APA), and the National Council on Measurement in Education (NCME) (2014), states that clinicians must act to establish fairness and accuracy in testing individuals with disabilities. These efforts are also mandated by relevant law, including Section 504 of the Rehabilitation Act (1973), the Individuals With Disabilities Education Act (IDEA, 1997), and the Americans With Disabilities Act (ADA, 1990) and ADA Amendments Act (2008).

There are a number of important issues related to psychological assessment of disabled people, including the overall approach to assessment, test selection, administration, interpretation, and documentation (Caplan & Shechter, 1995; Hill-Briggs, Dial, Morere, & Joyce, 2007). In this chapter, I will provide an overview of considerations for cultural competence for conducting psychological assessment with people with disabilities.

Several problems have been noted to affect the psychological assessment of disabled people including the presence of bias, unreliability, and lack of validity (AERA, APA, & NCME, 2014). Many disabilities, including physical, sensory, and intellectual disabilities, can affect aspects of assessment including performance on psychological and neurocognitive tests (Hill-Briggs et al., 2007). Another complicating factor is the high prevalence of comorbid conditions or secondary disabilities (Hill-Briggs et al., 2007). It is critical that the examiner consider the individual's disability, and how it may or may not relate to other functions, and delineate a strategy to ensure the appropriate construct is being measured (Olkin & Pledger, 2003). For example, some psychometric tests can be confounded by disability-related symptoms or characteristics such as fatigue and pain that could artificially inflate a measure of depression (R. B. Hughes, Robinson-Whelen, Taylor, Peterson, & Nosek, 2005; Radnitz, Bockian, & Moran, 2000). A motor functioning disability that affects fine motor control could produce results that falsely indicate cognitive impairment (Hill-Briggs et al., 2007). Examiners who do not take these issues into consideration risk drawing misleading inferences, reaching inaccurate conclusions, and making unsuitable treatment recommendations (Horin, Hernandez, & Donoso, 2012). Although quantitative assessment can yield valuable information (and some measures can be administered in standardized fashion—e.g., Wechsler Verbal subtests with the aforementioned person with tetraplegia), it is important to account for the limitations of psychometric practices such as summed scores and the ways in which scientifically derived scores can mislead (Caplan & Shechter, 1995; Lezak, 2002). Assessment results have real and serious implications for people with disabilities; receipt of required services or support can hinge on these findings, which affects disabled people's lives considerably.

## Universal Design

Universal design (UD) is a concept that was borrowed from barrier-free design in the field of architecture; as accessibility legislation evolved, architects were challenged to meet the needs of people with disabilities in ways that were both economical and appealing to businesses (Story, Mueller, & Mace, 1998). UD emerged when it became clear that improvements in accessibility not only reduced barriers for disabled people but also benefited everyone.

In 2012, a meme created by Craig Froehle to demonstrate the difference between the concepts of equality and equity "went viral" on the Internet (Froehle, 2016). He posted it to his blog, but as it was shared widely, several people adapted the meme, and one modification became a helpful visual aid to depict UD. The origin and source of this particular adapted image is unknown, but this version has three small pictures of three White people of different heights trying to watch a baseball game. In the first image, each of the three has one crate to stand on to see the game over a fence, representing "equality." The crate is superfluous for the tall person, but it enables the midheight person to see over the wooden fence; yet even with a crate, the shortest person still cannot see over the fence. This is a world without disability accommodations. In the second image, the tall person has no crate, the midheight person has one crate, and the shortest person has two crates, facilitating "equity." This is a world with reasonable accommodations. In the third image, all three people are standing on the ground, there are no crates, and the wooden fence has been replaced with a transparent chain-link fence; the caption reads, "the cause of inequity has been addressed and the systemic barrier removed." This is a world of UD, where the focus is on the interaction between the individual and the environment, and systems and

EQUALITY    EQUITY    LIBERATION

Credit: Center for Story-Based Strategy. (n.d.). Why we need to step into #the4thbox. Retrieved from: https://www.storybasedstrategy.org/the4thbox

FIGURE 8.1. Equality, equity, liberation.
*Credit:* A collaboration between the Center for Story-Based Strategy and the Interactive Institute for Social Change.

structures are created with access in mind. As a step further, the Center for Story-Based Strategy collaborated with the Interactive Institute for Social Change (n.d.) to illustrate a new version of the meme, as shown in Figure 8.1, using people of color and making the third image completely barrier free. In this image, there is no fence at all and the subtitle reads, "liberation."

The UD concept has now spread beyond mobility to encompass other categories of human ability such as cognition, vision, hearing and speech, and body function as well as other realms of access including education (Story et al., 1998). UD is a trending concept in the field of instructional design; UD means proactively valuing diversity and deliberately engaging with problem-solving practices to enable students of all cultures, backgrounds, and abilities to learn effectively (Edyburn, 2010). The UD approach to test development involves intentional consideration of individual differences in test design and creating testing environments. Implementing UD preserves the construct intended to be measured and does not compromise validity; in fact, Ketterlin-Geller (2005) recommended the use of rigorous methods such as differential item functioning (DIF) and item response theory (IRT) modeling to detect possible bias and help ensure accurate measurement of the construct. For guidance on the process of constructing a universally designed test, see Ketterlin-Geller (2005).

Much of the onus in improving access to fair quantitative measurement falls to test developers. The *Standards for Educational and Psychological Testing* encourage the use of UD processes, which allows for maximum usability regardless of membership in diverse groups (AERA, APA, & NCME, 2014). Universally designed tests emphasize clearly defined constructs, with carefully selected content, tasks, response methods, and testing procedures so that unrelated examinee factors, such as physical impairments, do not impede access or affect test validity (AERA, APA, & NCME, 2014). Even with advances in test development, psychologists who provide psychological assessment to persons with disabilities must be mindful to do so in a fair and unbiased manner.

## Assessment Planning

There are many considerations when planning to conduct psychological assessment with a disabled person. Consistent with a biopsychosocial model of disability, examiners should account for the interaction between the individual and his or her environment (Bruyère & Peterson, 2005). The most useful information that can be gleaned in the process of assessment is related to how the person functions over time, in varied situations, and in response to changing environmental demands (Bruyère, Van Looy, & Peterson, 2005; Reed et al., 2005). Sometimes disability can affect the process, such as in the case of disability-related fatigue or decreased stamina. Lezak (2002) notes that in such circumstances, the clinician may decide to prioritize the most important questions for examination or plan to break up the assessment into multiple shorter sessions. It is essential to take a collaborative approach with the disabled person and his or her family or support persons to get input as to the optimal strategy for completing the assessment process.

### Test Selection

The selection of tests and measurement tools is one of the most important parts of the assessment process and even more so in considering what to administer to individuals with disabilities (Pullin, 2002). In one study of psychological assessment practices, Horin et al. (2012) found that the majority of clinicians surveyed (62.7%) endorsed taking disability considerations into account when choosing assessment measures. Judicious test selection can allow the clinician to obtain the most valuable and accurate data (APA, 2012). Ideal tests will have an established record of valid use for people with disabilities, but this is rarely possible (Geisinger, 1998; Pullin, 2002). The APA (2012) advises that psychologists refrain from using tests without known or adequate validity for use with persons with disabilities. To decide whether or not an instrument is suitable for use with disabled people, clinicians must analyze the validity information regarding its use with people with particular disabilities, just as one would for any specific population (AERA, APA, & NCME, 2014). When considering using a measure developed for use with the general population with a disabled individual, clinicians should consult the technical manual and/or contact the publisher, who may be able to provide further information (Geisinger, 1998). Lezak (2002) emphasized the importance of clinicians having the freedom to explore the full range of human behavior during assessment. Often, assessment is reduced to the interpretation of a simple data set, but no statistically determined standards can capture the complexity of functioning and ability (Caplan & Shechter, 1995). As a result, quantitative measures ought to be supplemented by other approaches such as qualitative and functional assessments. It is because of the required level of intricacy and reasoning that psychologists receive advanced education to conduct assessment, and specialty training in areas such as rehabilitation and neuropsychology. Psychologists must be able to be creative and flexible in assessment of persons with disabilities instead of rigidly adhering to standardized instruments and available norms (Caplan & Schechter, 1995). To be responsive to diverse individuals whose characteristics may not be accurately reflected through examination through customary means, Lezak (2002) recommends assessment in the tradition of Luria (1966), whose approach was lauded for its creativity, flexibility, and applicability to intervention.

Disability status can considerably obscure the meaning of test results (APA, 2012). If the examiner intends to utilize an instrument to assess the extent of disability, such as achievement testing for an individual with a learning disability, there may be no threats to validity. However, if the disability is not the intended target of assessment but affects performance on tasks meant to measure a different construct, tests cannot be administered and interpreted in the same way as with nondisabled people, because the validity is compromised (Hill-Briggs et al., 2007). For example, someone whose upper extremities are affected by a spinal cord injury is likely to perform poorly on a pencil-and-paper measure of cognitive speed as a result of the requirement of fine motor skills.

*Norms*

One of the most difficult challenges in the assessment of people with disabilities is the issue of standardized norms in psychological testing (Horin et al., 2012). Most psychological and neurocognitive tests are normed on groups that do not include disabled people (Olkin, 1999). Ideally, instruments will include individuals with disabilities in the general norm groups or provide separate norms for disabled examinees. However, typically standardized assessment instruments lack appropriate norms for disability populations, in part because they are difficult to develop given the heterogeneity in the disability community and problems obtaining an adequate sample size for particular disabilities (Hill-Briggs et al., 2007).

The norms an examiner uses to evaluate an individual's scores will determine how the results are interpreted, so the exclusion of disabled persons from normative samples is highly problematic. Lezak (2002) points out the weaknesses of reliance on published norms; there are sometimes drastic inconsistencies between norms for closely related groups, such as age ranges. Furthermore, some norms cannot be applied to people who are not members of the majority or dominant groups on which norms were based, because they yield a distorted picture of functioning and prevent any detailed examination of subscales or subscores (Lezak, 2002).

Lezak (2002) points out that numerical scores with given statistical properties are hardly the only source of normative data. Again, alternative approaches such as ecological and functional assessment can provide rich data about performance on activities of daily living, self-directed behavior, recognition and awareness, directional sense, use of language, or other tasks. Lezak (2002) recommends that these practical behavioral assessments, though not a substitute for quantitative measures, can provide supplemental information, particularly when observations are replicable over time and across settings.

### Batteries

Some psychologists use established test batteries, or sets of measurement tools that have been rigorously normed and validated on large samples of people. Lezak (2002) notes a number of disadvantages to the use of standard batteries with persons with disabilities. First, because all measures are generally given to all examinees, batteries run the risk of either over- or undermeasuring neurocognitive performance and/or emotional issues. Second, the rigidity of batteries may make it difficult to add tests when early results suggest the need to assess a construct in more depth or to eliminate unnecessary tests if adequate information has been gleaned. Lezak (2002) contends that "without adding specialized examination techniques or tests as questions arise, relevant problems can be missed" (p. 342). Finally, test batteries make it more difficult to provide testing accommodations, discussed next in detail.

## Test Administration and Scoring

Most standardized measures require adherence to precise procedures for administration and scoring. Decisions to alter protocols require thoughtful consideration, information gathering, and ultimately disclosure and justification. However, alterations of test procedures do not necessarily compromise the validity of the administration. As rehabilitation and neuropsychologists know, the purpose of the assessment is to assess the patient's "best performance" (Caplan & Shechter, 1995;

Geisinger, 1998; Vanderploeg, 2000). As a result, sometimes modification of standardized test procedures for persons with disabilities is warranted. For example, an administration may be adapted for limit testing when assessing persons with severe impairments (Caplan & Shechter, 1995; Geisinger, 1998; Lezak, 2002; Vanderploeg, 2000). In other instances, alteration is not appropriate, such as when the purpose of the assessment is to measure the impact of disability-related factors or a test of technical skills applicable to specific job functions (AERA, APA, & NCME, 2014).

There are two types of alterations to the testing environment, procedures, format, or content. *Accommodations* are changes to improve access to the test that do not affect the particular construct being measured, whereas *modifications* do affect the identified construct (AERA, APA, & NCME, 2014). Consequently, a modification poses a threat to validity, whereas an accommodation does not. Psychologists must determine if accommodations are appropriate and differentiate between accommodations and modifications (APA, 2012). Comparability of test scores is preserved with an accommodation (AERA, APA, & NCME, 2014), so an accommodated measure should yield more valid results than if the same measure were not accommodated, so long as the accommodation does not fundamentally alter the construct that is being measured (APA, 2012). Adaptations can include (a) adjustments to the test format (e.g., oral instead of reading for blind individuals), (b) changing the response format, (c) additional time or rest breaks to complete testing, (d) omission of subtests, (e) use of alternate forms if available, and (f) modifying the testing setting (AERA, APA, & NCME, 2014).

Whenever a test administration or response format breaks from standardization, the validity of normative data and interpretation guidelines is compromised, and accurate interpretation depends entirely on advanced understanding of multifaceted influences including disability and other diversity variables (Hill-Briggs et al., 2007). Horin et al. (2012) found that the majority of test examiners studied reported they do not make adaptations to test administration, relying on standardization instructions to glean reliable and valid results. Administration of alternate test formats was the most commonly provided disability accommodation such as oral administration, enlarged print, or Braille (Horin et al., 2012). The authors also found that providers who endorsed having higher degrees of freedom in their ability to select tests reported more use of adaptations and modifications based on disability than those who endorsed less freedom, indicating that some psychologists are more comfortable deviating from the use of batteries and prescribed norms in the assessment process.

Psychologists should give careful consideration to the degree to which any adaptations could affect the validity of the assessment. Just as with selecting appropriate norms, psychologists should ascertain if a test publisher endorses the use of particular accommodations for people with certain disabilities (APA, 2012). There is limited research on the effects of test accommodations, so there are no readily available normative data for common modifications or standardized accommodations (Hill-Briggs et al., 2007; Sireci, Li, & Scarpati, 2003). For example, the Wechsler Adult Intelligence Scale, Fourth Edition (WAIS-IV) manual denotes that although accommodation for disability is allowed, there are no "disability-normative" data available for comparison (Wechsler, 2014). The WAIS-IV manual guides examiners to omit certain subtests and weight other subtests more heavily, depending on the particular person and his or her disability needs (Hill-Briggs et al., 2007; Horin et al., 2012; Wechsler, 2014).

A wide range of potential accommodations can facilitate accessibility to a measure, depending on the type and extent of the disability (AERA, APA, & NCME, 2014). Accommodations must be made on a case-by-case basis, rooted in information about disability and awareness of appropriate accommodations for each particular person's impairment(s) (Hill-Briggs et al., 2007). It is beneficial to minimize alterations to only what is necessary and preserve as much of the standardized content and process as possible. It is impossible to explore all of the possible strategies and combinations of methods that can be used to accommodate specific measures, because each accommodation is in response not only to a specific disability but also to individual differences, particular constructs, and the purpose of assessment (AERA, APA, & NCME, 2014).

A robust literature base exists regarding specific assessment challenges, such as providing motor-free neuropsychological assessment to people with spinal cord injury or other disabilities that affect upper extremity functioning (Hill-Briggs et al., 2007). For individuals with intellectual disabilities, pictorial representations of responses can be substituted for Likert-type scales (Hartley & MacLean, 2006). The purpose of accommodations is not to provide an unfair advantage, but rather to remove barriers that are not germane to the construct, in essence equaling the metaphorical playing field for people with disabilities (AERA, APA, & NCME, 2014). Some of the most commonly used assessment accommodations are listed in Table 8.1.

In some instances, more significant modifications that alter the testing construct are necessary to enable minimal access to a particular type of measurement (AERA, APA, & NCME, 2014). In this way, examiners can glean limited information regarding the individual's performance on the specific construct. In these cases, the construct has been affected, and interpretation should not be based on standardized norms or established cutoff scores (AERA, APA, & NCME, 2014). Essentially, a modification should be treated as a new instrument, with validation efforts

TABLE 8.1.

Examples of Assessment Accommodations

| | |
|---|---|
| Testing environment | Alternative seating options, arm- or footrests |
| | Size and position of table (variable height, tilt) |
| | Accessible room with adequate space, near restroom, food available |
| | Suitable lighting (including dimming for those bothered by bright lights) |
| Use of adaptive equipment | Weights or fasteners to secure materials |
| | Writing utensil grips or holders, handles, or clips |
| | Head stick, light beam, switching mechanism |
| Testing procedures | Extend timing or adjustment of time limits |
| | Page turning |
| | Use of an unaffected nondominant hand |
| | Rest breaks and positioning changes |
| | Schedule during optimal time of day with regard to physical discomfort |
| | Schedule brief sessions |
| | Select substitute tests or alternative assessments unaffected by disability |
| Presentation format | Text to Braille |
| | Oral administration and responding rather than self-administration |
| | Text or pictorial magnification |
| Test content | Use only portions of the test unaffected by disability |
| | Adjust items to lower reading level |
| | Skip problematic items |

undertaken and cautious interpretation through clinical judgment and knowledge gained through experience (Hill-Briggs et al., 2007).

The *Standards for Educational and Psychological Testing* recognizes that it is challenging and complicated to delineate an accommodation from a modification and to determine the comparability of scores, particularly when the research is so sparse (AERA, APA, & NCME, 2014). Furthermore, not every disabled person requires alterations when taking tests; many disabilities will not interfere with the purpose of testing. Professional experience, training, and judgment are essential in making such decisions.

## Interpretation and Report Writing

Interpretation of the test scores of persons with disabilities, particularly those that were administered with accommodations, requires (a) thorough knowledge about the examinee's disability, (b) a clear understanding of the construct measured by the test, and (c) insight into how the two factors interact. Horin et al. (2012) found that examiners were more willing to consider unique disability factors during the interpretation and report-writing aspects of assessment than they were to use accommodations during testing. Disability-specific information necessary for examiners includes disability etiology, age of onset, functional abilities, and comorbid health conditions or other disabilities (Hill-Briggs et al., 2007). All of these factors can influence interpretation (e.g., the examinee experienced pain during the assessment or was experiencing psychological distress).

Ethically, psychologists have a duty to note in assessment reports the use of any accommodation or modification, along with any interpretative cautions (APA, 2002, 2011). Culturally competent psychologists are thoughtful in the ways in which they do so. A carefully worded discussion should address the validity of the scores, rationale for interpretations, and intended uses of the results (AERA, APA, & NCME, 2014). If modifications were made that may have affected the reliability or the validity of test scores, so that the scores obtained are not comparable with those attained via standardized administrations, this should be clearly communicated to report consumers.

Some examiners use a technique called "flagging" test scores that resulted from either an accommodated or modified test administration by placing an asterisk next to them in the written report (AERA, APA, & NCME, 2014). The extent to which this practice is permissible under law is not entirely clear, but disability advocates vehemently object to flagging as a means of designating accommodated results (APA, 2012). Flagging may increase the likelihood of discrimination against people with disabilities, because their capabilities may be unfairly discounted. When it is substantiated that the scores from accommodated test administrations are comparable, it not appropriate to flag such scores (AERA, APA, & NCME, 2014). Lezak (2002) cautions that laypersons can misconstrue scores in ways that can harm disabled persons by denying them needed services or supports. She suggests psychologists use descriptors of performance levels and percentile ranges rather than including scores in assessment reports (Lezak, 2002), although there is as yet little consensus about the quantitative correlates of such labels (Caplan, 1995; Guilmette, Hagan, & Giuliano, 2008). In any case, examiners should communicate clearly the complexity of all contributing factors to assessment results, acknowledge the limitations of the findings, and discuss possible alternative hypotheses (Hill-Briggs et al., 2007).

## Assessing Deaf People

Psychologists who provide psychological assessment to Deaf people should be aware of Deaf culture and significant linguistic differences from non-Deaf people. Rather than someone with an audiological deficit, a Deaf person is a culturally diverse person whose identity can affect his or her assessment results (Freeman, 1989). Common issues are examiners' assumptions that solely using nonverbal tests, having a Deaf examinee read instructions, or involving an interpreter are adequate accommodation to account for the language barrier; this is not the case (Hill-Briggs et al., 2007).

Verbally mediated instruments should not be used with Deaf examinees, because lack of familiarity with spoken English can confound the results. Although it may seem like a person fluent in American Sign Language (ASL) could take a test in English by having an interpreter translate the material into ASL, this is not a valid way to measure his or her abilities (Hill-Briggs et al., 2007). Because of the complexities of language, such as sentence structure and the alphabet, it is not safe to assume a one-to-one correlation between ASL and English; consequently, the examiner could inadvertently measure something entirely different than intended (Hill-Briggs et al., 2007). Moreover, language can influence test performance, even if language proficiency is not explicitly required, such as an examinee who must read instructions to a math problem in English (Freeman, 1989).

Although Deaf individuals vary in their reading skills and may have oral abilities, people who primarily communicate in ASL or other sign languages or dialects should be tested in their native language, preferably by a fluent clinician (Hill-Briggs et al., 2007). If an interpreter is employed, he or she must have training in the process of psychological assessment and experience with mental health interpretation (AERA, APA, & NCME). Furthermore, the clinician must be familiar with the cultural background of the examinee and know how to utilize an interpreter competently (AERA, APA, & NCME, 2014; Hill-Briggs et al., 2007). Any time English is translated into ASL, the information has to be cognitively transformed, which can place some of the mental load onto the interpreter (Hill-Briggs et al., 2007). Furthermore, the interpreter may subtly adjust or supplement instructions and responses inadvertently for clarity or ease of understanding, which can lead to inaccuracies and distortions in test results (Hill-Briggs et al., 2007).

The Wechsler performance scales have been used extensively with the Deaf but permit only limited conclusions about intelligence (Hill-Briggs et al., 2007; Wechsler, 2014). Additionally, results of intelligence testing of the Deaf population have not consistently correlated with other related measures such as school performance (Freeman, 1989).

Hill-Briggs et al. (2007) recommend that examiners of Deaf individuals limit visual distractions in the testing setting and minimize auditory interference, because many Deaf people have some residual hearing. They also caution against having Deaf examinees close their eyes or wear a blindfold during perceptual-motor tasks; this alienates the individual from all means of communication and is considered culturally inappropriate.

Personality assessment of Deaf individuals is also affected by cultural considerations (Freeman, 1989; Hill-Briggs et al., 2007). When using conventional inventories (e.g., the Minnesota Multiphasic Personality Inventory [MMPI-2]), it is important to take into account verbal and reading skill level and English proficiency (Freeman, 1989). Results should be interpreted cautiously because of cultural differences; for example, endorsement of items about hearing voices or believing that the television is talking to oneself is not a valid indicator of psychotic thought processes in Deaf people (Hill-Briggs et al., 2007). Disjointed sentences or unusual syntax can also be false indicators of psychopathology (Freeman, 1989).

Other potential cultural misunderstandings when assessing a Deaf examinee include misinterpretation of dramatic movements and affect commonly utilized in Deaf culture to express emotion (Misiaszek et al., 1985). Moreover, Deaf people often have an above-average external locus of control and may be disconnected from mainstream media and society in favor of immersion in Deaf culture and companionship (Becker & Jauregui, 1985; Dowaliby, Burke, & McKee, 1983). According to Freeman (1989), Deaf people can be misconstrued as inflexible, odd, or self-centered, which can render unbiased diagnosis difficult (Holm, 1987). Effective communication is imperative during an assessment, but due to discomfort, either the examiner or the examinee may hesitate to disclose lack of understanding, leading to erroneous conclusions (Freeman, 1989). Providers conducting psychological assessment should work to enhance their knowledge and familiarity with Deaf culture and norms to be maximally effective.

## Assessing Blind People

Hill-Briggs et al. (2007) note that blind people and those with visual impairments are a heterogeneous population; indeed, like blindness, visual impairments have various congenital and acquired etiologies including trauma and disease. Providers must not amalgamate together all individuals who identify as blind or visually impaired. A standard instrument—the Comprehensive Vocational Evaluation System (CVES) battery (Hill-Briggs et al., 2007)—was developed to address some of the challenges in testing this population. Unlike traditional batteries, the CVES was created specifically to accommodate a low- to no-vision population, offering a relevant normative database not typically available for people with disabilities.

## High-Stakes Assessment

It is beyond the scope of this chapter to delve into the intricacies of specialized assessments for medicolegal purposes such as capacity to make medical decisions or manage finances, or parenting evaluations in custody disputes. However, these contexts are some of the most critical because the outcome of such evaluations can have drastic, and sometimes devastating, effects on disabled people. These assessments can be highly contentious (APA, 2012), and the lives of one or more people may be substantially affected by the results (e.g., custody loss, forfeiture of legal rights to make one's own medical decisions). Psychologists are challenged in these cases to balance ethical considerations that can at times seem to be in conflict with one another (APA, 2002). Examiners also must become aware of their own value system and consider that the values of their disabled patients may diverge markedly from their own (Bickenbach, 2012). It should not be assumed that disabled individuals cherish mainstream societal principles such as independence and self-sufficiency (Longmore, 2003). It is imperative, then, that special care is taken to ensure that the rights of disabled people are fully honored and diverse identities taken into consideration. In this way, psychologists may serve as effective advocates for their patients with disabilities.

One area that has been particularly problematic is that of custody evaluations where one parent has a disability. Parenting capacity examinations are far too often conducted without any attention to cultural considerations. For example, a parent with mobility limitations deserves to have a functional assessment in the home environment with appropriate accommodations in place (APA, 2012). Instead, examiners who evaluate only in an office setting can fall prey to stereotypical assumptions that the nondisabled parent is of higher quality on the basis of disability, or lack thereof (Benjet, Azar, & Kuersten-Hogan, 2003). Saini (2008) found that the majority of custody evaluation examiners have had no relevant disability-specific training in performing evaluations with parents with disabilities.

A 2012 report by the National Council on Disability (NCD) revealed that the rate of separation of children from their disabled parents is disproportionately high. Unfortunately, the process of determining custody is heavily based on assessments that are biased and on conjecture stemming from stereotypes (Andrews & Ayers, 2016; NCD, 2012). In family court proceedings disabled parents are rarely offered accommodations or adaptations that would be appropriate for their disability

(NCD, 2012). Even though adaptive parenting tools and supports could allow parents to function effectively, families are routinely and needlessly separated through the legal system (Andrews & Ayers, 2016).

Take, for example, the instance of parents with an intellectual disability, who are one of the disability groups most vulnerable to child custody loss (NCD, 2012). Stereotypes about the inability of intellectually disabled adults to care for children are widespread, but the literature does not support this contention; in fact, research suggests that most parents with intellectual disabilities, with appropriate support in place, are able to learn adequate skills to raise children (Andrews & Ayers, 2016). Psychologists trained in cultural aspects of disability are well equipped to provide fair and unbiased evaluations that allow intellectually disabled parents the opportunity to demonstrate their child-rearing abilities on equal footing with their nondisabled peers (APA, 2013).

## Application of the International Classification of Functioning, Disability, and Health

Recall from Chapter 2 that the 2001 World Health Organization (WHO) International Classification of Functioning, Disability, and Health (ICF) can be used to conceptualize disability through a biopsychosocial framework. The ICF can help clinicians formulate the ways in which impairments (e.g., spinal cord injury), activity limitations (e.g., upper and lower extremity mobility limitations), and participation restrictions (e.g., social isolation) shape a disabled examinee. The dynamic relation of these with the individual's contextual factors, including environment and personal characteristics, illustrates the domains that must be considered in the planning and execution of a culturally competent assessment. Through assessment, environmental factors such as technology and support services can be identified as means by which to improve the individual's life. Similarly, personal factors identified in an assessment (e.g., personality traits) can help a disabled person better understand him- or herself and allow health care providers to learn to intervene in ways that are both sensitive and effective. The ICF provides a comprehensive framework to guide understanding of assessment findings.

## Conclusion

To provide culturally competent assessment to people with disabilities, psychologists are encouraged to utilize multiple methods of evaluation and integrate data from several sources (APA, 2012). Quantitative, qualitative, ecological, and functional approaches can all contribute to a fuller picture of a disabled person's capabilities and attributes. The APA (2012) recommends that psychologists minimize bias by increasing awareness of their own prejudices about disability, explore all possible hypotheses about assessment results, and defer making conclusions until all data is available for integration (Sandoval, Frisby, Geisinger, Scheuneman, & Grenier, 1998).

In addressing the referral question, culturally competent psychologists balance pertinent psychometric, social, clinical, and disability-related issues with distinct individual characteristics (Mackelprang & Salsgiver, 2016; Schultz & Stewart, 2008). It is both a science and an art to integrate the multiple factors in the ICF into meaningful conclusions and recommendations. Instead of reductive and simplistic formulations, culturally competent health care providers endeavor to fully comprehend and meaningfully organize the complexities of the physical, psychological, and social aspects of the lives of persons with disabilities by increasing their training and relevant experience and consulting pertinent literature (Elliott & Umlauf, 1995; Groth-Marnat, 2009). It is crucial that each disabled person's strengths and weaknesses are given full and balanced consideration. Purely deficit-based approaches do not demonstrate cultural competence.

To achieve these outcomes, psychologists must have both the competence and the flexibility to be completely responsive to the needs of disabled examinees (Lezak, 2002; Luria, 1966). To be effective, examiners need to think outside the box and be willing to be creative. Progress has been made in test development, but the field is far from the complete adoption of UD (AERA, APA, & NCME, 2014). Persons with disabilities should be included in research on psychological testing so that better norms are developed (Hill-Briggs et al., 2007) and new instruments can be created to provide access to measurement for all.

There is something especially penetrative about a hurtful experience, such as being left out, which remains unseen by the social world; others continue their business with little sign of dissonance. Pains which are chronically disregarded are likely to become felt as personal shortcomings, as social contradictions are translated into problems of the body or personality"

—WATERMEYER AND SWARTZ (2016, pp. 274–275)

# 9   Providing Culturally Competent Intervention

MANY PSYCHOLOGISTS LACK sufficient knowledge about disability issues, likely because they have limited experience working with disabled clients (Olkin, 2017). Providers may feel discomfort working with disabled people and feel unsure about how to respond, resulting in vulnerability to making erroneous assumptions and potentially harming the therapeutic relationships (American Psychological Association [APA], 2012). In this chapter, I will discuss some general considerations for culturally competent psychological intervention with persons with disabilities. I will cover issues specific to disability and also discuss similarities between disabled clients and their nondisabled peers. Finally, I will review the evidence base for interventions applicable to disability populations. This chapter is not a list of disability etiquette strategies or a prescription for certain treatments. The goal is to provide a foundation from which to make clinical decisions in unique and complicated situations in a culturally effective manner.

## Ethical and Legal Issues

### Relevant Laws

Clinicians should know the relevant laws that affect patients with disabilities and protect their rights as consumers of health care, including psychological services (APA, 2012). Title III of the Americans With Disabilities Act (ADA) promotes accessibility for "places of public accommodations"—that is, any public or private practice that offers care to the public. This means that clinicians cannot ignore, deny services, exclude, or segregate those with disabilities. The same services should be offered to disabled and nondisabled persons alike; charging extra fees for making accommodations is rarely acceptable. For example, if a patient requires an American Sign Language (ASL) interpreter to receive therapy, the therapist should not charge the Deaf person for the interpreter (Leigh, Corbett, Gutman, & Morere, 1996). It also means that health care providers must eliminate barriers to access to care to the extent that it is "readily achievable" based on the size and resources of the business (ADA, 1990). Federal tax credits that can cover up to half of the cost of modification to enhance accessibility to persons with disabilities are available to small businesses.

The "readily achievable" language is one of several regrettable gray areas in the ADA that make it difficult to enforce. Another potential loophole is language that suggests providers may not need to meet ADA standards if doing so causes an "undue burden" or "fundamentally alters" the service. Unfortunately, recent legislation—the ADA Education and Reform Act of 2018 that passed in the House of Representatives on February 15, 2018, on a 225-to-192 vote—has threatened to erode the ADA even further. This bill requires that those wishing to sue businesses in federal court over an ADA public accommodations violation must first deliver a written notice to that business detailing the illegal barrier(s) to access. That business then has 60 days to devise a plan to address the complaints and an additional 60 days to take action. Proponents say the legislation is aimed at curbing unscrupulous lawyers who seek profit by threatening businesses with litigation without actually seeking to improve access. It is unclear how the bill will fare in the U.S. Senate, but activists say the bill, if enacted, would essentially gut the ADA's provisions dealing with public accommodations by removing any incentive that businesses have to comply with the law before a complaint is filed. The Consortium for Citizens With Disabilities, a coalition of disability rights organizations, issued a statement that argued, "We know of no other law that outlaws discrimination but permits entities to discriminate with impunity until victims experience that discrimination and educate the entities perpetrating it about their obligations not to discriminate" (Consortium for Citizens With Disabilities, 2017).

*Ethical Standards*

Clients with disabilities must provide consent in the manner prescribed for all patients by Standards 3.10, 9.03, and 10.01 of the APA (2002) ethics code, with the exception of specified activities such as the evaluation of decisional capacity (e.g., in cases of severe neurocognitive disorders; APA, 2012). Special considerations include communication barriers and the use of interpreters discussed earlier, using consent language that the client can reasonably understand, and respectfully evaluating the need for consent by medical or legal guardians (APA, 2012). Providers should explain the right to confidentiality and privacy to their clients and other parties who may accompany them (e.g., interpreter, personal attendant, family members, or significant other; APA, 2012). Providers should carefully assess the extent of decisional capacity and use accommodations judiciously to elicit autonomous, informed decisions (APA, 2012). If accommodations can produce informed decisions, these supports should be used to obtain individuals' informed consent (Kerkhoff & Hanson, 2015). In instances where informed decision making is not possible, ethical practice calls for the inclusion of decisional surrogates to exercise "substituted judgment"; Kerkhoff and Hanson (2015) advise providers to work to understand and address the views of disability among surrogates. These types of ethical dilemmas are especially difficult when surrogate values about life with a disability are denigrating or negativistic.

Becoming aware of disability as a diversity factor and responding appropriately is vital to ethical practice. Further, psychologists must obtain the required competencies when diversity such as disability is relevant to the effective implementation of services (Cornish et al., 2008). The APA ethics code (APA, 2002) addresses competence in Standard 2.01. Given that one fifth of the U.S. population is estimated to have a disability, it is incumbent upon psychologists to gain cultural competence in working with disabled persons (APA, 2012). Providers should be aware of and attend to the importance of language choices (discussed in depth in Chapter 5).

Although it is always important to practice only within the bounds of one's competence, providers should strive to adopt cultural humility with disabled populations. Even highly trained and experienced professionals need continuing education in assessing and treating persons with disabilities, accommodations, evolving technology, and federal and local laws governing disability issues (APA, 2012).

## General Considerations

The most important consideration in working with disabled people is for clients to be at the center of their own care. There are varied definitions of patient-centered care, and health care in the United States has struggled to balance professionalism and consumerism (Berwick, 2009). Rehabilitation health care providers have worked effectively in teams for decades to coordinate care for people with disabilities (Sinclair, Lingard, & Mohabeer, 2009). The best definition of patient-centered care that I have found is "the experience (to the extent the informed, individual patient desires it) of transparency, individualization, recognition, respect, dignity, and choice in all matters, without exception, related to one's person, circumstances, and relationships in health care" (Berwick, 2009, pp. w560–w561).

Clinicians who approach people with disabilities as partners and collaborators are in a better position to support their clients' goals and aspirations (Wright, 1983). By maximizing client involvement in treatment planning and decision making, disabled patients experience empowerment and increased self-determination (Barry & Edgman-Levitan, 2012). Clinicians should consider how disability culture and other linguistic and cultural identities, independently or in combination, may affect their clients' life experience and presenting problems. Each person should be treated as a unique individual with the shared experience of being human (Kerkhoff & Hanson, 2015). Rather than depending on a uniform approach for all clients with disabilities, customized treatment can reduce stereotyping and help prevent ethical problems in treatment while embodying a core ethical tenet: respect toward disabled clients (APA, 2012; Kerkhoff & Hanson, 2015). Respect for human dignity among those with disabilities is also a foundational principle of rehabilitation psychology (Wright, 1983).

*Space Issues*

Physical space considerations are more than simply a legal requirement. Accessible space allows disabled people to enter and move about while receiving care or services (Artman & Daniels, 2010). Starting from the outside, the presence of adequate disabled parking spaces and well-marked and barrier-free pathways to buildings are not just conveniences (APA, 2012). These features provide a welcoming and affirming experience for disabled clients (Leigh, Powers, Vash, & Nettles, 2004). There are many obvious building considerations, such as doorways wide enough for wheelchair access, automatic openers or easily manipulated handles, adequate lighting, accessible bathrooms, and ramps and elevators (Artman & Daniels, 2010). When these features are absent, it communicates to disabled people that they do not belong there and can make them feel like a burden or hassle to be accommodated (Leigh, Powers, Vash, & Nettles, 2004). Safety exits such as fire stairwells may have accessible options available, such as an escape chair, but often no one actually knows how to use them (APA, 2012). Health care providers should assume that some of their clientele will be disabled. Office locations with nearby accessible public transportation enhance access to services for clients with disabilities (APA, 2012).

Health care providers without an accessible space could conduct sessions in a mutually convenient accessible location or refer the client to an accessible practice (Artman & Daniels, 2010). Although practical, these solutions merely perpetuate segregation and discrimination. On a recent professional listserv discussion, a question was raised about whether or not a clinician should obtain a liability waiver from a client who can only climb stairs by sitting down and moving up one step at a time while in a building without an elevator. My response was to ask the clinician to imagine what it would be like for a disabled client to come to see a mental health care provider, which in and of itself is not an easy task; then imagine the client can get in the building only to realize that the only way to the therapy office is up a flight of stairs; and finally imagine the pressure that person feels to try to make it work, or the compulsion to apologize for causing a hassle if the therapist offers to see the client in an alternate location. People with disabilities are socialized to apologize for our bodies and the inconveniences created by them (Mpofu, Chronister, Johnson, & Denham, 2012). The disabled client is always in the "power-down position" relative to the health care provider. Culturally competent clinicians must be allies who take action, even when there are financial implications. If a health care provider is unwilling to intentionally move to an accessible office space, I believe that for the sake of transparency, it should be advertised that the practice is inaccessible to people with mobility disabilities. There is nothing more frustrating than taking the time and effort to attend an appointment only to find out that people with disabilities are not welcome there. In contrast, allies can make known their commitment to an inclusive atmosphere by advertising willingness to make reasonable accommodations and to welcome service animals.

*Assumptions*

Because disability has historically been framed as an individual and medical problem, instead of a cultural identity, clinicians often assume that psychological distress is inevitable for disabled people (Watermeyer & Swartz, 2016). As a result of the spread effect, diagnostic overshadowing can occur (Wright, 1983); that is, clinicians overfocus on impairment or overemphasize the importance of disability (APA, 2012). It is important not to assume that disability issues are the basis for the client seeking psychological services (Artman & Daniels, 2010). It is easy to wrongly presume that a client with a disability wishes to focus primarily on the disability or its effects (Olkin, 2002; Olkin & Pledger, 2003). Conversely, clinicians may dismiss or invalidate disability experiences, which can adversely affect the therapeutic alliance (Olkin, 1999). It is critical for clinicians to recognize that individuals respond to disability in varied ways (Leigh, Powers, Vash, & Nettles, 2004). Clinicians who make assumptions about specific linear process or "stages of acceptance" risk overlooking the impact of life circumstances, personality characteristics, and the interaction between disability and environment, all of which are likely to affect one's response to disability.

*Communication*

An important issue in working with disabled clients is verbal and nonverbal communication. For example, therapists can misperceive negative emotional expressions as maladjustment to disability, rather than as a reasonable response to painful experiences or continued oppressive exclusion (Artman & Daniels, 2010). The way that a client with a disability speaks or moves his or her body may also result in misunderstandings. For example, facial expressions may be involuntary or can have multiple meanings, reflecting not only possible underlying psychological issues but also responses to factors such as chronic pain or memory problems. Among sign language users, facial expressions can convey many nuances of meaning (Leigh, Powers, Vash, & Nettles, 2004). Body language may or may not reflect disability-related needs. Some individuals frequently change positions in their wheelchairs to prevent pressure sores, but adjusting position can also be a response to lighting or temperature changes. In learning conventional psychotherapy and clinical interviewing techniques, providers are often taught to interpret such movements psychologically; for example, shifting in one's seat may also be a sign of boredom, anxiety, or discomfort discussing the topic at hand. Similarly, verbal and nonverbal messages may conflict in some patients with disabilities because of impairments such as partial facial paralysis. Clinicians can easily misinterpret the amount or type of manifest emotion and undervalue or ignore a client's input (Artman & Daniels, 2010). These examples illustrate why it is so important for providers to ask clients directly about their experiences and ensure that clear communication occurs.

It may take extra time to communicate effectively with a client who has a disability. With patience, health care providers can enhance their own skills and accommodate their clients' communication needs. It is always important to ask patients about their communication preferences rather than make assumptions. A common pitfall among outsiders is to focus on an ASL interpreter, rather than sustaining eye contact with a Deaf person (Leigh, Corbett, Gutman, & Morere, 1996). Sometimes speech is affected by disability (e.g., dysarthria following stroke) and difficult for clinicians to understand. This can elicit anxiety and impatience, but it is important never to pretend to understand something that is not clear or rush a client through efforts to communicate. Communication choices of disabled clients should be respected and honored. Although it may seem more efficient to depend on a family member or personal care attendant to translate, this practice is considered culturally rude and dismissive toward the disabled client, not to mention raises concerns related to privacy and confidentiality. Much like getting to know someone with a foreign accent, communication between two individuals becomes easier with practice and familiarity. A person with language processing disabilities may better understand when clinicians articulate words clearly and pause between statements. Clinicians should avoid speaking in loud, dramatic, or condescending ways. Communication is arguably the most essential task of psychotherapy, so it is critical to ensure accurate representation of the client in determining assessment outcomes, treatment preferences, and therapy procedures.

## Assistance

Health care providers should feel free to ask clients with disabilities if they need assistance with a task, but clinicians should not volunteer to help without permission. Rather, health care providers may ask for particular instructions on how to be most helpful. For example, a blind client may request specific descriptions to enhance their awareness of the immediate environment. Be thoughtful about use of language, and ask clients about their preferences. Pay attention to the language choices of individuals in referring to their disability. For example, if a client refers to herself as autistic, a clinician might open a discussion about what being autistic means to that client and how use of identity-first language fits into her worldview. It is helpful to try to validate the client and minimize clinician bias and misperception about the client's disability. Although the clinician may be an expert in a certain therapy or a type of disability, patients are always experts about their own experience.

## Tailored Sessions

Clinicians may need to consider unconventional methods to suit the needs of disabled clients. Fatigue or pain may make it difficult to tolerate a 45- to 50-minute therapy session (Olkin, 2002; Olkin & Pledger, 2003). In other cases, the burden of travel can dictate longer and less frequent sessions. Telephone or video sessions are another option to improve access to mental health care for patients with disabilities. Clinicians are encouraged to be flexible about the length, number, nature, and frequency of sessions based on the stamina, attention span, processing ability, and transportation resources of disabled clients (Artman & Daniels, 2010).

Adaptations range from physical changes to specific modifications to the therapy itself (Hurley, Tomasulo, & Pfadt, 1998), and studies have shown that individuals with a wide range of intellectual and cognitive abilities can participate in and benefit from psychotherapy (Prigatano, 1991; Prout & Browning, 2011; Willner, 2005). Lewis, Lewis, and Davies (2016) found through qualitative investigation of the experiences of intellectually disabled participants in cognitive-behavioral therapy that they found the intervention useful, although difficult. Psychotherapy by nature is challenging and requires motivation; despite traditional doctrine that people with cognitive limitations cannot benefit from therapy, recent literature suggests that they should not be excluded on the basis of disability (Lewis et al., 2016). Box 9.1 lists several accommodations that can be useful in therapy to promote the full participation and benefit for clients with disabilities. Obviously, not all of these approaches are appropriate for every disabled client. Many patients will need no accommodations, whereas others may require several.

BOX 9.1.
ADAPTIVE STRATEGIES AND ACCOMMODATIONS FOR PSYCHOTHERAPY

Offer flexibility of session length, frequency, and time
Supply materials to promote comfort such as a blanket or pillow
Refrain from wearing strong scents, such as perfume
Provide visual aids and written summaries
Audio-record sessions
Simplify complex interventions into smaller chunks
Modify language to reduce level of vocabulary
Use shorter sentences and simple words
Add experiential components to traditional techniques
Assign homework assignments in written or drawn form
Increase structure and directiveness in session
Clearly outline treatment course and expectations
Involve social supports with permission
Be mindful of relational dynamics in session
Refer to peer-led support networks and groups
Take a disability-affirmative stance
Consider telephone or video sessions

## Clinician Thoughts and Feelings

Clinicians should engage in self-reflection concerning their own disability-related thoughts and emotions. Health care providers may feel anxious, fearful, vulnerable, and even repulsed when working with disabled clients (APA, 2012). Exposure to someone with a disability can bring up personal fears of vulnerability and mortality (Artman & Daniels, 2010). Clinicians may harbor critical judgments about clients who sustained disability as a result of reckless behavior, such as driving while intoxicated; these thoughts may make it difficult to empathize and foster emotional distance from the client (Artman & Daniels, 2010; Olkin, 2017). It is important to be aware of and address such feelings (Olkin, 1999). Similarly, clinicians should refrain from asking questions or broaching topics that are motivated by personal curiosity rather than clinical relevance (Artman & Daniels, 2010). Self-examination is crucial; cultural humility requires health care providers to examine their own preconceptions, beliefs, and emotional reactions toward persons with disabilities (Cornish et al., 2008).

## Positive Psychology

Early work in the Lewinian tradition showed that individuals demonstrate great variability in response to disability, and that by shifting the focus of their values to emphasize preserved positive traits and abilities, people could mitigate the negative impact of disability (D. S. Dunn & Dougherty, 2005; Elliott, Kurylo, & Rivera, 2002). Wright (1983) discovered that many disabled people found meaning in their experiences and could transform their perceptions of worth and humanity. In fact, research has now established that stress need not result in adversity but may actually lead to positive growth (Somerfield & McCrae, 2000). This process can take many forms for people with disabilities, from reprioritization of life goals and spiritual development to exploration of new values (D. S. Dunn & Dougherty, 2005); in these instances, disabled people are not simply coping or surviving, but thriving (Elliott et al., 2002; McMillen & Cook, 2003).

Although traditional models and psychological approaches to disability are deficit based (Wehmeyer, 2013), it is important for providers to assess each client's strengths and incorporate them into interventions (Buntinx, 2013). Interventions that consider the personal strengths of a disabled client increase self-worth, empowerment, and resilience (Wehmeyer, 2013). Encouraging clients to elicit personal strengths through self-reflection or use of formal tools may be helpful (D. S. Dunn & Dougherty, 2005). The Values in Action (VIA) Survey of Character Strengths, for example, is a free psychometrically sound inventory available online that can be used to learn about one's positive characteristics (Seligman, Park, & Peterson, 2004). Buntinx (2013) emphasizes that providers must center interventions around the ambitions, aspirations, and goals of disabled clients rather than what providers may think clients need or want (Elliott et al., 2002).

Integrating the tenets of positive psychology through patient-centered care and empowerment increases the likelihood that interventions will be effective (Elliott et al., 2002). Rather than pathologizing disability and fostering dependence, positive psychology approaches help clients (re)discover their own abilities and enable them to utilize skills learned in therapy and generalize them in other areas of their lives long after rehabilitation is complete and psychotherapy has been completed (Kerkhoff & Hanson, 2015).

## Evidence-Based Interventions

### Adult Interventions

There are very few evidence-based psychotherapies (EBPs) that have been developed for or adequately tested with adults with disabilities (Artman & Daniels, 2010).

"Disability" may be an exclusion factor in clinical intervention research, which makes it impossible to know if EBPs are efficacious for them, or even clinically indicated. There are some exceptions to this rule, most notably the robust evidence base for cognitive-behavioral therapy for chronic pain (CBT-CP). Several small-scale or pilot studies have investigated specific EBPs for certain disability groups, such as coping effectiveness training for persons with spinal cord injuries (Duchnick, Letsch, & Curtiss, 2009), eye movement desensitization and reprocessing (EMDR) for posttraumatic stress disorder (PTSD) with people with intellectual disability (Jowett et al., 2016), and cognitive-behavioral therapy for depression with clients who have multiple sclerosis (MS; Gottberg et al., 2016; A. P. Turner et al., 2016). This research is useful for specific interventions with certain groups but limited in overall applicability to the larger disability community.

On the other hand, CBT-CP was developed for people with disabling chronic pain conditions based on robust evidence that cognitive and behavioral factors significantly predict physical, social, and emotional functioning in this population (Ehde, Dillworth, & Turner, 2014). CBT-CP is composed of several strategies to help clients increase functioning, reduce maladaptive thoughts and emotional distress, and develop tools to help manage pain (J. A. Turner, Holtzman, & Mancl, 2007). CBT-CP is a good treatment option because it has few risks or side effects, unlike invasive treatments or medication, and it has consistently been shown to be effective with a wide range of clients with pain; however, the typical effect sizes are relatively modest in relation to treatment outcomes (Ehde et al., 2014). Clinically, the way in which CBT-CP is delivered is particularly important, given disability cultural factors. Like many clients with disabilities, those with chronic pain often mistrust the medical establishment and may feel invalidated by past experiences receiving treatment. The likelihood of success is fostered by aligning oneself with the client and carefully helping him or her to reprioritize values, explore new ways of coping, and begin to consider an identity as someone with an invisible disability. For many clients, the term *disability* has been synonymous with *inability*, and it can be empowering to learn that there are ways in which persons with disabilities live fully and capably. In my experience, CBT-CP is particularly effective in group format, because patients are able to connect with others who have faced similar challenges and can start to identify with the disability community.

More research is needed to help clinicians understand the experiences of people with disabilities in treatment. CBT, for example, is a demanding process that requires planning and work, and the quality of the therapeutic relationship is crucial to the client's response to treatment (Gottberg et al., 2016). Clients with disabilities deserve to be treated by clinicians who have the knowledge, skills, and ability to be effective with this population.

## Child Interventions

In contrast to adult psychotherapies, there are numerous intervention approaches designed specifically for children and adolescents with disabilities, especially those with developmental and mental health disabilities. Although a full review of these approaches is beyond the scope of this chapter, one approach in particular warrants mentioning: applied behavioral analysis (ABA) for autism. ABA is important because it represents a contemporary clash between the science of psychology and the culture of disability. ABA was developed in the 1960s by O. Ivar Lovaas at the University of California Los Angeles (UCLA); he blended behaviorism, observational coding, and antecedent and consequence analysis with single-subject design to create a comprehensive and empirically supported intervention meant to increase social and adaptive functioning skills among children with autism (Smith & Eikeseth, 2011). Indeed, decades of research have demonstrated relatively robust effects of ABA on increased receptive and expressive language skills, daily living abilities, and social functioning in autistic children (Virues-Ortega, 2010). Concurrently, the neurodiversity movement has rejected pathological definitions of autism and rejects many of the tenets of ABA, most essentially that autistic behaviors such as self-stimulatory behavior ("stimming") should be a focus of change at all (Collier, 2012; Kapp, Gillespie-Lynch, Sherman, & Hutman, 2012). Controversy abounds in discourse about finding a cure for autism, how to address autistic behaviors that are dangerous or harmful, and the role of nonautistics (often parents of autistic children) in research, advocacy, and intervention (Jaarsma & Welin, 2012). Both movements—ABA and neurodiversity—are moving full steam ahead, and it is yet to be determined if there is a way in which they can work together to optimize quality of life for those with autism.

## Disability-Affirmative Therapy

Rhoda Olkin, a disabled psychologist, published a seminal work in 1999 called "What Psychotherapists Should Know About Disability" (Olkin, 1999). In that volume, Olkin began to lay the groundwork for what she later termed *disability-affirmative therapy*, or DAT (Olkin, 2007, 2017). Olkin describes DAT as a template for case formulation consisting of principles that can be applied to psychotherapy with disabled clients. The first component of DAT is nine areas of exploration with clients and/or their families to contextualize the experience of disability. These nine areas consist of developmental history, current disability status, models of disability, other demographic and cultural identities, disability culture and community, social interactions, microaggressions, emotion management, and relational intimacy (Olkin, 2017).

Second, DAT involves a therapist stance that Olkin (2017) developed from various sources including gay affirmative therapy. DAT, rather than a technique or approach, is more a framework for understanding clients. Olkin's (2017) DAT assumes that disability is not inherently pathological and that it has value and meaning; her framework encourages clients to develop an affirmation of disability identity by finding mentors with disabilities, becoming involved with the disability community, and engaging in positive reframing of stigmatized traits. Olkin (2017) argues that by engaging with other disabled people, clients can connect with others who have faced similar life experiences, find role models, become exposed to disability cultural icons, and learn about novel assistive technologies and ways of functioning. By exploring the experience of microaggressions directly with clients, Olkin postulates that disabled clients can gain greater perspective on their own emotional reactions to such instances and better determine effective responses.

Strengths of the DAT framework include an emphasis on helping clients recognize and contextualize oppressive experiences, fostering connection with the disability community and culture, and normalizing and validating emotional responses that are typically pathologized or not tolerated from disabled people such as rage (Olkin, 2017). The primary shortcoming of DAT, noted by Olkin herself, is that there is no real empirical basis for it. This is reflective of the field itself and how evidence-based treatments for people with disabilities remain in their infancy; Olkin, with a wealth of personal and professional experience, has pioneered advances in psychotherapy for disabled persons and has arguably made the most practical and meaningful contributions to clinical work in disability since Wright (1983). Theoretically, DAT is grounded in the biopsychosocial model of disability and informed by social psychology (e.g., D. S. Dunn, 2015). The next logical step is to test out DAT hypotheses with empirical scrutiny.

## Disability and Trauma

The concepts of disability and trauma are interwoven in several ways. First, people can become disabled as a result of trauma, such as an injury or accident (Watermeyer & Swart, 2016). Some disabled people develop PTSD following acute medical incidents that were experienced as life threatening (Shalev, Schreiber, Galai, & Melmed, 1993). Second, disabled people are exposed to different types of trauma; they are more likely to experience abuse or assault than nondisabled people. Third, people with disabilities are vulnerable to the effects of chronic microaggressions and minority stress.

Watermeyer and Swartz (2016) point out that people who acquire disabilities can experience a loss of control that can result in self-blame as a defense against the conclusion that the world is unpredictable or dangerous. As discussed earlier, health care providers and broader society may either overtly or covertly place blame for disability on the disabled person, particularly if any associated behavior is considered reckless (Watermeyer & Swartz, 2016). For example, it is common to be asked by laypersons whether one was a smoker upon disclosing a diagnosis of throat or lung cancer. A psychodynamic explanation would hold that society projects its own fears about uncertainty and safety in an unpredictable world by blaming the victim. Damage to the self may exist in a harmful alliance with struggles to restore trust in what has become an unsafe, unpredictable world (Watermeyer & Swartz, 2016). Similarly, responses to disability within one's family and social network have been described secondary traumatization; indeed, in some instances caregivers were found to be as or more upset about the disability than the disabled person (Elliott, Shewchuk, & Richards, 2001). As a result, disabled people can feel pressure to reassure others and, in doing so, subjugate their own emotional experiences (Watermeyer & Swartz, 2016).

## Violence and Abuse

People with disabilities are more vulnerable to violence and abuse when compared to the nondisabled population (Saxton et al., 2001; Saxton, McNeff, Powers, Curry, & Limont, 2006). Disabled people are perceived to be powerless and easily exploited, and may be physically dependent, socially isolated, and/or sexually naïve (APA, 2012; Hassouneh-Phillips & Curry, 2002). Perpetrators have diminished risk of being discovered; people with disabilities are less likely to be believed if they do report abuse or neglect (K. Hughes et al., 2012; Sobsey, 2014). Children and adolescents with disabilities are over three times more likely to be abused or neglected than their peers without disabilities (L. Jones et al., 2012). Disabled adults are 1.5 times more likely than nondisabled adults to experience multiple episodes of violence and longer duration of abuse (APA, 2012; K. Hughes et al., 2012). The risk level increases significantly for specific disability types including intellectual and mental health disabilities (Sobsey, 2014). People with cognitive disabilities are the most vulnerable to violence of any group of persons with disabilities (Harrell, 2014). Women with disabilities, especially older women, are also at elevated risk of abuse (APA, 2012; Williams & Colvin, 2016). Men with disabilities experience similar rates and types of abuse, but it often goes unrecognized (Saxton et al., 2006).

Culturally competent clinicians are aware of the signs, symptoms, and dynamics of disability-related violence including unique areas of vulnerability (R. B. Hughes et al., 2010; Slayter, 2009). Disability-specific abuse can include under- or overadministration of medications, involuntary confinement, withholding or dismantling of assistive equipment (e.g., wheelchairs), and refusing to provide or allow personal assistance for essential daily living activities such as eating and personal hygiene (Hassouneh-Phillips & Curry, 2002; R. B. Hughes et al., 2011). It can be more difficult for disabled persons to leave intimate relationships in which the partner is the perpetrator of abuse (Slayter, 2009); similarly, disabled survivors of abuse almost always know the perpetrator and are often dependent on him or her for care, whether in institutional or community dwellings (Powers et al., 2002).

Health care providers should routinely screen disabled people for abuse and/ or neglect and intervene appropriately when such is discovered (APA, 2012). It is important to learn state mandatory reporting requirements for violence against people with disabilities including children, older adults, and dependent adults (APA, 2012). Whenever possible, it is best to involve the survivor throughout the reporting process (Nosek, Hughes, & Taylor, 2004). Clinicians should document the history of abuse and neglect and discuss safety planning with clients such as having a safe retreat, backup personal care assistance, and social supports (Nosek et al., 2004). It is crucial to address the potential long-term consequences of reporting on disabled clients, including possible deleterious effects on quality of care and displacement or homelessness (Nosek et al., 2004). These complexities can require additional effort to arrange alternative services or enlist the assistance of other professionals or service agencies (Slayter, 2009).

Many domestic violence resource centers or shelters are not accessible to people with disabilities, so clinicians are encouraged to proactively locate and provide contact information for accessible local domestic violence and sexual assault programs. Local disability service providers or advocacy groups (e.g., Centers for Independent Living; ADAPT chapters) can also be helpful resources. Robinson-Whelen and colleagues (2014) developed a safety awareness program for women with disabilities consisting of abuse awareness, knowledge, safety skills, safety self-efficacy, social support, and safety-promoting behavior in a peer-led group. These components could be adapted for individual use with clients with disabilities or replicated in other settings.

## Cumulative Microaggressions and Minority Stress

Like other marginalized groups, disabled people experience microaggressions, which were explored in depth in Chapter 3. Only in the last couple of decades have researchers started to focus on the cumulative effects of microaggressions; associations have been found with negative physical and mental health outcomes, contributing to health disparities in diverse groups including members of lesbian, gay, bisexual, transgender, queer-plus (LGBTQ+) communities and racial and ethnic minorities (e.g., Sue et al., 2007; Torres & Taknint, 2015). However, there is a notable literature gap about the cumulative impact over time of microaggressions toward persons with disabilities. Similarly, although work in the area of minority stress theory and race-based stress and trauma work have made great strides in understanding how stress stemming from prejudice and discrimination harms culturally and linguistically diverse people (Carter, 2007; Meyer, 1995), we know very little empirically about the ways in which disabled people are harmed. Nonetheless, we can draw upon the reflections of those with the lived experience of disability.

To live with disability is to inhabit a world where you are constantly "othered," and where barriers to full participation are regularly encountered (Watermeyer & Swartz, 2016). In this way cumulative microaggressions and repeated traumas can become chronic stressors. It can become difficult for people with disabilities to accurately assess their own worth and level of achievement, given societal messages and a low bar for accomplishment (APA, 2012; Kerkhoff & Hanson, 2015). Disability demands facing some of the most difficult and eschewed human experiences such as shame, dependency, and loss, and as a result, many disabled people live in survival mode (Watermeyer and Swartz, 2016). The work of psychotherapy is in many ways a luxury that disabled people can rarely afford, both literally and figuratively. It is stressful to try not to internalize ableist rhetoric because it is so insidious. Internalized ableism makes it very difficult for disabled people to develop self-compassion in therapy. Watermeyer and Swartz (2016) summarize this phenomenon clearly:

> Disabled people, through having to survive in the face of chronic discrimination, may suffer the ongoing effects of symbolic violence directed at self-identity. These experiences are often invisible to others, as even the most prejudiced ideas about disability are seldom recognized as such. Patronizing responses are likely to be viewed as kindness, although having the capacity to obliterate one's dignity and legitimacy as an adult, an equal. The combination of such treatment with material deprivation and individualizing, medical logic can create a psychological environment in which it is extremely difficult to clearly see prejudice for what it is, and hold firmly to one's worth. (p. 274)

## Suicide

Russell, Turner, and Joiner (2009) found that disability is associated with a greater lifetime occurrence of suicidal ideation among a large and diverse sample of adults. Disabled people are four times more likely to have attempted suicide than nondisabled people (Meltzer et al., 2012). In a systematic review, Nagraj and Omar (2015) found that adolescents with physical, intellectual, and learning disabilities were significantly more likely to attempt suicide than adolescents without physical disabilities. People with disabilities are at higher risk for suicide than their nondisabled peers (Giannini et al., 2010), and disabled people have higher rates of mood disorders, which are associated with suicidality (Meltzer et al., 2012). As a result, people with disabilities who are depressed are believed to be particularly vulnerable to death by suicide (Lund, Nadorff, & Seader, 2016). Several important sociodemographic risk factors for attempted suicide among disabled people are listed in Box 9.2.

Some studies have found that disability predicts suicidality even when controlling for depression, indicating that clinicians should take special care to assess disabled clients for suicide risk (Lund, Nadorff, & Seader, 2016). Fässberg and colleagues (2016) noted that disability, physical illnesses, and functional limitations are associated with suicidal behavior in older adults. Khazem, Jahn, Cukrowicz, and Anestis (2015) found that disabled people who report higher self-perceived burdensomeness are at higher risk for suicidal ideation. This finding is particularly important because burdensomeness is one of the pervasive negative stereotypes about disability.

Lund, Nadorff, Winer, and Seader (2016) found that suicide was viewed by members of society as significantly more acceptable for persons with disabilities than for nondisabled people. Hypotheses include hopelessness about the permanency of disability and bias against disability as such an undesirable state that it warrants suicide (Lund, Nadorff, Winer, & Seader, 2016). The authors found that acceptability

---

BOX 9.2.
SOCIODEMOGRAPHIC RISK FACTORS FOR ATTEMPTED SUICIDE AMONG DISABLED PERSONS

Female sex
Younger age
Lower education
Low income
Unmarried status
Unemployment
Physical health problems
Debt
Difficulty with activities of daily living, especially of high cognitive content
Social isolation

of suicide was higher for physical disabilities and chronic illnesses than it was for psychiatric disabilities, an interesting finding in light of other research that people with psychiatric disabilities are at higher risk of suicide than those with nonpsychiatric disabilities (Lund, Nadorff, & Seader, 2016). This may represent a mismatch between the perceptions of insiders and outsiders about quality of life.

Findings related to the acceptability of suicidality for people with disabilities are troubling on several levels. First, it conveys a negative message about the worth of disabled people in the eyes of society (APA, 2012). Second, it may give credence to the rationale of suicidal persons with disabilities of feeling burdensome and hopeless (Lund, Nadorff, & Seader, 2016). Clinicians may even share these sentiments about acceptability of suicide in the context of different types of disabilities. Thus, they must be aware of their own biases and consider the ways in which societal attitudes affect perceptions of quality of life (APA, 2012; Lund, Nadorff, & Seader, 2016).

It is important for clinicians to understand the suicide risk factors that affect disabled clients and take steps to prevent suicide and ensure client safety. Suicide prevention efforts must extend beyond treatment of depression and include assessment of other risk factors such as poor impulse control and history of dangerous behavior (Lund, Nadorff, & Seader, 2016). Finally, certain emotional states, including feelings of burdensomeness, hopelessness, and worthlessness, should be considered specific risk factors for suicide among disabled clients (Charlifue & Gerhart, 1991; Serafini, Pompili, Forte, Amore, & Girardi, 2014). These and other affective, cognitive, and behavioral risk factors for attempted suicide among people with disabilities are listed in Box 9.3.

---

BOX 9.3.
AFFECTIVE, COGNITIVE, AND BEHAVIORAL RISK FACTORS FOR
ATTEMPTED SUICIDE AMONG DISABLED PERSONS

Depression
Feelings of burdensomeness
Hopelessness
Feelings of worthlessness
Despondency, apathy, withdrawal
Anger or agitation
Alcohol abuse
Expressions of shame
Destructive or dangerous behavior
Relational discord
Greater perceived discrimination

## Sexuality

Many in society erroneously believe that adults with disabilities usually do not have intimate relationships (APA, 2012). We already know that disabled people experience discrimination based on disability when trying to form romantic relationships (see Chapter 3). Psychologists are encouraged to recognize that all adults with disabilities have the right to sexual intimacy, partnership, marriage, and a family, and that most disabled people have the capacity to engage in these relationships (O'Toole & Doe, 2002). A full exploration of issues relating to sexuality and disability is beyond the scope of this chapter, but issues of sexuality are important to consider when working with people with disabilities. As discussed in Chapter 3, people with disabilities are often desexualized by society. Expressions of sexuality from disabled persons may be met with hostility, discomfort, or even disgust (East & Orchard, 2014). As a result, it can be very difficult for disabled clients to achieve sexual health (Owens & De Than, 2015).

Furthermore, unfamiliarity with disability, stereotypes, and discomfort with discussion of issues such as sexual intercourse and sexuality among health care and medical providers can lead to neglect of topics like sexual behavior, contraceptives, sexually transmitted infections (STIs), reproductive capacity, and assisted reproductive technology (ART; O'Toole & Doe, 2002). It is problematic when clinicians overfocus on disability at the expense of important health topics such as sexual health, because disabled people deserve to have accurate information about sexuality to make personal choices about behavior (Owens & De Than, 2015). It is incumbent upon health care providers to at least broach the topic even if the client does not raise it.

According to the World Health Organization (WHO, 2006), sexual health is "a state of physical, emotional, mental, and social wellbeing in relation to sexuality" (p. 5) Importantly, this definition is not simply the absence of disease or dysfunction, but rather emphasizes safety and pleasure. Like nondisabled people, individuals with disabilities may have a limited scope of understanding of sexual pleasure and experiences. Because disabled people are less likely to receive adequate information and education about sexuality, their concept of sexual activity may be limited to sexual intercourse between men and women (O'Toole & Doe, 2002). It can be empowering for disabled people to broaden their concept of sexuality to understand that there are many means of finding sexual pleasure, with or without partners (Mona, Cameron, & Clemency Cordes, 2017; Owens & De Than, 2015).

Many disability and rehabilitation providers have basic knowledge about one of the earliest sexual discussion models used with disabled clients. The PLISSIT model (Annon, 1976) consists of a progressive intervention cycle wherein the provider first grants permission to discuss intimacy topics. The next stage would be to provide limited information about sexual issues and to offer specific suggestions, if applicable. Finally, providers may offer or refer clients for intensive therapy as needed (Annon, 1976). Criticisms of the PLISSIT model include its linearity, that permission giving is too implicit and only offered once, and that it may allow providers to assume that there is no need to discuss sexuality after the model has been followed. In response to these criticisms, B. Taylor and Davis (2007) developed the Extended-PLISSIT (Ex-PLISSIT) model, which emphasizes the need for repeated permission giving throughout intervention and client contact. The authors operationalize permission giving and clearly state that it should involve normalization of sexuality (B. Taylor & Davis, 2007). Providers following the Ex-PLISSIT model are not to assume that the client has no concerns if none are brought up (B. Taylor & Davis, 2007). Overall, Ex-PLISSIT is cyclical and better captures sexual needs throughout the lifespan. It puts more responsibility on providers to foster an atmosphere of trust and safety in which to address intimacy issues. Finally, Ex-PLISSIT promotes self-reflection about the provider's own assumptions and attitudes toward sexuality and disability, and how those may affect dynamics with clients (B. Taylor & Davis, 2007).

Mona et al. (2017) developed a set of disability and sexuality health care competency model competencies (DASH-CM) that encompasses the attitudes, knowledge, and skills providers need to effectively address sexual health issues with disabled clients. In addition to competencies in knowledge of sexual functioning and the impact on sexuality of various disability-producing diagnoses, Mona et al. (2017) assert that providers should also have a solid understanding of disability, and in particular that "exploring sexuality among people with disabilities is necessary culturally" (p. 1006). They also emphasize the importance of intersectionality of other diverse identities including sexual orientation, gender, and sexual behavior (Mona et al., 2017).

In all treatment contexts but especially when addressing sexuality, it is important that clinicians establish and maintain appropriate professional boundaries, remain within the bounds of their own competence, and refer clients to other health care providers when indicated, thoughtfully and in ways that do not promote shame. For a full discussion of sexual accessibility and strategies and techniques to enhance sexual pleasure for persons with disabilities, see Mona and colleagues (2014) and Owens and De Than (2015).

## Conclusion

This chapter has covered major ethical and legal concerns for working with disabled clients as well as general considerations for providing effective intervention in a culturally competent manner. It is important that providers are prepared to address disability-related aspects of issues such as exposure to trauma, suicidality, and sexuality, but providers will frequently find that clients with disabilities present for psychotherapy for many of the same reasons as nondisabled clients: to enhance their awareness, functioning, and life satisfaction (Norcross, 2005).

There is no point doing research just for the sake of research.
—"OONAGH," cited in Kitchin (2000)

# 10 Conducting Culturally Competent Disability Research

FOR THE PAST several decades, there has been much discussion about a shift in paradigms of disability research and inquiry. This change parallels the evolution of disability models (discussed in Chapter 2) from the domination of the medical model to the development and implementation of the social and diversity models. Modest efforts have been made to examine the social and environmental factors affecting persons with disabilities (Blair & Minkler, 2009; Scotch, 2002). Inclusive methodology such as participatory action research (PAR) now appears more frequently in mainstream scientific publications (Kramer, Kramer, García-Iriarte, & Hammel, 2011). However, there remains a disconnection between disability research and the disability community (Ehde et al., 2013). Disability research has historically been, and largely remains, the domain of nondisabled academics (Kitchin, 2000). In this chapter, I will discuss the progress that has been made toward a more sociopolitical research perspective, inclusion of disabled persons in the research process, and specifically how PAR is well suited for disability research.

## History of Disability Research

Traditional disability research in the past was based on the medical model and conventional scientific methods; thus, disabled participants (i.e., subjects) were the object of investigation (Stodden et al., 2003). Such research was often conducted in hospitals or clinical settings and analyzed program data and results of national surveys (Stodden et al., 2003). The focus was primarily on diagnosis and treatment and the prevention of disability (K. E. McDonald & Raymaker, 2013; Scotch, 2002). Fine and Asch (1988) published an important critique of disability research in which they accused researchers of overemphasizing the medical aspects of disability and holding the assumption that impairment was the root of problems and that people with disabilities were in need of help and social support. Disabled people were portrayed as victims, and disability was viewed as the central or lone identity of participants.

Almost 20 years later, an issue of *American Psychologist* was devoted to a call for psychology to truly embrace the "new paradigm" (Gill, Kewman, & Brannon, 2003; Olkin & Pledger, 2003; Tate & Pledger, 2003). Gill et al. (2003) explained that the "new paradigm" stemmed from the movement of disabled scholars to redefine disability as a social construction and promote the social model to use disability research to create sociopolitical change. Olkin and Pledger (2003) called for disability and rehabilitation researchers to expand their perspective from disability as a solely personal phenomenon to encompass familial, political, and societal aspects of disability. Indeed, Tate and Pledger (2003) endorsed "new research directions" that emphasize consumer involvement in research within a holistic socioecological perspective of disability (p. 293). They appealed to the field to "acknowledge the dynamic interaction between the person and the environment, to be aware of the importance of consumer participation in the planning, implementation, and evaluation of research activities and interventions strategies, and to recognize the limitations of traditional, more medically oriented, definitions and measures of disability" (p. 289).

Another 15 years have passed, and I am struck by the truth that this paradigm is not new, and that despite a long history of espousing the importance of including persons with disabilities in research about them and demonstrations of the merits of such studies (Berghs, Atkin, Graham, Hatton, & Thomas, 2016), contemporary rehabilitation intervention research rarely includes disabled people meaningfully in the research process (Ehde et al., 2013). As a result, difficulties in translating such research to practice, effectively disseminating findings, and facilitating implementation are just as problematic now as they ever were (Ehde et al., 2013).

Social sciences such as anthropology, sociology, and political science first used observational and qualitative research methods to study disability (Gill et al., 2003), and early rehabilitation psychologists emphasized the importance of environmental factors from the start (Ehde et al., 2013; Fine & Asch, 1988). Yet the quest for rigorous, experimental research methodologies has dominated rehabilitation and disability research for decades; some argue that adherence to strict behavioral science standards is due to the field's desire to be perceived as legitimately scientific and on par with the status of medicine and "hard" sciences (D. S. Dunn & Elliott, 2008; Scotch, 2002). D. S. Dunn and Elliott (2008), however, point out that the definition of science includes not only empirical study but also theoretical development.

Rehabilitation and disability research has only recently, slowly, and perhaps reluctantly (Tate & Pledger 2003) started to acknowledge the importance of theory-driven research and the value of qualitative, community, and consumer-involved research methods (Scotch, 2002). In spite of evidence supporting the merits of inclusion approaches, Berghs and colleagues (2016) found from their review that most contemporary intervention studies lacked participatory designs. They found remaining evidence of patronizing approaches among some researchers whose "view of research was out of touch with the disability movement; intersectionality and more rights-based approaches; developments in cultural competence; and efforts to tackle discrimination" (p. 68).

## Challenges of Disability Research

Disability and rehabilitation research can be incredibly rich as a result of the great breadth and complexity of the disabled population; however, these same factors also make this field of inquiry very challenging. D. S. Dunn and Elliott (2008) point out that there has been a persistent gap in coherent theory to drive disability and rehabilitation research forward. In their review of the literature, Berghs and colleagues (2016) observed that theoretical connections were seldom made among identified differences, disability and health models, diagnoses and impairments, and outcome measurements. Olkin and Pledger noted in 2003 that the field was wanting for unified theories and models that are sequenced and build on previous knowledge, evolving as new information is gained.

Johnston and colleagues (2009) along with D. S. Dunn and Elliott (2008) noted that disability and rehabilitation research is by nature an interdisciplinary field and accordingly must examine a wide range of personal, systemic, and environmental contributors to the phenomenon of disability. Proponents of the "new paradigm" have stressed the need to address policy, employment, cultural, health, and economic implications (Olkin & Pledger, 2003). Other academic fields are unlikely to face this same level of complexity (D. S. Dunn & Elliott, 2008).

Because the disability population is so diverse and profoundly affected by multiple contextual factors, it can be difficult to obtain large participant samples for studies at multiple sites (Ehde et al., 2013; Johnston et al., 2009). Disabled people, especially those who are also culturally and/or linguistically diverse, can be difficult to recruit and retain in research for several reasons, not the least of which is the barrier of mistrust (Blair & Minkler, 2009). The field has made a clear commitment to improving the lives of disabled people and empowering people with disabilities, at least in part through enlisting them to participate in research (Johnston et al., 2009; Tate & Pledger, 2003). The nature of disability sometimes calls for adaptations such as assistive technology or other accommodations to enable the inclusion of disabled persons in research, but these modifications are not consistently provided (Johnston et al., 2009), thereby adding another uncontrolled variable.

The larger scientific and research communities have instituted measures of research quality and methodological rigor based on grading systems by which to determine the contribution of studies to evidence-based practice (Johnston et al., 2009). Using grading systems to evaluate the quality of various study parameters can foster excellence in research and encourage judicious use of resources (Berghs et al., 2016). There are grading systems available to determine the strongest evidence for meta-analyses and systematic reviews of the literature. Indeed, an important criticism of disability and rehabilitation research has been a lack of empirical data to inform evidence-based practice (Ehde et al., 2013; Olkin & Pledger, 2003). However, the grading systems used for research studies heavily favor basic scientific methodologies that are best utilized in large homogenous studies with robust control groups and masked (i.e., "blind") random assignment of participants, such as randomized controlled trials (RCTs) of the effectiveness of medications (Ehde et al., 2013; Johnston et al., 2009). As a result, these types of studies are more attractive to funding sources than those that utilize alternative methodology. Johnston and colleagues (2009) summarize it best:

> For many of the current research problems in disability and rehabilitation however, the usual or optimal solution will not be a large RCT. The best research design is not always the largest or most rigorous one possible; it is rather the one that will most advance knowledge on the basis of the state of prior research and development and resource constraints. (p. 5)

Therein lies the problem: The research designs and methodologies that best capture the complexity of disability and allow for consumer participation are perceived as less rigorous and will fare less well under evidence-grading methods that may determine funding (Johnston et al., 2009). It is not simple to mask treatment conditions or ethically establish control groups when people have diverse needs and their lives are directly or significantly affected by their participation or lack thereof. Objective empiricism certainly has its strengths and its place in research, but the sheer complexity and nuance surrounding disability demands a focus on the subjective human experience, including social and environmental marginalization

(Scotch, 2002). Ehde and colleagues (2013) contend that participatory approaches can be used effectively throughout the research process to complement and enhance scientific rigor, and may improve the overall success and usefulness of disability and rehabilitation research.

Funding is a significant barrier to the type of disability and rehabilitation research that researchers and regulatory bodies have repeatedly called for. Congress and other governing agencies determine funding priorities, and although those very organizations espouse the importance of consumer participation in research, there is nonetheless a general failure to include people with disabilities in high-level positions of authority responsible for funding decisions (Olkin & Pledger, 2003). Much of disability and rehabilitation research has been dependent on federal funding, but inconsistencies in priorities and direction in the context of scarce financial resources have hampered the ability of researchers to produce sustained lines of research (Olkin & Pledger, 2003). Johnston and colleagues (2009) reflected that although funding opportunities are more available for smaller scale and pilot projects, financial constraints often limit the rigor with which researchers can study and use the most well-respected methodologies (Berghs et al., 2016). Funding sources can also stifle creativity and inclusion by imposing stringent criteria, timelines, and policies about use of resources (Conder, Milner, & Mirfin-Veitch, 2011).

## Inclusion in Research

Virtually all government and disability organizations that fund research agree that participants as stakeholders should have a role in the research process (National Institute on Disability and Rehabilitation Research [NIDILRR], 2017). Most researchers acknowledge that including disabled persons in research about them provides more relevant and applicable results, and some argue that consumer participation enhances both the ethical strength and the evidence base of research design (Berghs et al., 2016).

Because scientific inquiry of disability issues is so steeped in medical and deficit-based perspectives, some researchers may not believe that disabled people have the interest or capability to contribute meaningfully to research (Radermacher, Sonn, Keys, & Duckett, 2010). Questions have been raised about the competency and qualifications of disabled participants (Tate & Pledger, 2003), but the body of literature that addresses optimal consumer participation remains largely separate from mainstream disability and rehabilitation inquiry (Balcazar, Keys, Kaplan, & Suarez-Balcazar, 1998). Researchers vary considerably in their approach to the type and extent of the consumer role (Barnes, 2008), although many create no role at all for consumers. It appears likely that researchers will increasingly be required to involve consumers in their projects (Johnston et al., 2009; NIDILRR, 2017; Tate & Pledger, 2003), opening the door to more creative and unconventional approaches to disability research (K. E. McDonald & Raymaker, 2013).

Disability and rehabilitation researchers would likely identify the purpose of their research as a way to increase the field's understanding of the target populations, establish effective interventions to alleviate problems, and measure the success of these efforts (Ehde et al., 2013). In other words, most disability research is undertaken with the motivation to *help* people with disabilities. From the participant side, that certainly does not always seem like the case. First of all, there is typically very little potential for personal gain for participants in behavioral and social science research. Researchers have exploited disabled people in the past (Kitchin, 2000). Disabled research participants have been used for the purpose of research that is perceived to have mostly benefited the researchers themselves instead of members of the disability community (Barnes, 2008; K. E. McDonald & Raymaker, 2013). Some scholars have argued that disability research has only served to reinforce social status disparities and power differentials between the nondisabled and disabled (Barnes, 2008; Kitchin, 2000). As a result, many members of the disability community are understandably wary of researchers.

Kitchin (2000) conducted interviews with disabled laypeople about their perceptions of research and participation; many participants reported that disability research is alienating and disempowering because they perceive that researchers are capitalizing on their knowledge and experiences, some of which is quite personal or even private (Kitchin, 2000). They were suspicious of researchers' motives, especially nondisabled researchers, and wondered if any real action resulted from research studies (Kitchin, 2000). However, Kitchin (2000) also discovered that participants believed that research, if conducted differently, could be very useful to advance the lives of disabled people. Participants favored a partnership model wherein academic researchers and disability community members worked collaboratively (Kitchin, 2000).

It is important to explore the values of target communities and their members; the attitudes held by the research team may not be congruent with the goals and focus of the community (Stodden et al., 2003). It is not often that a research project begins with direct contact with a group of disabled stakeholders to discuss their priorities and identified needs (K. E. McDonald & Raymaker, 2013), yet that is exactly the approach that is most likely to be effective in gaining community buy-in, soliciting and retaining participants, and gathering accurate data (Radermacher et al., 2010). Communities want to know how their research participation can be mutually beneficial, and they deserve the opportunity to share in the results and take away something meaningful (K. E. McDonald & Raymaker, 2013). Disability research still has ground to gain in actively *listening* to the disability community (Olkin & Pledger, 2003).

It is critical, as in all other areas of cultural competency, that researchers examine and understand their own personal biases and use self-awareness to grow and learn (Stodden et al., 2003). Take, for example, a study exploring levels of distress among Latinx parents of children with Down syndrome. Does the research team consider measurement of environmental and social factors that may influence distress, or do they focus solely on individual factors such as parenting style and severity of disability? Have they thought about whether their findings hold risk of stigmatizing or harming people with Down syndrome or their families? Do they consider efforts to prevent the birth of people with Down syndrome to be harmful? Does the primary investigator have personal relationships with people with Down syndrome? Does he or she have a disability? Is he or she Latinx? Would the primary investigator continue a pregnancy after receiving a fetal diagnosis of developmental disability? There are not always right answers to such questions, but certainly the right exists for them to be pondered.

Researchers are challenged to involve disabled people in research respectfully. There are many roles for disabled people in scientific inquiry—as principal investigators, research assistants, project managers, study therapists, consultants, writers, reviewers, and more. Most important, disabled people should be respected, treated with dignity, provided autonomy, and allowed self-determination (K. E. McDonald & Raymaker, 2013). It is crucial that research does not simply select one disabled person to be a "token" member of the research team. Involvement of disabled persons will only be effective if their participation is genuine (Kramer et al., 2011); people with disabilities are frequently patronized, and if inclusion efforts are perceived as inauthentic, relationships may be damaged and progress thwarted (K. E. McDonald & Raymaker, 2013). To improve research to better represent the knowledge and experience of disabled people, approaches must be both emancipatory, promoting sociopolitical change, and empowering, promoting the well-being of those who participate (Kitchin, 2000).

## Researchers With Disabilities

Olkin (1999; Olkin & Pledger, 2003) has been a staunch advocate for the need for more disability and rehabilitation researchers to be disabled themselves. Other scholars also assert that one of the best ways for this to occur is for more people with disabilities to receive mentorship and encouragement to become investigators

(Kitchin, 2000). There are a few important points to consider about this issue. First of all, Olkin is entirely correct that people with disabilities are severely underrepresented in research and health service psychology, and although the representation levels of trainees from other diverse identities are trending upward, disability representation remains stagnant (Andrews & Lund, 2015). Olkin (1999; Olkin & Pledger, 2003) argues that disabled researchers "bring a different consciousness to disability research" (p. 299). She contends that researchers with disabilities would be more inclusive, advocate for disability inclusion in other types of research, be attentive to those with intersecting identities, and foster better relationships with the disability community. Barnes (2008), however, points out that being disabled does not guarantee that one will be inclusive or oriented toward social justice issues. I do not disagree, and as discussed in Chapter 6, the extent to which one identifies as disabled and affiliates with the disability community is highly variable. That said, and as articulated by Olkin and Pledger (2003), there are no other areas of diversity study that are so unrepresentative of the people being served or studied. Imagine if the *Journal of Black Psychology* was filled with articles by almost all White researchers and reviewed by a predominantly White editorial board, or that the leadership of the Society for the Psychology of Women was made up mostly of men. We know from the need to implement affirmative action policies that diverse representation will not improve without targeted efforts to provide marginalized people with opportunities to succeed. In that way, it is crucial for disability representation to increase in disability and rehabilitation research. Disabled people deserve to see others like themselves in these roles and have the chance to fill them.

## Participatory Action Research

PAR is not a new phenomenon, and despite the scarcity of its use in rehabilitation psychology research, its history is rich, steeped in the work of foundational rehabilitation psychology theorists (Ehde et al., 2013; G. Nelson, Ochocka, Griffin, & Lord, 1998). PAR has consistently been traced to the social psychological principles of Kurt Lewin and his proteges (Torre, Fine, Stoudt, & Fox, 2012); Lewin purportedly espoused that the most effective means to understand social systems was to try to change them; this is the premise of action research (G. Nelson et al., 1998). Tamara Dembo emphasized the difference between disability insiders and outsiders, showing an early understanding of the importance of the lived experience of disability (Ehde et al., 2013), which is the foundation of participatory research.

Blending action research and participatory approaches, PAR is a process of partnering with individuals and communities to explore and improve complex social, psychological, behavioral, or health problems (G. Nelson et al., 1998). Sometimes referred to as emancipatory research (Barnes, 2008), PAR is not a methodology, but rather a specific approach to the research process; as such, it can be utilized with both quantitative and qualitative research methods (Balcazar et al., 1998).

There are several different definitions of PAR, but all criteria share these core tenets (Balcazar et al., 1998; Blair & Minkler, 2009; Conder et al., 2011; Minkler et al., 2002; Maciver et al., 2013; G. Nelson et al., 1998; Stodden et al., 2003; Torre et al., 2012):

1. Consumer involvement: Stakeholders influence all phases of the research process.
2. Cooperative: All involved collaborate to share decision-making power and hold mutual ownership of the project.
3. Empowering: PAR respects consumers to use valuable knowledge to improve their own communities.
4. Facilitates change: PAR aims to effect sociopolitical transformation.

The goals of PAR include improving the validity and cultural relevance of research via consumer participation, empowering consumers to create and employ knowledge to enrich their lives, producing research congruent with community priorities, and strengthening consumer awareness of their own abilities to act as agents of change (Conder et al., 2011; Minkler et al., 2002; Stodden et al., 2003). Torre et al. (2012) argue that PAR "lifts responsibility for social problems off the backs of individuals who have paid the greatest price for injustice and exposes the social and political conditions that produce and justify injustice" (p. 179).

*Consumer Involvement*

PAR deliberately obscures the distinction between the researcher and the researched (Minkler et al., 2002). Generally PAR promotes the maximum participation of people whose identities and lives are affected by the topic studied, so for disability and rehabilitation research, this would be persons with disabilities (G. Nelson et al., 1998). In this way, PAR recognizes the unique knowledge and abilities of people with the lived experiences of disability (Balcazar et al., 1998). Ehde and colleagues (2013) also recommend the involvement of other important stakeholders including medical and health care providers, disability advocacy organizations, representatives from funding sources, and those directly involved in enacting legislation and policy, which is advantageous for research to have an impact at the systems level (Gill et al., 2003). However, it is important to understand that various stakeholders have differing and sometimes conflicting interests, so the research team should clarify roles and goals from the outset. Gill et al. (2003) advocate for research collaboration with both consumers and policymakers and wisely observe that the "mutual suspicions, prejudices, and biases of these groups will necessarily result in a bumpy relationship that can only be sustained by perseverance and the understanding that such broad-based efforts are more likely to bring about significant advances in disability policy" (p. 311).

In PAR, stakeholders should be involved throughout the research process, from gathering to interpreting and disseminating data (G. Nelson et al., 1998), not simply consulted once or twice. PAR strives for the inclusion of experiential participation of people with disabilities during the implementation of research (Balcazar et al., 1998). Disabled people deserve the opportunity to contribute to the formulation of research questions, influencing the broader disability and rehabilitation research agenda directly (Ehde et al., 2013; Olkin & Pledger, 2003; Tate & Pledger 2003). Involvement throughout the process facilitates shared ownership of research and allows stakeholders to advocate for policy based on scientific findings (Ehde et al., 2013). Balcazar et al. (1998) argue that the most important aspect of the participation of people with disabilities is that they help determine actions necessary to solve problems that affect them and their communities.

*Cooperative*

PAR participants share power and decision making equally and have mutual ownership of the project (G. Nelson et al., 1998). Essentially, consumer stakeholders collaborate with academics to become coresearchers (Balcazar et al., 1998). This philosophy completely contradicts that of traditional research, where significant power differences exist between researchers and participants being studied. To achieve an equal distribution of power, researchers must be willing to relinquish some control and allow participants shared decision-making power (Balcazar et al., 1998). G. Nelson et al. (1998) suggest discarding labels and titles to cultivate an atmosphere of connection and consideration and form supportive relationships despite differences.

Essentially, the role of the researcher shifts from expert to facilitator of team communication and inquiry (G. Nelson et al., 1998). Doing PAR work inclusively in groups can counterbalance power differentials by focusing on group strengths in an environment of respectful social support (Kramer et al., 2011). Communication in PAR is reciprocal, with ongoing feedback loops between team members. Ehde and colleagues (2013) point out that the goal of PAR is to build balanced relationships *with* affected stakeholders by changing the dynamic to research done *with* persons with disabilities, rather than research *for* or *on* them.

## Empowering

A major purpose of PAR is to empower consumers to partner with researchers to improve understanding of relevant problems and develop solutions to improve their own communities and increase control over their lives (Balcazar et al., 1998; G. Nelson et al., 1998). To empower disabled people, it is essential that they are respected and valued; in other words, researchers need to recognize that people with disabilities themselves are capable of finding solutions to important problems. In PAR, all team members demonstrate respect for the unique and different strengths of fellow team members. Researchers must be open to colearning, believe that disabled participants add value to the process, and appreciate a range of different forms of participation (Conder et al., 2011; G. Nelson et al., 1998).

Many PAR disability researchers emphasize that it is crucial to include intersecting identities like race, ethnicity, gender, sexual orientation, socioeconomic status, and other aspects of cultural and linguistic diversity. Because these individuals with disabilities have traditionally been sidelined within the disability right movements, PAR provides an opportunity to give voice to the most disenfranchised people with disabilities (Balcazar et al., 1998; Minkler et al., 2002). PAR can elevate the relevance and applicability of research products in these communities (Balcazar et al., 1998). Because participants gain a stake in the quality of the research through their involvement, research results are more likely to reflect an authentic portrayal of their lived experience, so the findings are more likely to be accepted by community members (Balcazar et al., 1998).

PAR involves learning from the experiences of one another, respecting one another's needs and concerns, and recognizing one another's strengths (Conder et al., 2011). To accomplish this, disabled participants need to be fully supported so that they are enabled to participate, meaning that the structures and research processes in place promote understanding of people with disabilities (Conder et al., 2011; Maciver et al., 2013). Balcazar et al. (1998) note that PAR involvement can allow disabled people to become aware of their own capabilities and strengths. Likewise, at the community level, PAR can foster community building and dialogue (G. Nelson et al., 1998).

## Facilitates Change

PAR differs from traditional research in that it is undertaken with the purpose of taking action to create social transformation (G Nelson et al., 1998). D. S. Dunn and Elliott (2008) point out that rehabilitation psychology is particularly well positioned to affect health and public policy issues. This alters the way that researchers design studies and select research questions; PAR researchers also must reflect on the purpose of the research, who is likely to benefit from it, who could be harmed or put at risk, and whether the research could result in sociopolitical change (Olkin & Pledger, 2003; Torre et al., 2012). G. Nelson et al. (1998) consider one of the strengths of PAR to be its ability to develop and build local systems. Ehde and colleagues (2013) argue that PAR is consistent with the service and advocacy goals of rehabilitation and disability intervention research and that PAR has a role to play in developing evidence-based practice interventions. As noted by Blair and Minkler (2009), PAR includes both research and action, so the process does not end at the publication of findings but proceeds to facilitate the translational work of research findings to practice (Ehde et al., 2013).

## The PAR Process

PAR requires a process of cycles; research teams may add or emphasize certain phases or sequences, but all PAR research should have a continuous feedback loop where new knowledge constantly informs action and where stakeholder influence is invited and utilized throughout the process. The Lewinian tradition includes organized cycles of problem definition, fact finding, goal setting, action, and evaluation to generate new knowledge and solutions (G. Nelson et al., 1998). Maciver and colleagues (2013) emphasize investigation, reflection, and exploration of community knowledge and perceptions. Ehde and colleagues (2013) developed a model of ways that PAR can be utilized during several phases of disability and rehabilitation research, including agenda setting, design, implementation, dissemination, and sustainability. Figure 10.1 illustrates the cyclical nature and participation from stakeholders in PAR throughout the research process. The experiences of disabled persons and their communities are centered in this model, empowering them with input and control at every stage.

## Validity

One concern that has been raised about participatory research has already been discussed earlier—the scientific qualifications and capabilities of disabled people to contribute to research (Tate & Pledger, 2003). The other main issue raised in objection is that inclusion of participants in research processes could threaten the scientific rigor of studies (Balcazar et al., 1998).

PAR enhances validity in certain ways—for one, ecologically. Ecological validity is a form of external validity that represents the real-world applicability of research findings (Blair & Minkler, 2009; Torre et al., 2012). Some scholars have argued that PAR provides expert validity, but not the type that academics are used to; in PAR, the experts are the people with the lived experience, not those with the most

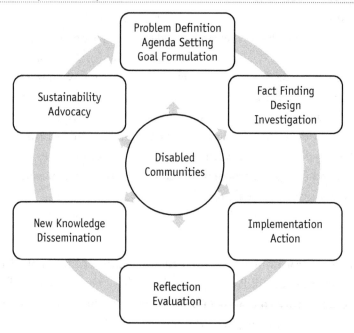

FIGURE 10.1. Participatory action research continuous feedback loop.

education or status (Blair & Minkler, 2009). Others contend that PAR has impact validity, in that it can be evaluated by the extent to which it creates change (Torre et al., 2012).

Another aspect of external validity is the extent to which research is welcomed, perceived as relevant, and actually utilized or implemented by stakeholders (Balcazar et al., 1998; Blair & Minkler, 2009). The impact of such high local or community relevance, however, is that it reduces the generalizability of findings to other settings (Blair & Minkler, 2009). PAR researchers would argue that the trade-off is worthwhile, because the work is much more ecologically important and can be replicated to transfer to other settings or populations (Blair & Minkler, 2009).

Researchers often reject the notion of removing barriers between the researchers and the researched, believing that releasing some control of the research process compromises the integrity of the study (Kitchin, 2000). This may stem from the assumption that PAR is a methodology—a type of qualitative or "soft" approach, which is a clear misunderstanding. PAR can be used with various methodologies including quantitative research (Balcazar et al., 1998). Kitchin (2000) aptly points out that consumer inclusion need not preclude the use of rigorous scientific methods, only that there are additional coresearchers involved. As he put it, "there is a renegotiation of the relationship between the researcher and researched, rather than a radical overhaul of the scientific procedures underlying the research" (p. 40). Unlike traditional research, PAR participants are encouraged to ask questions, verify information, and suggest alternative interpretations, which some would argue actually increases scientific rigor (Balcazar et al., 1998; Kitchin, 2000).

It is also important to note that researchers utilizing PAR must carefully attend to the methodology and intent of the study. There are a number of specific procedures and strategies that PAR researchers and people with disabilities use to facilitate partnered research (see K. E. McDonald & Raymaker, 2013), and disabled participants can "ground the interpretation of data in lived experiences" (Kramer et al., 2011, p. 264).

*Difficulties*

Of course, PAR is not without difficulties, barriers, and ethical questions. Some examples of challenging issues are intracommunity conflict, issues of inclusion and exclusion, insider/outsider tension, and difficult decisions about how to take action based on result (Minkler et al., 2002). Many researchers find it difficult to connect with disability communities and form meaningful relationships with consumer participants (Balcazar et al., 1998). Other researchers struggle with the concept of transferring power to consumer coresearchers; academics are typically most comfortable in the role of expert, holding decision-making power. Similarly, researchers may be uncomfortable with the idea of receiving criticism from community members when their intent is to help the community. PAR researchers must embody cultural humility and be willing to honor the expertise of those with the lived experience and to unpack the difference between intent and impact. Another barrier can be the length of the PAR process; it is not unusual for a PAR project to take several years to complete (Balcazar et al., 1998); however, institutions may place pressure on researchers to meet deadlines or publish results. Action also has consequences; it is possible for groups, agencies, or legislators to become hostile or resistant to consumer-driven changes and advocacy efforts (Balcazar et al., 1998). Researchers must weigh the potential benefits and drawbacks of the research circumstances to determine whether PAR should be utilized.

Balcazar et al. (1998) poignantly hypothesize that some of the misconceptions and reluctance to adopt PAR occur because "most researchers do not experience the conditions that oppress individuals with disabilities and do not fully share their sense of urgency about transforming their social reality" (p. 110).

## Health Disparities/Public Health

People with disabilities are increasingly being recognized as a population that experiences health disparities and deserves attention from public health researchers.

Health and disability are often related but not synonymous—one can be in good health and also disabled. When disability is equated with poor health, efforts at health promotion and disease prevention are undermined (U.S. Office of the Surgeon General Office on Disability, 2005). Health disparities are avoidable population health outcome differences related to historical social, economic, or environmental marginalization (Krahn, Walker, & Correa-De-Araujo, 2015).

Contributing to the inadequate attention and research dedicated to health disparities in the disabled population is routine dismissal of clear health differences between disabled and nondisabled people based on the assumption that disability-related impairments account for the discrepancies (Krahn et al., 2015). However, there are numerous examples of how disabled people have disproportionately poorer health than their nondisabled peers beyond the variance attributed to impairment itself. Disabled people have higher rates of behavioral risk factors for poor health outcomes, including smoking, low levels of physical activity, and obesity; they are also at heightened risk of both unintentional injury and violence (Krahn et al., 2015). Despite a greater incidence of chronic diseases than the nondisabled population, people with disabilities are considerably less apt to undergo preventive care such as cancer screenings, immunizations, mammograms, and Pap tests (U.S. Office of the Surgeon General Office on Disability, 2005). It is a vicious cycle wherein disabled people systematically experience poverty, inaccessibility, and discrimination, leading to economic and social disadvantages that result in behavioral lifestyle risk factors and diminished mental health, only exacerbating existing and causing more chronic illnesses, poorer health, and additional functional limitations (Krahn et al., 2015).

Part of the problem with disability and public health research is that data collection tools often leave out disability as a demographic factor, such as gender or race. Alternatively, disability may be assessed, but the definition and inclusion criteria are inconsistent and variable, making it impossible to compare data across studies (Stodden et al., 2003). There is great need to improve knowledge through the use of standardized disability identifiers to permit comparison of data and investigate intragroup differences such as type of disability and the experiences of people with disabilities who are culturally and linguistically diverse (Stodden et al., 2003; Krahn et al., 2015). Similarly, despite Americans With Disabilities Act (ADA) legislation that mandates accessibility compliance, there are no overarching means for assessing the accessibility of facilities or medical equipment or collecting data about compliance (Krahn et al., 2015). Without these practices in place, it is impossible to give appropriate attention and direct resources efficiently toward alleviating these disparities.

Another main contributor to health disparities for disabled people is active and passive exclusion from public health and biomedical research studies (Hamilton et al., 2017; Radermacher et al., 2010). Some researchers consider this to be an unintended consequence of oversight because of overprotective attitudes toward those at risk for exploitation (Krahn et al., 2015; K. E. McDonald & Raymaker, 2013). A major concern among researchers is how to include participants who are perceived to lack the capacity to understand information or communicate decisions; rather than developing resources or making revisions to help participants understand and make informed decisions about participation, they are instead simply excluded from research about them or that affects them. There remains a gap in existing research on evidence-based practices to support consent and capacity judgments. K. E. McDonald and Raymaker (2013) provide a comprehensive list of strategies for facilitating inclusive disability public health research, useful for all types of research with disabled people.

Health disparities among people with disabilities require legislative reform to improve access to care. Cost is a significant factor among other contributors to exclusion such as transportation barriers and lack of access to facilities and health care providers (Krahn et al., 2015). Although disabled people are covered by health insurance at similar rates as nondisabled counterparts, they are less likely to hold private coverage and bear the out-of-pocket cost of high copayments for medical supplies and equipment (Krahn et al., 2015; U.S. Office of the Surgeon General Office on Disability, 2005). The Patient Protection and Affordable Care Act of 2010 (ACA) is extremely important and culturally relevant to the disability community. Key provisions include prohibition of denial of coverage based on preexisting conditions, elimination of lifetime caps on benefits, and expansion of the Medicaid program to cover many disabled Americans who were not previously eligible (Patient Protection and Affordable Care Act, 2010). It is important to note that some state governments and governors elected not to enact the expansion of Medicaid within their states (Price & Eibner, 2013). Recent legislative threats to repeal the ACA and judicial decisions weakening its reach have left disability activists fearful that the overall health of the disability community may further decline in the future (Lindner, Rowland, Spurlock, Dorn, & Davis, 2018).

## Directions Forward

Traditional rehabilitation research has often disregarded the value of diverse cultural characteristics (Stodden et al., 2003). The field has focused heavily on fostering the independence and self-sufficiency of disabled people. Although independence is important to many and a core Western and White American value, disability culture embraces interdependency, and many culturally and linguistically diverse families hold a collectivist perspective (Stodden et al., 2003). It is important to understand the cultural salience of disability within specific cultures and utilize outcome measures of success that can accommodate varying values and goals (Radermacher et al., 2010; Stodden et al., 2003). For example, if return to employment is the primary outcome measure in a study, a participant who did not go back to work would not be considered successful; however, depending on the individual's cultural and personal value system, success may have indeed been achieved, for example, in his or her new role as a stay-at-home parent. Likewise, a participant who returned to work could be persistently depressed and experiencing recurrent suicidal ideation yet considered to have been successfully rehabilitated.

Culturally competent research must allow for flexibility to achieve its purpose. For example, traditional data collection tools such as surveys may be entirely inappropriate for members of cultures whose primary means of conveying information is through oral tradition, those who cannot read or write, and people who are linguistically diverse (Balcazar et al., 1998; Stodden et al., 2003). Culturally competent researchers are aware that certain groups of persons with disabilities are particularly marginalized even within the disability community itself, including people of color, members of the lesbian, gay, bisexual, transgender, queer-plus (LGBTQ+) population, and immigrants with disabilities (among others), and take deliberate steps to select participants to give voice to those groups (Minkler et al., 2002).

Figure 10.2 illustrates a decision aid tool (IDEAS) developed by Berghs and colleagues (2016) that emphasizes five aspects of cultural sensitivity: inclusion, dignity, equity, accessibility, and intersectionality. In each of these areas, researchers must

| I | D | E | A | S |
|---|---|---|---|---|
| Inclusion | Dignity | Equity | Accessibility | Intersectionality |
| How were people included? | How was dignity ensured? | How were long- and short-term equity achieved in terms of inclusion and dignity, and in terms of contributing to policies that tackle inequalities for people with impairments? | Was accessibility thought about? | Did the research involve people with different types of impairments, from different ethnic groups, different ages, women, children and young people? |

FIGURE 10.2.  IDEAS decision aid tool.

Credit: Berghs, M. J., Atkin, K. M., Graham, H. M., Hatton, C., & Thomas, C. (2016). Implications for public health research of models and theories of disability: A scoping study and evidence synthesis. *Public Health Research, 4*(8), 103, Box 5.

answer important questions to ensure that their process is inclusive, both of disability and of intersecting identities, and that it upholds the dignity of participants, is relevant to policy and advocacy, and is fully accessible. Berghs and colleagues (2016) also developed a more comprehensive checklist for researchers to assess for cultural competence in disability research. This checklist, shown in Table 10.1, expands upon the concepts included in the IDEAS tool and also considers the analytical framework of research. In other words, researchers are challenged to consider the ways in which disability is framed in their work and pushed to consider sociopolitical issues that may influence their findings.

## Conclusion

The challenges facing disability and rehabilitation research are significant, but they could be lessened by collective advocacy by researchers across disciplines, involvement with policymakers, and inclusion of stakeholders. D. S. Dunn and Elliott (2008) summarized the needed balance nicely: "Rehabilitation psychology benefits from a judicious mix of scientific rigor and real-world vigor" (p. 255). Researchers may be reluctant to adopt what can seem like radical changes given funding difficulties; decades of literature have demonstrated that inclusive research is effective yet is a long-term investment that does not pay off right away (Berghs et al., 2016). Instead, disability and rehabilitation research appear to be caught in a vicious cycle; if the field is still struggling to implement consumer participation 10 or 15 years from now, there is risk for the possibilities of stagnation, poorly informed evidence bases, faulty understandings, ineffective responses, and squandered resources.

At long last, it is time for disability and rehabilitation researchers to fully collaborate with consumers and other stakeholders who should be involved in all aspects of research, including planning, conducting, evaluating, interpreting, disseminating, and applying research findings (Stodden et al., 2003). D. S. Dunn and Elliott (2008) encourage researchers to use quantitative and experimental methods whenever possible but to be open to qualitative methods when they best fit the research question and existing knowledge base. When possible, researchers should use more than one method to build and refine theories and facilitate sustainable lines of research (D. S. Dunn & Elliott, 2008).

PAR and other participant-focused or ethnographic approaches promote sociopolitical change; they can empower people with disabilities but will only do so if utilized by researchers. Disability and rehabilitation research must finally move beyond a constrictive focus on the individual experience of disability (Olkin & Pledger, 2003) and instead return to its roots—the Lewinian tradition—where the

TABLE 10.1.

Checklist for Researchers to Ensure Cultural Competence in Disability Research

| | |
|---|---|
| Inclusion | Is it possible for the research to engage in coproduction or to involve disabled stakeholders in the development of the research question or design? What are the implications of participation? |
| Dignity | How well is the research likely to reflect the diverse experiences of disability? Is it important that it does? To what extent does the research either generically or specifically touch on issues related to the experiences of disabled people? How, for example, can disability sensitivity be ensured in design? What ethical issues need to be considered? Are the theoretical and empirical implications of using particular types of measures made explicit? |
| Equity | How well will the research contribute to improving the conditions for health for people with a range of different impairments, conditions, and/or mental health issues? Does it link to social entitlements for well-being and/or enabling social environments? What models of disability/impairment inform the research? Is there a discussion of universality and generalizability and, in particular, the extent to which the research can be said to reflect disability experiences? If not, is this acknowledged and the implications for the evidence base considered? |
| Accessibility | Has the intervention, and the study through which it will be evaluated, been designed with accessibility in mind? What adjustments are necessary and feasible to ensure accessibility? Are disabled participants needlessly excluded? How well does the research, for example, engage with those who use nonverbal communication strategies or who have cognitive impairments and/or learning disabilities? |
| Intersectionality | Does the existing evidence suggest that there is a gap in the literature linked to health inequalities? How well does the research connect to comorbidities and intersectionality? How well will it articulate the link between gender, age, socioeconomic class, sexuality, geography, disability, or ethnicity? |
| Analytical framework | How well does the research provide a meaningful analysis of disabling experiences in a way that links to theoretical perspectives/causal framework underpinning the intervention? Are there any disability-oriented recommendations that other researchers could learn from or that are important to the evaluation of the intervention? Does it acknowledge that people with disabilities can "flourish" rather than see disability as a burden? Does it consider how a disabling social and political environment might explain experiences? |

environmental and social factors are just as important as the personal (G. Nelson et al., 1998; Torre et al., 2012). Accessibility and accommodations must be routinely assessed and supports put in place to facilitate the full participation of disabled people at every level of the research hierarchy (Olkin & Pledger, 2003; Stodden et al., 2003). Investigators need to ask important questions about equity and how public policy is facilitating, improving, or ignoring the condition of disabled people in our society (Stodden et al., 2003). Disability and rehabilitation researchers should leverage their abilities and commit to taking action to dismantle oppressive structures and processes that disempower disabled people far more than any impairment.

# References

Alamo, H. L. (2015). The x-ing of language: The case AGAINST "Latinx." *Latino Rebels*. Retrieved from http://www.latinorebels.com/2015/12/12/the-x-ing-of-language-the-case-against-latinix/

Albert, A. B., Jacobs, H. E., & Siperstein, G. N. (2016). Sticks, stones, and stigma: Student bystander behavior in response to hearing the word "retard." *Intellectual and Developmental Disabilities, 54*(6), 391–401. doi:10.1352/1934-9556-54.6.391

Albrecht, G. L., & Devlieger, P. J. (1999). The disability paradox: High quality of life against all odds. *Social Science & Medicine, 48*(8), 977–988. doi:10.1016/s0277-9536(98)00411-0

Albrecht, G. L., Seelman, K. D., & Bury, M. (2001). *Handbook of disability studies*. Thousand Oaks, CA: Sage Publications.

Allport, G. W. (1954). *The nature of prejudice*. Cambridge, MA: Perseus Books.

Altman, B. (2001). Disability definitions, models, classification schemes, and applications. In G. Albrecht, K. Seelman, & M. Bury (Eds.), *Handbook of disability studies* (pp. 97–122). Thousand Oaks, CA: Sage.

American Educational Research Association, American Psychological Association, National Council on Measurement in Education, & Joint Committee on Standards for Educational and Psychological Testing. (2014). *Standards for educational and psychological testing*. Washington, DC: American Educational Research Association.

American Psychological Association. (2002). Ethical principles of psychologists and code of conduct. *American Psychologist, 57*, 1060–1073. doi:10.1037/0003-066x.57.12.1060

American Psychological Association. (2008). Resolution on the Americans with Disabilities Act. Retrieved from http://www.apastyle.org/manual/related/redirects/disabilities-act.aspx

American Psychological Association. (2010). *Publication manual of the American Psychological Association* (6th ed.). Washington, DC: Author.

American Psychological Association. (2011). *Training students with disabilities in testing and assessment.* Washington, DC: Author.

American Psychological Association. (2012). Guidelines for assessment of and intervention with persons with disabilities. *American Psychologist, 67,* 43–62. http://dx.doi.org/10.1037/a0025892

American Psychological Association. (2013). Guidelines for psychological evaluations in child protection matters. *American Psychologist, 68*(1), 20–31. doi:10.1037/a0029891

Americans with Disabilities Act of 1990, Pub. L. No. 101-336, 104 Stat. 328 (1990).

Andrews, E. E., & Ayers, K. A. (2016). Parenting with disability: Experiences of disabled women. In S. Miles-Cohen & C. Signore (Eds.), *Eliminating inequities for women with disabilities: An agenda for health and wellness* (pp. 209–225). Washington, DC: American Psychological Association. doi:10.1037/14943-000

Andrews, E. E., & Elliott, T. (2014). Physical rehabilitation programs. In C. L. Hunter, C. M. Hunter, & R. Kessler (Eds.), *Handbook of clinical psychology in medical settings: Evidence based assessment and intervention* (2nd ed., pp. 673–690). New York, NY: Springer.

Andrews, E. E., Forber-Pratt, A. J., Mona, L. R., Lund, E. M., Pilarski, C. R., & Balter, R. (2019). #SaytheWord: A disability culture commentary on the erasure of "disability." *Rehabilitation Psychology.* Advance online publication. http://dx.doi.org/10.1037/rep0000258

Andrews, E., Kuemmel, A., Williams, J., Pilarski, C. R., Dunn, M., & Lund, E. M. (2013). Providing culturally competent supervision to trainees with disabilities in rehabilitation settings. *Rehabilitation Psychology, 58*(3), 233–244. doi:10.1037/a0033338

Andrews, E. E., & Lund, E. M. (2015). Disability in psychology training: Where are we? *Training and Education in Professional Psychology, 9*(3), 210–217. doi:10.1037/tep0000085

Ando, S., Clement, S., Barley, E. A., & Thornicroft, G. (2011). The simulation of hallucinations to reduce the stigma of schizophrenia: a systematic review. *Schizophrenia Research, 133*(1-3), 8–16. doi:10.1016/j.schres.2011.09.011

Annon, J. S. (1976). The PLISSIT model: A proposed conceptual scheme for the behavioral treatment of sexual problems. *Journal of Sex Education and Therapy, 2*(1), 1–15. doi:10.1080/01614576.1976.11074483

Antonak, R. F. (1982). Development and psychometric analysis of the Scale of Attitudes Toward Disabled Persons. *Journal of Applied Rehabilitation Counseling, 13*(2), 22–29.

Antonak, R. F., & Livneh, H. (2000). Measurement of attitudes towards persons with disabilities. *Disability and Rehabilitation, 22*(5), 211–224. doi:10.1080/096382800296782

Artman, L. K., & Daniels, J. A. (2010). Disability and psychotherapy practice: Cultural competence and practical tips. *Professional Psychology: Research & Practice, 41,* 442–448. doi:10.1037/a0020864

Asch, A., & Rousso, H. (1985). Therapists with disabilities: Theoretical and clinical issues. *Psychology Journal for the Study of Interpersonal Processes, 48,* 1–12. doi:10.1080/00332747.1985.11024263

Aspinall, P. J. (2002). Collective terminology to describe the minority ethnic population: The persistence of confusion and ambiguity in usage. *Sociology, 36*(4), 803–816. doi:10.1177/0038038502036004401

Atanelov, L., Stiens, S. A., & Young, M. A. (2015). History of physical medicine and rehabilitation and its ethical dimensions. *AMA Journal of Ethics, 17*(6), 568–574. doi:10.1001/journalofethics.2015.17.6.mhst1-1506

Au, K. W., & Man, D. W. (2006). Attitudes toward people with disabilities: A comparison between health care professionals and students. *International Journal of Rehabilitation Research, 29*(2), 155–160. doi:10.1097/01.mrr.0000210048.09668.ab

Balcazar, F. E., Keys, C. B., Kaplan, D. L., & Suarez-Balcazar, Y. (1998). Participatory action research and people with disabilities: Principles and challenges. *Canadian Journal of Rehabilitation, 12*, 105–112. doi:10.1037/10726-000

Balcazar, F. E., Suarez-Balcazar, Y., & Taylor-Ritzler, T. (2009). Cultural competence: Development of a conceptual framework. *Disability and Rehabilitation, 31*(14), 1153–1160. doi:10.1080/09638280902773752

Barnes, C. (2008). An ethical agenda in disability research: Rhetoric or reality? In D. M. Mertens & P. E. Ginsberg (Eds.), *The handbook of social research ethics* (pp. 458–473). London, UK: Sage. doi:10.4135/9781483348971.n29

Barnes, E. (2014). Valuing disability, causing disability. *Ethics, 125*(1), 88–113. doi:10.1086/677021

Barry, M. J., & Edgman-Levitan, S. (2012). Shared decision making—the pinnacle of patient-centered care. *New England Journal of Medicine, 366*(9), 780–781. doi:10.1056/nejmp1109283

Bau, A. (1999). Providing culturally competent services to visually impaired persons. *Journal of Visual Impairment & Blindness, 93*(5), 291–297.

Baynton, D. C. (2006). Defect: A selective reinterpretation of American immigration history. In N. J. Hirschmann & B. Linker (Eds.), *Civil disabilities* (pp. 44–64). doi:10.9783/9780812290530.44

Beach, M. C., Price, E. G., Gary, T. L., Robinson, K. A., Gozu, A., Palacio, A., . . . Powe, N. R. (2005). Cultural competency: A systematic review of health care provider educational interventions. *Medical Care, 43*(4), 356–373. doi:10.1097/01.mlr.0000156861.58905.96

Becker, G., & Jauregui, J. K. (1985). The invisible isolation of deaf women: Its effect on social awareness. In M. J. Deegan & N. A. Brooks (Eds.), *Women and disability: The double handicap* (pp. 23–36). New Brunswick, NJ: Transaction Books.

Bell, C. (2010). Is disability studies actually white disability studies? In L. J. Davis (Ed.), *The disability studies reader* (pp. 374–382). New York, NY: Taylor & Francis.

Belt, R. (2016). Contemporary voting rights controversies through the lens of disability. *Stanford Law Review, 68*, 1491–1552.

Benjet, C., Azar, S. T., & Kuersten-Hogan, R. (2003). Evaluating the parental fitness of psychiatrically diagnosed individuals: Advocating a functional-contextual analysis of parenting. *Journal of Family Psychology, 17*(2), 238–251. doi:10.1037/0893-3200.17.2.238

Berghs, M. J., Atkin, K. M., Graham, H. M., Hatton, C., & Thomas, C. (2016). Implications for public health research of models and theories of disability: A scoping study and evidence synthesis. *Public Health Research, 4*(8), 1–166. doi:10.3310/phr04080

Berwick, D. M. (2009). What "patient-centered" should mean: Confessions of an extremist. *Health Affairs, 28*(4), w555–w565. doi:10.1377/hlthaff.28.4.w555

Betancourt, J. R., Green, A. R., Carrillo, M. J. E., & IIa, O. A. F. (2003). Defining cultural competence: A practical framework for addressing racial/ethnic disparities in health and health care. *Public Health Reports, 118*, 293–302. doi:10.1093/phr/118.4.293

Bickenbach, J. (2012). Ethics, disability and the international classification of functioning, disability and health. *American Journal of Physical Medicine & Rehabilitation, 91*(13), S163–S167. doi:10.1097/phm.0b013e31823d5487

Bickenbach, J. (2014). Reconciling the capability approach and the ICF. *ALTER-European Journal of Disability Research/Revue Européenne de Recherche sur le Handicap, 8*(1), 10–23. doi:10.1016/j.alter.2013.08.003

Bickford, J. O. (2004). Preferences of individuals with visual impairments for the use of person-first language. *Rehabilitation Education for Blindness and Visual Impairment, 36,* 120–126. doi:10.3200/revu.36.3.120-126

Blackie, D. (2014). Disability, dependency, and the family in the early United States. In S. Burch & M. Rembis (Eds.), *Disability histories* (pp. 17–34). Champaign, IL: University of Illinois Press.

Blair, T., & Minkler, M. (2009). Participatory action research with older adults: Key principles in practice. *The Gerontologist, 49*(5), 651–662. doi:10.1093/geront/gnp049

Blanck, P. D., & Millender, M. (2000). Before civil rights: Civil war pensions and the politics of disability in America, *Alabama Law Review, 52,* 1–50.

Blaska, J. (1993). The power of language: Speak and write using "person first." *Perspectives on Disability,* 25–32.

Block, P., & Friedner, M. (2017). Teaching disability studies in the era of Trump. Somatosphere. Retrieved from http://somatosphere.net/2017/08/teaching-disability-studies-in-the-era-of-trump.html

Bock, G. (1983). Racism and sexism in Nazi Germany: Motherhood, compulsory sterilization, and the state. *Signs: Journal of Women in Culture and Society, 8*(3), 400–421.

Bogart, K. R. (2014). The role of disability self-concept in adaptation to congenital or acquired disability. *Rehabilitation Psychology, 59*(1), 107–115. doi:10.1037/a0035800

Bogart, K. R. (2015). Disability identity predicts lower anxiety and depression in multiple sclerosis. *Rehabilitation Psychology, 60*(1), 105–109. doi:10.1037/rep0000029

Bogart, K. R., Rottenstein, A., Lund, E. M., & Bouchard, L. (2017). Who self-identifies as disabled? An examination of impairment and contextual predictors. *Rehabilitation Psychology, 62*(4), 553–562. doi:10.1037/rep0000132

Bogdan, R. (1988). *Freakshow: Presenting human oddities for amusement and profit.* Chicago, IL: University of Chicago Press.

Branson, J., & Miller, D. (2002). *Damned for their difference: The cultural construction of Deaf people as" disabled:" A sociological history.* Washington, DC: Gallaudet University Press.

Brault, M. W. (2012). Americans With Disabilities: 2010. Current Population Reports, U.S. Census Bureau, Washington, DC. Retrieved from http://www.includevt.org/wp-content/uploads/2016/07/2010_Census_Disability_Data.pdf

Brew-Parrish, V. (2004). The wrong message—Still. *Ragged Edge Online.* Retrieved from http://www.raggededgemagazine.com/focus/wrongmessage04.html

Brock, D. (2005). Preventing genetically transmissible diseases while respecting persons with disabilities. In D. Wasserman, R. Wachbroit, & J. Bickenbach (Eds.), *Quality of life and human difference: Genetic testing, health care, and disability* (pp. 67–100). Cambridge, MA: Cambridge University Press.

Brostrand, H. L. (2006). Tilting at windmills: Changing attitudes toward people with disabilities. *Journal of Rehabilitation, 72*(1), 4–9.

Brown, K. (2018). Saying Stephen Hawking is "free" from his wheelchair is ableist. *Teen Vogue.* Retrieved from https://www.teenvogue.com/story/stephen-hawking-free-from-his-wheelchair-ableist

Brown, L. (2012). Identity-first language. Autistic self-advocacy network. Retrieved from http://autisticadvocacy.org/identity-first-language/

Brown, S. E. (1995). A celebration of diversity: An introductory, annotated bibliography about disability culture. *Disability Studies Quarterly, 15*(4), 36–55.

Brown, S. E. (1996). Disability culture: A fact sheet. Retrieved from www.independentliving.org/docs3/brown96a.html

Brown, S. E. (2001). Disability Culture - Independent Living Institute newsletter. Retrieved from http://www.independentliving.org/newsletter/12-01.html#anchor1

Brown, S. (2002). What is disability culture? *Disability Studies Quarterly, 22*(2), 34–50.

Brown, S. E. (2015). Disability Culture and the ADA. *Disability Studies Quarterly, 35*(3).

Brueggemann, B. J. (2013). Disability studies/disability culture. In M. L. Wehmeyer (Ed.), *Oxford handbook of positive psychology and disability* (pp. 279–299). New York, NY: Oxford University Press.

Bruyère, S. M., & Peterson, D. B. (2005). Introduction to the Special Section on the International Classification of Functioning, Disability and Health: Implications for Rehabilitation Psychology. *Rehabilitation Psychology, 50*(2), 103–104. doi:10.1037/0090-5550.50.2.103

Bruyère, S. M., Van Looy, S. A., & Peterson, D. B. (2005). The International Classification of Functioning, Disability and Health: Contemporary literature overview. *Rehabilitation Psychology, 50*(2), 113–121.

Bruyère, S. M., Erickson, W. A., & VanLooy, S. (2004). Comparative study of workplace policy and practices contributing to disability nondiscrimination. *Rehabilitation Psychology, 49*(1), 28–38. doi:10.1037/0090-5550.49.1.28

Bryant, M. S. (2017). *Confronting the "good death": Nazi euthanasia on trial, 1945–1953.* Boulder, CO: University Press of Colorado. doi:10.26530/oapen_625241

Buntinx, W. H. (2013). Understanding disability: A strengths-based approach. In M. L. Wehmeyer (Ed.), *The Oxford handbook of positive psychology and disability* (pp. 7–18). New York, NY: Oxford University Press.

Burch, S., & Sutherland, I. (2006). Who's not yet here? American disability history. *Radical History Review,* (94), 127–147. doi:10.1215/01636545-2006-94-127

Byrom, B. (2001). A pupil and a patient: Hospital-schools in progressive America. In P. K. Longmore & L. Umansky (Eds.), *The new disability history: American perspectives* (pp. 133–156). New York, NY: New York University Press.

Caldwell, J. (2011). Disability identity of leaders in the self-advocacy movement. *Intellectual and Developmental Disabilities, 49,* 316–346. doi:10.1352/1934-9556.

Campinha-Bacote, J. (2002). The process of cultural competence in the delivery of health-care services: A model of care. *Journal of Transcultural Nursing, 13*(3), 181–184. doi:10.1177/10459602013003003

Caplan, B. (1995). Choose your words! Division 22 Presidential Address. *Rehabilitation Psychology, 40,* 233–240. doi:10.1037/h0092829

Caplan, B., & Shechter, J. (1993). Reflections on the "depressed," "unrealistic," "inappropriate," "manipulative," "unmotivated," "noncompliant," "denying," "maladjusted," "regressed," etc patient. *Archives of Physical Medicine and Rehabilitation, 74,* 1123–1124. doi:10.1016/0003-9993(93)90074-K

Caplan, B., & Shechter, J. (1995). The role of nonstandard neuropsychological assessment in rehabilitation: History, rationale, and examples. In L. Cushman & M. Scherer (Eds.), *Psychological assessment in medical rehabilitation* (pp. 359–391). Washington, DC: American Psychological Association.

Carden-Coyne, A. (2007). Ungrateful bodies: Rehabilitation, resistance and disabled American veterans of the First World War. *European Review of History—Revue européenne d'Histoire, 14*(4), 543–565. doi:10.1080/13507480701752185

Carey, A. C. (1998). Gender and compulsory sterilization programs in America: 1907–1950. *Journal of Historical Sociology, 11*(1), 74–105. doi:10.1111/1467-6443.00054

Carter, R. T. (2007). Racism and psychological and emotional injury: Recognizing and assessing race-based traumatic stress. *Counseling Psychologist, 35*(1), 13–105. doi:10.1177/0011000006292033

Carter-Long, L. (2017). Nothing feels real a third of the time. Transcript of Ouch Talk Show presented by Kate Monaghan and Simon Minty. British Broadcasting Company. Retrieved from https://www.bbc.com/news/disability-42223698

Center for Community Health and Development. (2017). *Chapter 27, Section 7: Building culturally competent organizations*. Lawrence, KS: University of Kansas. Retrieved from the Community Tool Box: http://ctb.ku.edu/en/table-of-contents/assessment/assessing-community-needs-and-resources/conduct-concerns-surveys/main

Center for Story-Based Strategy & Interactive Institute for Social Change. (n.d.). Why we need to step into #the4thbox. Retrieved from https://www.storybasedstrategy.org/the4thotoxlo

Centers for Disease Control and Prevention. (2018). New ads from former smokers. Retrieved from https://www.cdc.gov/features/smokers-stories/index.html

Centers for Disease Control and Prevention. (n.d.). Communicating with and about people with disabilities. Retrieved from https://www.cdc.gov/ncbddd/disabilityandhealth/pdf/disabilityposter_photos.pdf

Chalfin, F. (2014). The role of a visible/visual disability in the clinical dyad: Issues of visibility/invisibility for the client and clinician. *Psychoanalytic Social Work, 21*(1–2), 121–132. doi:10.1080/15228878.2013.834265

Chan, F., Strauser, D., Maher, P., Lee, E. J., Jones, R., & Johnson, E. T. (2010). Demand-side factors related to employment of people with disabilities: A survey of employers in the Midwest region of the United States. *Journal of Occupational Rehabilitation, 20*(4), 412–419. doi:10.1007/s10926-010-9252-6

Chandler, D. (1994). The Sapir-Whorf hypothesis. Retrieved from http://www.aber.ac.uk/media/Documents/short/whorf.html

Charlifue, S. W., & Gerhart, K. A. (1991). Behavioral and demographic predictors of suicide after traumatic spinal cord injury. *Archives of Physical Medicine and Rehabilitation, 72*(7), 488–492.

Charlton, J. I. (1998). *Nothing about us without us: Disability oppression and empowerment.* Berkeley, CA: University of California Press. doi:10.1525/california/9780520207950.003.0001

Charmaz, K. (1994). Identity dilemmas of chronically ill men. *Sociological Quarterly, 35*(2), 269–288. doi:10.1111/j.1533-8525.1994.tb00410.x

Charmaz, K. (1995). The body, identity, and self. *Sociological Quarterly, 36*(4), 657–680. doi:10.1111/j.1533-8525.1995.tb00459.x

Chen, R. K., Brodwin, M. G., Cardoso, E., & Chan, F. (2002). Attitudes towards people with disabilities in the social context of dating and marriage: A comparison of American, Taiwanese and Singaporean college students. *Journal of Rehabilitation, 68*, 5–11.

Chipps, J. A., Simpson, B., & Brysiewicz, P. (2008). The effectiveness of cultural-competence training for health professionals in community-based rehabilitation: A systematic review of literature. *Worldviews on Evidence-Based Nursing, 5*(2), 85–94. doi:10.1111/j.1741-6787.2008.00117.x

Chiriboga, D. A., & Hernandez, M. (2015). Multicultural competence in geropsychology. In P. A. Lichtenberg, B. T. Mast, B. D. Carpenter & J. E. Loebach Wetherell (Eds.), *APA handbook of clinical geropsychology, Vol. 1: History and status of the field and perspectives on aging* (pp. 379–419). Washington, DC: American Psychological Association. doi:10.1037/14458-016

Christiansen, J. B., & Barnartt, S. N. (2003). *Deaf president now!: The 1988 revolution at Gallaudet University*. Washington, DC: Gallaudet University Press.

Church, D. (2011). Freakery, cult films, and the problem of ambivalence. *Journal of Film and Video, 63*(1), 3–17. doi:10.1353/jfv.2011.0003

Civil Rights Act of 1964. Pub. Law No. 88–352. (1964).

Civil Rights Act of 1968. Pub. Law No. 90–284. (1968).

Clare, E. (2015). *Exile and pride: Disability, queerness, and liberation*. Durham, NC: Duke University Press.

Clark, D. A. (2006). Capability approach. In D. A. Clark (Ed.), *The Elgar companion to development studies* (pp. 32–44). Cheltenham, UK: Edward Elgar Publishing.

Colker, R. (2001). Winning and losing under the Americans With Disabilities Act. *Ohio State Law Journal, 62*, 239–278. doi:10.2139/ssrn.262832

Collier, R. (2012). Person-first language: Noble intent but to what effect? *Canadian Medical Association Journal, 184*(18), 1977–1978. doi:10.1503/cmaj.109-4319

Comas-Diaz, L. (2001). Hispanics, Latinos, or Americanos: The evolution of identity. *Cultural Diversity and Ethnic Minority Psychology, 7*(2), 115–120. doi:10.1037/10999809.7.2.115

Conder, J., Milner, P., & Mirfin-Veitch, B. (2011). Reflections on a participatory project: The rewards and challenges for the lead researchers. *Journal of Intellectual and Developmental Disability, 36*(1), 39–48. doi:10.3109/13668250.2010.548753

Conroy, C. (2012). Freaks and not freaks: Theatre and the making of crip identity. *Lambda Nordica: The Journal of LGBT Studies, 17*(1-2), 168–193.

Consortium for Citizens with Disabilities. (2017). Re: CCD rights TF and allies letter of opposition to the Americans With Disabilities Act (ADA). Education and Reform Act of 2017 (H.R. 620). Retrieved from http://disabilityrights-law.org/sites/default/files/documents/Letter-Opposition-ADA-Education-Reform-Act-2017.pdf

Cook, J. W., Jr. (1996). Of men, missing links, and nondescripts: The strange career of PT Barnum's "What is it?" exhibition. In R. G. Thomson (Ed.), *Freakery: Cultural spectacles of the extraordinary body* (pp. 139–157). New York, NY: New York University Press.

Cornish, J. A. E., Gorgens, K. A., Monson, S. P., Olkin, R., Palombi, B. J., & Abels, A. V. (2008). Perspectives on ethical practice with people who have disabilities. *Professional Psychology: Research and Practice, 39*(5), 488–497. doi:10.1037/a0013092

Corrigan, P. W., & Miller, F. E. (2004). Shame, blame, and contamination: A review of the impact of mental illness stigma on family members. *Journal of Mental Health, 13*(6), 537–548.

Cox, T. (1994). A comment on the language of diversity. *Organization, 1*(1), 51–58. doi:10.1177/135050849400100109

Croom, A. M. (2015). Slurs, stereotypes, and in-equality: a critical review of "How Epithets and Stereotypes are Racially Unequal." *Language Sciences, 52*, 139–154. doi:10.1016/j.langsci.2014.03.001

Cross, T. L., Bazron, B. J., Dennis, K. W., & Isaacs, M. R. (1989). *Towards a culturally competent system of care: A monograph on effective services for minority children who are severely emotionally disturbed*. Washington, DC: CASSP Technical Assistance Center, Georgetown University Child Development Center.

Cross, W. E., Jr. (1995). The psychology of nigrescence: Revising the Cross model. In J. G. Ponterotto, J. M. Casas, L. A. Suzuki, & C. M. Alexander (Eds.), *Handbook of multicultural counseling* (pp. 93–122). Thousand Oaks, CA: Sage Publications.

Crow, L. (1996). Including all of our lives: Renewing the social model of disability. In J. Morris (Ed.), *Encounters with strangers*. London, UK: Women's Press.

Crow, L. (2000). Helen Keller: Rethinking the problematic icon. *Disability & Society, 15*(6), 845–859. doi:10.1080/713662010

Darling, R. B. (2003). Toward a model of changing disability identities: A proposed typology and research agenda. *Disability & Society, 18*, 881–895. doi:10.1080/0968759032000127308

Darling, R. B., & Heckert, D. A. (2010). Orientation toward disability: Differences over the lifecourse. *International Journal of Disability, Development and Education, 57*, 131–143. doi:10.1080/10349121003750489

Darling, R. B. (2013). *Disability and identity: Negotiating self in a changing society*. Boulder, CO: Lynne Rienner Publishers.

Davis, L. J. (Ed.). (2006). *The disability studies reader*. New York, NY: Taylor & Francis.

Davis, L. J. (2015). *Enabling acts: The hidden story of how the Americans With Disabilities Act gave the largest US minority its rights*. Boston, MA: Beacon Press.

Davis, L. (2005). Assisted suicide and the rights of the disabled. All Things Considered, National Public Radio. Retrieved from https://www.npr.org/templates/story/story.php?storyId=4866181

Deal, M. (2003). Disabled people's attitudes toward other impairment groups: A hierarchy of impairments. *Disability & Society, 18*(7), 897–910. doi:10.1080/0968759032000127317

Deal, M. (2006). *Attitudes of disabled people toward other disabled people and impairment groups* (Unpublished doctoral dissertation). City University, London, UK.

DeJong, G. (1979). Independent living: From social movement to analytic paradigm. *Archives of Physical Medicine & Rehabilitation, 60*, 435–446.

Dembo, T. (1982). Some problems in rehabilitation as seen by a Lewinian. *Journal of Social Issues, 38*(1), 131–139. doi:10.1111/j.1540-4560.1982.tb00848.x

Devlieger, P. (2005, October). Generating a cultural model of disability. Paper presented at 19th Congress of the European Federation of Associations of Teachers of the Deaf (FEAPDA). Geneva, Switzerland.

Di Giulio, G. (2003). Sexuality and people living with physical or developmental disabilities: A review of key issues. *Canadian Journal of Human Sexuality, 12*(1), 53.

Dijkers, M. P., & Greenwald, B. D. (2012). Functional assessment in traumatic brain injury rehabilitation. In N. D. Zasler, D. I. Katz, & R. D. Zafonte (Eds.), *Brain injury medicine: Principles and practice* (2nd ed., pp. 301–318). New York, NY: Demos Medical Publishing.

Diller, L. (2005). Pushing the frames of reference in traumatic brain injury rehabilitation. *Archives of Physical Medicine & Rehabilitation, 86*(6), 1075–1080. doi:10.1016/j.apmr.2004.11.009

Donaldson, M. S., Corrigan, J. M., & Kohn, L. T. (Eds.). (2000). *To err is human: Building a safer health system* (Vol. 6). Washington, DC: National Academies Press.

Dowaliby, F. J., Burke, N. E., & McKee, B. G. (1983). A comparison of hearing-impaired and normally hearing students on locus of control, people orientation, and study habits and attitudes. *American Annals of the Deaf, 128*, 53–59. doi:10.1353/aad.2112.0001

Duchnick, J. J., Letsch, E. A., & Curtiss, G. (2009). Coping effectiveness training during acute rehabilitation of spinal cord injury/dysfunction: A randomized clinical trial. *Rehabilitation Psychology, 54*(2), 123–132. doi:10.1037/a0015571

Duffy, J., & Dorner, R. (2011). The pathos of "Mindblindness": Autism, science, and sadness in "Theory of Mind" narratives. *Journal of Literary & Cultural Disability Studies, 5*(2), 201–216. doi:10.3828/jlcds.2011.16

Dunn, A. M. (2002). Culture competence and the primary care provider. *Journal of Pediatric Health Care, 16*, 105–111. doi:10.1016/s0891-5245(02)38851-5

Dunn, D. S. (2015). *The social psychology of disability.* New York, NY: Oxford University Press.

Dunn, D. S., & Andrews, E. E. (2015). Person-first and identity-first language: Developing psychologists' cultural competence using disability language. *American Psychologist, 70*(3), 255–264. doi:10.1037/a0038636

Dunn, D. S., & Burcaw, S. (2013). Disability identity: Exploring narratives accounts of disability. *Rehabilitation Psychology, 58*, 148–157. doi:10.1037/a0031691

Dunn, D. S., & Dougherty, S. B. (2005). Prospects for a positive psychology of rehabilitation. *Rehabilitation Psychology, 50*(3), 305–311. doi:10.1037/0090-5550.50.3.305

Dunn, D. S., & Elliott, T. R. (2005). Revisiting a constructive classic: wright's physical disability: A psychosocial approach. *Rehabilitation Psychology, 50*, 183–189. doi: 10.1037/0090-5550.50.2.183

Dunn, D. S., & Elliott, T. R. (2008). The place and promise of theory in rehabilitation psychology research. *Rehabilitation Psychology, 53*(3), 254–267. doi:10.1037/a0012962

Dunn, M. (2011). Discourses of disability and clinical ethics support. *Clinical Ethics, 6*(1), 32–38. doi:10.1258/ce.2011.011006

East, L. J., & Orchard, T. R. (2014). Somebody else's job: Experiences of sex education among health professionals, parents and adolescents with physical disabilities in southwestern Ontario. *Sexuality and Disability, 32*(3), 335–350. doi:10.1007/s11195-013-9289-5

Eddey, G. E., & Robey, K. L. (2005). Considering the culture of disability in cultural competence education. *Academic Medicine, 80*(7), 706–712. doi:10.1097/00001888-200507000-00019

Education for All Handicapped Children Act of 1975. Pub. L. No. 94–142. (1975).

Edyburn, D. L. (2010). Would you recognize universal design for learning if you saw it? Ten propositions for new directions for the second decade of UDL. *Learning Disability Quarterly, 33*(1), 33–41. doi:10.1177/073194871003300103

Ehde, D. M. (2010). Application of positive psychology to rehabilitation psychology. In R. G. Frank, M. Rosenthal, & B. Caplan (Eds.), *Handbook of rehabilitation psychology* (pp. 417–424). Washington, DC: American Psychological Association. doi:10.1037/15972-029

Ehde, D. M., Dillworth, T. M., & Turner, J. A. (2014). Cognitive-behavioral therapy for individuals with chronic pain: Efficacy, innovations, and directions for research. *American Psychologist, 69*(2), 153–166. doi:10.1037/a0035747

Ehde, D. M., Wegener, S. T., Williams, R. M., Ephraim, P. L., Stevenson, J. E., Isenberg, P. J., & MacKenzie, E. J. (2013). Developing, testing, and sustaining rehabilitation interventions via participatory action research. *Archives of Physical Medicine and Rehabilitation, 94*(1), S30–S42. doi:10.1016/j.apmr.2012.10.025

Elementary and Secondary Education Act of 1965. Pub. L. No. 80-10. (1965).

Elliott, T., & Andrews, E. E. (2016). Physical rehabilitation facilities. In J. C. Norcross, G. R. VandenBos, & D. K. Freedheim (Eds.), *APA handbook of clinical psychology*, Vol. I: *Clinical psychology: Roots and branches* (M. M. Domenech Rodriguez, Assoc Ed.). Washington, DC: American Psychological Association.

Elliott, T. R., Kurylo, M., & Rivera, P. (2002). Positive growth following acquired physical disability. In C. R. Snyder & S. J. Lopez (Eds.), *Handbook of positive psychology* (pp. 687–698). New York, NY: Oxford University Press.

Elliott, T. R., & Umlauf, R. L. (1995). Measurement of personality and psychopathology following acquired physical disability. In L. A. Cushman & M. J. Scherer (Eds.), *Psychological assessment in medical rehabilitation* (pp. 325–358). Washington, DC: American Psychological Association.

Elliott, T. R., Shewchuk, R. M., & Richards, J. S. (2001). Family caregiver social problem-solving abilities and adjustment during the initial year of the caregiving role. *Journal of Counseling Psychology, 48*(2), 223–232. doi:10.1037/0022-0167.48.2.223

Ellis-Hill, C., Payne, S., & Ward, C. (2008). Using stroke to explore the Life Thread Model: An alternative approach to understanding rehabilitation following an acquired disability. *Disability and Rehabilitation: An International, Multidisciplinary Journal, 30*(2), 150–159. doi:10.1080/09638280701195462

Erikson, E. H. (1950). *Childhood and society* (2nd ed.). New York, NY: W. W. Norton and Company.

Erikson, E. H. (1968). *Identity: Youth and crisis.* New York, NY: W. W. Norton and Company.

Evans, J. (2004). Why the medical model needs disability studies (and vice-versa): A perspective from rehabilitation psychology. *Disability Studies Quarterly, 24*(4), 93–98. doi:10.18061/dsq. v24i4.893

Evans, S. E. (2004). *Forgotten crimes: The Holocaust and people with disabilities.* Chicago, IL: Ivan R. Dee Publishing.

Fässberg, M. M., Cheung, G., Canetto, S. S., Erlangsen, A., Lapierre, S., Lindner, R., . . . Duberstein, P. (2016). A systematic review of physical illness, functional disability, and suicidal behaviour among older adults. *Aging & Mental Health, 20*(2), 166–194. doi:10.1080/ 13607863.2015.1083945

Feldman, D., Gordon, P. A., White, M. J., & Weber, C. (2002). The effects of people-first language and demographic variables on beliefs, attitudes and behavioral intentions toward people with disabilities. *Journal of Applied Rehabilitation Counseling, 33*(3), 18–25.

Fine, M., & Asch, A. (1988). Disability beyond stigma: Social interaction, discrimination, and activism. *Journal of Social Issues, 44*(1), 3–21. doi:10.1111/j.1540-4560.1988.tb02045.x

Finkelstein, V. (1998). Emancipating disability studies. In T. Shakespeare (Ed.), *The disability reader: Social science perspectives* (pp. 28–49). London, UK: Cassell.

Fisher-Borne, M., Cain, J. M., & Martin, S. L. (2015). From mastery to accountability: Cultural humility as an alternative to cultural competence. *Social Work Education, 34*(2), 165–181. doi:10.1080/02615479.2014.977244

Fiske, S. T., Cuddy, A. J., & Glick, P. (2007). Universal dimensions of social cognition: Warmth and competence. *Trends in Cognitive Sciences, 11*(2), 77–83. doi:10.1016/j.tics.2006.11.005

Fiske, S. T., Xu, J., Cuddy, A. C., & Glick, P. (1999). (Dis)respecting versus (dis)liking: Status and interdependence predict ambivalent stereotypes of competence and warmth. *Journal of Social Issues, 55*(3), 473–489. doi:10.1111/0022-4537.00128

Flower, A., Burns, M. K., & Bottsford-Miller, N. A. (2007). Meta-analysis of disability simulation research. *Remedial and Special Education, 28*(2), 72–79. doi:10.1177/07419325070280020601

Forber-Pratt, A. J., Lyew, D. A., Mueller, C., & Samples, L. B. (2017). Disability identity development: A systematic review of the literature. *Rehabilitation Psychology, 62*(2), 198–207. doi:10.1037/rep0000134

Forber-Pratt, A. J., Lyew, D. A., Samples, L. B., & Mueller, C. (2017, April). Application of models of disability identity development to creating a new measure: Preliminary findings. Paper presented at the American Educational Research Association (Disability Studies in Education SIG), San Antonio, TX.

Forber-Pratt, A. J., Mueller, C. O., & Andrews, E. E. (2018). Disability identity and allyship in rehabilitation psychology: Sit, stand, sign, and show up. *Rehabilitation Psychology.* Advance online publication. doi:10.1037/rep0000256

Forber-Pratt, A. J., Zape, M., & Merrin, G. J. (2018, August). Construction & preliminary validation of the Disability Identity Development Scale (DIDS). Paper presented at the Annual Convention of the American Psychological Association (Division 22—Rehabilitation Psychology), San Francisco, CA.

Forber-Pratt, A. J., & Zape, M. P. (2017). Disability identity development model: Voices from the ADA-generation. *Disability and Health Journal, 10*(2), 350–355. doi:10.1016/j.dhjo.2016.12.013

Frank, A. W. (1993). The rhetoric of self-change: Illness experience as narrative. *Sociological Quarterly, 34*(1), 39–52. doi:10.1111/j.1533-8525.1993.tb00129.x

Frank, D. W., & Beane, L. L. (2015). How the ADA was passed. *The Federal Lawyer,* 62–63.

Frederick, A. (2015). Between stigma and mother-blame: Blind mothers' experiences in USA hospital postnatal care. *Sociology of Health & Illness, 37*(8), 1127–1141. doi:10.1111/1467-9566.12286

Freeman, S. T. (1989). Cultural and linguistic bias in mental health evaluations of deaf people. *Rehabilitation Psychology, 34*(1), 51–63. doi:10.1037/0090-5550.34.1.51

Friedland, J. (1998). Occupational therapy and rehabilitation: An awkward alliance. *American Journal of Occupational Therapy, 52*(5), 373–380. doi:10.5014/ajot.52.5.373

Friedman, C. (2016). Outdated language: Use of "mental retardation" in Medicaid HCBS waivers post-Rosa's Law. *Intellectual and Developmental Disabilities, 54*(5), 342–353. doi:10.1352/1934-9556-54.5.342

Froehle, C. (2016). The evolution of an accidental meme: How one little graphic became shared and adapted by millions. Retrieved from https://medium.com/@CRAiG/the-evolution-of-an-accidental-meme-ddc4e139e0e4

Gallaudet University. (n.d.). *History of Gallaudet University.* Retrieved from http://www.gallaudet.edu/history.html

Galer, D. (2016). Packing disability into the historian's toolbox: On the merits of labour histories of disability. *Labour/Le Travail, 77*(1), 257–262. doi:10.1353/llt.2016.0008

Galvin, R. (2003). The making of the disabled identity: A linguistic analysis of marginalisation. *Disability Studies Quarterly, 23*(2), 149–178. doi:10.18061/dsq.v23i2.421

Gaylord-Ross, R., & Browder, D. (1991). Functional assessment: Dynamic and domain properties. In L. H. Meyer, C. A. Peck, & L. Brown (Eds.), *Critical issues in the lives of people with severe disabilities* (pp. 45–66). Baltimore, MD: Paul H. Brookes.

Geisinger, K. F. (1998). Psychometric issues in test interpretation. In J. H. Sandoval, C. L. Frisby, K. F. Geisinger, J. D. Scheuneman, & J. R. Grenier (Eds.), *Test interpretation and diversity: Achieving equity in assessment* (pp. 17–30). Washington, DC: American Psychological Association.

Gelfman, R., Peters, D. J., Opitz, J. L., & Folz, T. J. (1997). The history of physical medicine and rehabilitation as recorded in the diary of Dr. Frank Krusen: Part 3. Consolidating the position

(1948–1953). *Archives of Physical Medicine & Rehabilitation, 78*(5), 556–561. doi:10.1016/s0003-9993(97)90178-7

Gernsbacher, M. A. (2017). Editorial perspective: The use of person-first language in scholarly writing may accentuate stigma. *Journal of Child Psychology and Psychiatry, 58*(7), 859–861. doi:10.1111/jcpp.12706

Giannini, M. J., Bergmark, B., Kreshover, S., Elias, E., Plummer, C., & O'Keefe, E. (2010). Understanding suicide and disability through three major disabling conditions: Intellectual disability, spinal cord injury, and multiple sclerosis. *Disability and Health Journal, 3*(2), 74–78. doi:10.1016/j.dhjo.2009.09.001

Gibson, J. (2006). Disability and clinical competency: An introduction. *California Psychologist, 39*, 6–10.

Gill, C. J. (1987). A new social perspective on disability and its implications for rehabilitation. *Occupational Therapy in Health Care, 4*(1), 49–55. doi:10.1080/j003v04n01_05

Gill, C. J. (1995). A psychological view of disability culture. *Disability Studies Quarterly, 15*(4), 15–19.

Gill, C. (1997). Four types of integration in disability identity development. *Journal of Vocational Rehabilitation, 9*, 39–46. doi:10.1016/s1052-2263(97)00020-2

Gill, C. J. (2001). Divided understanding: The social experience of disability. In G. L. Albrecht, K. D. Seelman, & M. Bury (Eds.), *Handbook of disability studies* (pp. 351–372). Thousand Oaks, CA: Sage Publication.

Gill, C. J. (2010). No, we don't think our doctors are out to get us: Responding to the straw man distortions of disability rights arguments against assisted suicide. *Disability and Health Journal, 3*, 31–38. doi:0.1016/j.dhjo.2009.10.003

Gill, C., Kewman, D. G., & Brannon, R. W. (2003). Transforming psychological practice and society: Policies that reflect the new paradigm. *American Psychologist, 58*, 305–312. doi:10.1037/0003-066X.58.4.305

Gilson, S. F., Tusler, A., & Gill, C. (1997). Ethnographic research in disability identity: Self-determination and community. *Journal of Vocational Rehabilitation, 9*, 7–17.

Goffman, E. (1963). *Stigma: Notes on the management of spoiled identity.* Englewood Cliffs, NJ: Prentice Hall.

Golden, M., & Zoanni, T. (2010). Killing us softly: The dangers of legalizing assisted suicide. *Disability and Health Journal, 3*(1), 16–30. doi:10.1016/j.dhjo.2009.08.006

Goldman, C. D. (1982). Architectural barriers: A perspective on progress. *Western New England Law Review, 5*(3), 465–493.

Goldman, A. S., Schmalstieg, E. J., Freeman, D. H., Jr., Goldman, D. A., & Schmalstieg, F. C., Jr. (2003). What was the cause of Franklin Delano Roosevelt's paralytic illness? *Journal of Medical Biography, 11*(4), 232–240. doi:10.1177/096777200301100412

Goodley, D. (2016). *Disability studies: An interdisciplinary introduction* (2nd ed.). Thousand Oaks, CA: Sage Publications.

Gottberg, K., Chruzander, C., Backenroth, G., Johansson, S., Ahlström, G., & Ytterberg, C. (2016). Individual face-to-face cognitive behavioural therapy in multiple sclerosis: A qualitative study. *Journal of Clinical Psychology, 72*(7), 651–662. doi:10.1002/jclp.22288

Gould, S. J. (1985). Carrie Buck's daughter. *Constitutional Commentary, 2*, 331–339.

Gouvier, W. D., & Coon, R. C. (2002). Misconceptions, discrimination, and disabling language: Synthesis and review. *Applied Neuropsychology, 9*, 48–57. doi:10.1207/S15324826AN0901_6

Granello, D. H., & Gibbs, T. A. (2016). The power of language and labels: "The mentally ill" versus "People with mental illnesses." *Journal of Counseling & Development, 94*(1), 31–40. doi:10.1002/jcad.12059

Green, S., Davis, C., Karshmer, E., Marsh, P., & Straight, B. (2005). Living stigma: The impact of labeling, stereotyping, separation, status loss, and discrimination in the lives of individuals with disabilities and their families. *Sociological Inquiry, 75,* 197–215. doi:10.1111/j.1475-682x.2005.00119.x

Groce, N. E., & Zola, I. K. (1993). Multiculturalism, chronic illness, and disability. *Pediatrics, 91*(5), 1048–1055.

Groth-Marnat, G. (2009). *Handbook of psychological assessment* (5th ed.). Hoboken, NJ: John Wiley & Sons.

Grue, J. (2016). The problem with inspiration porn: A tentative definition and a provisional critique. *Disability & Society, 31*(6), 838–849. doi:10.1080/09687599.2016.1205473

Guerra, G., & Orbea, G. (2015). The argument against the use of the term "Latinx." *The Phoenix.* Retrieved from: https://swarthmorephoenix.com/2015/11/19/the-argument-against-the-use-of-the-term-latinx/

Guilmette, T. J., Hagan, L. D., & Giuliano, A. J. (2008). Assigning qualitative descriptions to test scores in neuropsychology: Forensic implications. *Clinical Neuropsychologist, 22*(1), 122–139.

Hadley, B. J. (2008). Mobilising the monster: modern disabled performers' manipulation of the freakshow. *M/C Journal, 11*(3), 1–7.

Hahn, H. (1988). The politics of physical differences: Disability and discrimination. *Journal of Social Issues, 44,* 39–47. doi:10.1111/j.1540-4560.1988.tb02047.x

Hahn, H., & Beualaurier, R. L. (2001). Attitudes towards disabilities: A research note on activist with disabilities. *Journal of Disabilities Policy Studies, 12,* 40–46. doi:10.1177/104420730101200105

Hahn, H., & Belt, T. L. (2004). Disability identity and attitudes towards a cure in a sample of disabled activists. *Journal of Health and Social Behavior, 45,* 453–464. doi:10.1177/002214650404500407

Haller, B., & Ralph, S. (2003). John Callahan's Pelswick cartoon and a new phase of disability humor. *Disability Studies Quarterly, 23*(3). Retrieved from http://www.dsqsds.org/article/view/431/608. doi:10.18061/dsq.v23i3/4.431

Hamilton, J., Ingham, B., McKinnon, I., Parr, J. R., Tam, L. Y. C., & Le Couteur, A. (2017). Mental capacity to consent to research? Experiences of consenting adults with intellectual disabilities and/or autism to research. *British Journal of Learning Disabilities, 45*(4), 230–237. doi:10.1111/bld.12198

Harrell, E. (2014). Crime against persons with disabilities, 2009–2012—Statistical tables. U.S. Department of Justice, Office of Justice Programs, Bureau of Justice Statistics.

Hartley, S. L., & MacLean, W. E. (2006). A review of the reliability and validity of Likert-type scales for people with intellectual disability. *Journal of Intellectual Disability Research, 50*(11), 813–827. doi:10.1111/j.1365-2788.2006.00844.x

Hassouneh-Phillips, D., & Curry, M. A. (2002). Abuse of women with disabilities: State of the science. *Rehabilitation Counseling Bulletin, 45*(2), 96–104. doi:10.1177/003435520204500204

Hayes, M., & Black, R. (2003). Troubling signs: Disability, Hollywood movies and the construction of a discourse of pity. *Disability Studies Quarterly, 23*(2). doi:10.18061/dsq.v23i2.419

Heinemann, A. W. (1995). Measures of coping and reaction to disability. In L. A. Cushman & M. J. Scherer (Eds.), *Psychological assessment in medical rehabilitation* (pp. 39–99). Washington, DC: American Psychological Association.

Helms, J. E. (Ed.). (1990). *Contributions in Afro-American and African studies, No. 129. Black and White racial identity: Theory, research, and practice.* New York, NY: Greenwood Press.

Hendren, S. (n.d.). On boundedness: FAQs about the accessible icon. Abler. Retrieved from http://ablersite.org/2013/07/12/on-boundedness-faqsabout-the-accessible-icon/

Herbert, J. T. (2000). Simulation as a learning method to facilitate disability awareness. *Journal of Experiential Education, 23*(1), 5–11. doi:10.1177/105382590002300102

Hergenrather, K., & Rhodes, S. (2007). Exploring undergraduate student attitudes toward persons with disabilities application of the disability social relationship scale. *Rehabilitation Counseling Bulletin, 50*(2), 66–75. doi:10.1177/00343552070500020501

Hewstone, M. (2003). Panacea for prejudice. *Psychologist, 16*(7), 352–355.

Hershey, L. (1994). Wade Blank's liberated community. In B. Shaw (Ed.), *The ragged edge: The disability experience from the pages of the first fifteen years of The Disability Rag* (pp. 145–155). Louisville, KY: Advocado Press.

Hickel, K. W. (2001). Medicine, bureaucracy, and social welfare: The politics of disability compensation for American veterans of World War I. In P. K. Longmore & L. Umansky (Eds.), *The new disability history: American perspectives* (pp. 236–267). New York, NY: New York University Press.

Hill-Briggs, F., Dial, J. G., Morere, D. A., & Joyce, A. (2007). Neuropsychological assessment of persons with physical disability, visual impairment or blindness, and hearing impairment or deafness. *Archives of Clinical Neuropsychology, 22*, 389–404. doi:10.1016/j.acn.2007.01.013

Hoffman, L. C. (2013). An employment opportunity or a discrimination dilemma: Sheltered workshops and the employment of the disabled. *University of Pennsylvania Journal of Law & Social Change, 16*, 151–179.

Hogan, D. J. (2014). *The Wizard of Oz FAQ: All that's left to know about life, according to Oz.* Milwaukee, WI: Applause Theatre & Cinema Books.

Hogg, M. A., & Abrams, D. (1988). *Social identifications: A social psychology of intergroup relations and group processes.* London, UK: Routledge.

Hojati, A. (2012). A study of euphemisms in the context of English-speaking media. *International Journal of Linguistics, 4*(4), 552–562. doi:10.5296/ijl.v4i4.2933

Holm, C. S. (1987). Testing for values with the Deaf: The language/cultural effect. *Journal of Rehabilitation of the Deaf, 20*, 1–9.

Hopkins, S. (n.d.). Meaning of Symbol. Retrieved from: https://www.3elove.com/pages/meaning-of-symbol

Horin, E. V., Hernandez, B., & Donoso, O. A. (2012). Behind closed doors: Assessing individuals from diverse backgrounds. *Journal of Vocational Rehabilitation, 37*(2), 87–97.

Houck, D. W., & Kiewe, A. (2003). *FDR's body politics: The rhetoric of disability.* College Station, TX: Texas A&M University Press.

Hughes, K., Bellis, M. A., Jones, L., Wood, S., Bates, G., Eckley, L., . . . Officer, A. (2012). Prevalence and risk of violence against adults with disabilities: A systematic review and meta-analysis of observational studies. *Lancet, 379*(9826), 1621–1629. doi:10.1016/s0140-6736(11)61851-5

Hughes, R. B., Lund, E. M., Gabrielli, J., Powers, L. E., & Curry, M. A. (2011). Prevalence of interpersonal violence against community-living adults with disabilities: A literature review. *Rehabilitation Psychology, 56*(4), 302–319. doi:10.1037/a0025620

Hughes, R. B., Robinson-Whelen, S., Pepper, A. C., Gabrielli, J., Lund, E. M., Legerski, J., et al. (2010). Development of a safety awareness group intervention for women with diverse disabilities: A pilot study. *Rehabilitation Psychology, 55*(3), 263–271. doi:10.1037/a0019916

Hughes, R. B., Robinson-Whelen, S., Taylor, H. B., Peterson, N. J., & Nosek, M. A. (2005). Characteristics of depressed and nondepressed women with physical disabilities. *Archives of Physical Medicine and Rehabilitation, 86,* 473–479. doi:10.1016/j.apmr.2004.06.068

Hunt, B., & Hunt, C. S. (2000). Attitudes toward people with disabilities: A comparison of undergraduate rehabilitation and business majors. *Rehabilitation Education, 14*(3), 269–283.

Hunt, E., & Agnoli, F. (1991). The Whorfian hypothesis: A cognitive psychology perspective. *Psychological Review, 98*(3), 377–389. doi:10.1037/0033-295x.98.3.377

Hurley, A., Tomasulo, D. J., & Pfadt, A. G. (1998). Individual and group psychotherapy approaches for persons with intellectual disabilities and developmental disabilities. *Journal of Developmental and Physical Disabilities, 10,* 365–386. doi:10.1023/a:1021806605662

Iezzoni, L. I., McCarthy, E. P., Davis, R. B., & Siebens, H. (2000). Mobility problems and perceptions of disability by self-respondents and proxy respondents. *Medical Care, 38*(10), 1051–1057. doi:10.1097/00005650-200010000-00009

Individuals with Disabilities Education Act Amendments of 1997. Pub. L. No. 105–17. (1997).

Iredale, R. (2000). Eugenics and its relevance to contemporary health care. *Nursing Ethics, 7*(3), 205–214. doi:10.1177/096973300000700303

Isaacson, M. (2014). Clarifying concepts: Cultural humility or competency. *Journal of Professional Nursing, 30*(3), 251–258.

Ishige, N., & Hayashi, N. (2005). Occupation and social experience: Factors influencing attitude towards people with schizophrenia. *Psychiatry and Clinical Neurosciences, 59*(1), 89–95. doi:10.1111/j.1440-1819.2005.01337.x

Jaarsma, P., & Welin, S. (2012). Autism as a natural human variation: Reflections on the claims of the neurodiversity movement. *Health Care Analysis, 20*(1), 20–30. doi:10.1007/s10728-011-0169-9

Jambeck, J. R., Andrady, A., Geyer, R., Narayan, R., Perryman, M., Siegler, T., ... Lavender Law, K. (2015). Plastic waste inputs from land into the ocean. *Science, 347,* 768–771. doi:10.1126/science.1260352

Jennings, A. (2016). *Engendering and regendering disability: Gender and disability activism in postwar America.* In S. Burch & M. Rembis (Eds.), *Disability histories* (pp. 345–363). Champaign, IL: University of Illinois Press.

Johnson, H. M. (2003). Unspeakable conversations. *New York Times Magazine.* Retrieved from https://www.nytimes.com/2003/02/16/magazine/unspeakable-conversations.html

Johnson, J. (2013). Negotiating autism as an epidemic of discourse. *Disability Studies Quarterly, 33*(2). doi:10.18061/dsq.v33i2.3716

Johnson, M. (1998). PRIDE & IDENTITY Part 2 of an interview with Nadina LaSpina and Daniel Robert. *Electric EDGE* (Web Edition of The Ragged Edge), March/April.

Johnson, M. (2006). *Disability awareness—Do it right! Your all-in-one-how-to-guide.* Louisville, KY: Advocado Press.

Johnson, M. (2007). Before its time: Public perception of disability rights, the Americans With Disabilities Act, and the future of access and accommodation. *Washington University Journal of Law & Policy, 23,* 121–150.

Johnston, M. V., Vanderheiden, G. C., Farkas, M. D., Rogers, E. S., Summers, J. A., & Westbrook, J. D. (2009*). The challenge of evidence in disability and rehabilitation research and practice: A position paper.* National Center for the Dissemination of Disability Research (NCDDR). Austin, TX: SEDL.

Joint Commission. (2010). *Advancing effective communication, cultural competence, and patient- and family-centered care: A roadmap for hospitals.* Oakbrook Terrace, IL: Author.

Jones, E. E., & Nisbett, R. E. (1971). The actor and the observer: Divergent perceptions of the causes of behavior. In E. E. Jones, D. Kanouse, H. H. Kelley, R. E. Nisbett, S. Valins, & B. Weiner (Eds.), *Attribution: Perceiving the causes of behavior* (pp. 79–94). Morristown, NJ: General Learning Press.

Jones, L., Bellis, M. A., Wood, S., Hughes, K., McCoy, E., Eckley, L., et al. (2012). Prevalence and risk of violence against children with disabilities: A systematic review and meta-analysis of observational studies. *Lancet, 380*(9845), 899–907. doi:10.1016/s0140-6736(12)60692-8

Jowett, S., Karatzias, T., Brown, M., Grieve, A., Paterson, D., & Walley, R. (2016). Eye movement desensitization and reprocessing (EMDR) for DSM–5 posttraumatic stress disorder (PTSD) in adults with intellectual disabilities: A case study review. *Psychological Trauma: Theory, Research, Practice, and Policy, 8*(6), 709–719. doi:10.1037/tra0000101

Kaplan, R. (2002). Quality of life: An outcomes perspective. *Archives of Physical Medicine and Rehabilitation, 83*(2), S44–S50. doi:10.1053/apmr.2002.36955

Kapp, S. K., Gillespie-Lynch, K., Sherman, L. E., & Hutman, T. (2012). Deficit, difference, or both? Autism and neurodiversity. *Developmental Psychology, 49*(1), 59–71. doi:10.1037/a0028353

Kaye, H. S., Harrington, C., & LaPlante, M. P. (2010). Long-term care: Who gets it, who provides it, who pays, and how much? *Health Affairs, 29*(1), 11–21. doi:10.1377/hlthaff.2009.0535

Keller, R. M., & Galgay, C. E. (2010). Microaggressive experiences of people with disabilities. In D. W. Sue (Ed.), *Microaggressions and marginality: Manifestation, dynamics, and impact* (pp. 241–268). Hoboken, NJ: John Wiley & Sons.

Kelley-Moore, J. A., Schumacher, J. G., Kahana, E., & Kahana, B. (2006). When do older adults become "disabled"? Social and health antecedents of perceived disability in a panel study of the oldest old. *Journal of Health and Social Behavior, 47*(2), 126–141. doi:10.1177/002214650604700203

Kelly, M. P., & Barker, M. (2016). Why is changing health-related behaviour so difficult? *Public Health, 136,* 109–116. doi:10.1016/j.puhe.2016.03.030

Kemp, N. T., & Mallinckrodt, B. (1996). Impact of professional training on case conceptualization of clients with a disability. *Professional Psychology: Research and Practice, 27*(4), 378–385. doi:10.1037/0735-7028.27.4.378

Kendall, E., & Buys, N. (1998). An integrated model of psychological adjustment following acquired disability. *Journal of Rehabilitation, 64*(3), 16.

Kendregan, C. P. (1966). Sixty years of compulsory eugenic sterilization: Three generations of imbeciles and the constitution of the United States. *Chicago-Kent Law Review, 43,* 123–145.

Kennedy, J., Wood, E. G., & Frieden, L. (2017). Disparities in insurance coverage, health services use, and access following implementation of the Affordable Care Act: A comparison of disabled and nondisabled working-age adults. *INQUIRY: The Journal of Health Care Organization, Provision, and Financing, 54,* 1–10. doi:10.1177/0046958017734031

Kerkhoff, T. R., & Hanson, S. L. (2015). Disability culture: An ethics perspective. In J. M. Uomoto & T. M. Wong (Eds.), *Multicultural neurorehabilitation: Clinical principles for rehabilitation professionals* (pp. 169–202). New York, NY: Springer.

Ketterlin-Geller, L. R. (2005). Knowing what all students know: Procedures for developing universal design for assessment. *Journal of Technology, Learning, and Assessment, 4*(2). Retrieved from http://ejournals.bc.edu/ojs/index.php/jtla/article/download/1649/1491

Khazem, L. R., Jahn, D. R., Cukrowicz, K. C., & Anestis, M. D. (2015). Physical disability and the interpersonal theory of suicide. *Death Studies, 39*(10), 641–646. doi:10.1080/07481187.2015.1047061

Kitchin, R. (2000). The researched opinions on research: Disabled people and disability research. *Disability & Society, 15*(1), 25–47. doi:10.1080/09687590025757

Kleinman, A., & Benson, P. (2006). Anthropology in the clinic: The problem of cultural competency and how to fix it. *PLoS Medicine, 3,* e294. doi:10.1371/journal.pmed.0030294

Koehler-Pentacoff, E. (2015). *The missing Kennedy: Rosemary Kennedy and the secret bonds of four women.* Baltimore, MD: Bancroft Press.

Krahn, G. L., Walker, D. K., & Correa-De-Araujo, R. (2015). Persons with disabilities as an unrecognized health disparity population. *American Journal of Public Health, 105*(S2), S198–S206. doi:10.2105/ajph.2014.302182

Kramer, J. M., Kramer, J. C., García-Iriarte, E., & Hammel, J. (2011). Following through to the end: The use of inclusive strategies to analyse and interpret data in participatory action research with individuals with intellectual disabilities. *Journal of Applied Research in Intellectual Disabilities, 24*(3), 263–273. doi:10.1111/j.1468-3148.2010.00602.x

Kraus, L., Lauer, E., Coleman, R., & Houtenville, A. (2018). *2017 Disability statistics annual report.* Durham, NH: University of New Hampshire.

Krishnamurthy, R., VandeCreek, L., Kaslow, N. J., Tazeau, Y. N., Milville, M. L., Kerns, R., et al. (2004). Achieving competency in psychological assessment: Directions for education and training. *Journal of Clinical Psychology, 80,* 725–739. doi:10.1002/jclp.20010

Kubler-Ross, E. (1968). *On death and dying.* New York, NY: Macmillan.

Kuppers, P. (2007). Outsides: Disability culture nature poetry. *Journal of Literary & Cultural Disability Studies, 1*(1), 22–33. doi:10.3828/jlcds.1.1.4

Lalvani, P., & Broderick, A. A. (2013). Institutionalized ableism and the misguided "Disability Awareness Day": Transformative pedagogies for teacher education. *Equity & Excellence in Education, 46*(4), 468–483. doi:10.1080/10665684.2013.838484

Landsman, G. (1999). Does God give special kids to special parents? In L. L. Layne (Ed.), *Transformative motherhood: On giving and getting in a consumer culture* (pp. 133–155). New York, NY: New York University Press.

Lane, H. L. (2002). Do deaf people have a disability? *Sign Language Studies, 2*(4), 356–379. doi:10.1353/sls.2002.0019

Langlois, J. A., Maggi, S., Harris, T., Simonsick, E. M., Ferrucci, L., Pavan, M., . . . Enzi, G. (1996). Self-report of difficulty in performing functional activities identifies a broad range of disability in old age. *Journal of the American Geriatrics Society, 44*(12), 1421–1428. doi:10.1111/j.1532-5415.1996.tb04065.x

Larson, K. C. (2015). *Rosemary: The hidden Kennedy daughter.* Boston, MA: Houghton Mifflin Harcourt.

Lawrie, P. (2018). Race, Work, and Disability in Progressive Era United States. In M. Rembis, C. Kudlick, & K. E. Nielsen (Eds.), *The Oxford Handbook of Disability History* (pp. 229–246). New York: Oxford University Press.

Leigh, I. W., Corbett, C. A., Gutman, V., & Morere, D. A. (1996). Providing psychological services to deaf individuals: A response to new perceptions of diversity. *Professional Psychology: Research and Practice, 27*(4), 364–371. doi:10.1037/0735-7028.27.4.364

Leigh, I. W., Powers, L., Vash, C., & Nettles, R. (2004). Survey of psychological services to clients with disabilities: The need for awareness. *Rehabilitation Psychology, 49*(1), 48–54. doi:10.1037/0090-5550.49.1.48

Lenze, E. J., Rogers, J. C., Martire, L. M., Mulsant, B. H., Rollman, B. L., Dew, M. A., . . . Reynolds, C. F., III. (2001). The association of late-life depression and anxiety with physical disability: A review of the literature and prospectus for future research. *American Journal of Geriatric Psychiatry, 9*(2), 113–135. doi:10.1097/00019442-200105000-00004

Lewis, N., Lewis, K., & Davies, B. (2016). "I don't feel trapped anymore. . . I feel like a bird": People with learning disabilities experience of psychological therapy. *Journal of Applied Research in Intellectual Disabilities, 29*(5), 445–454. doi:10.1111/jar.12199

Lezak, M. D. (2002). Responsive assessment and the freedom to think for ourselves. *Rehabilitation Psychology, 47*(3), 339–353. doi:10.1037/0090-5550.47.3.339

Li, L., & Moore, D. (1998). Acceptance of disability and its correlates. *Journal of Social Psychology, 138*(1), 13–25. doi:10.1080/00224549809600349

Lindner, S., Rowland, R., Spurlock, M., Dorn, S., & Davis, M. (2018). "Canaries in the mine . . . " the impact of Affordable Care Act implementation on people with disabilities: Evidence from interviews with disability advocates. *Disability and Health Journal, 11*(1), 86–92. doi:10.1016/j.dhjo.2017.04.003

Link, B. G., & Phelan, J. C. (2001). Conceptualizing stigma. *Annual Review of Sociology, 27*(1), 363–385. doi:10.1146/annurev.soc.27.1.363

Linkowski, D. C. (1971). Acceptance of Disability Scale. PsycTESTS Dataset. doi:10.1037/t15375-000

Linton, S. (1998). *Claiming disability: Knowledge and identity.* New York, NY: New York University Press.

Livneh, H. (1982). On the origins of negative attitudes toward people with disabilities. *Rehabilitation Literature, 43*, 338–347. doi:10.1891/9780826161628.0002

Livneh, H. (1986). A unified approach to existing models of adaptation to disability: I. A model adaptation. *Journal of Applied Rehabilitation Counseling, 17*(1), 5–16, 56.

Livneh, H., & Antonak, R. F. (2005). Psychosocial adaptation to chronic illness and disability: A primer for counselors. *Journal of Counseling & Development, 83*(1), 12–20. doi:10.1002/j.1556-6678.2005.tb00575.x

Livneh, H., Lott, S., & Antonak, R. (2004). Patterns of psychosocial adaptation to chronic illness and disability: A cluster analytic approach. *Psychology, Health & Medicine, 9*(4), 411–430. doi:10.1080/1354850042000267030

Lombardo, P. A. (2003). Facing Carrie Buck. *Hastings Center Report, 33*(2), 14–17. doi:10.2307/3528148

Long, A. (2008). Introducing the new and improved Americans with Disabilities Act: Assessing the ADA Amendments Act of 2008. *Northwestern University Law Review Colloquy, 103*, 217–229.

Longmore, P. K. (1985). A note on language and the social identity of disabled people. *American Behavioral Scientist, 28*(3), 419–423. doi:10.1177/000276485028003009

Longmore, P. (1987). Uncovering the hidden history of disabled people. *Reviews in American History, 15*(3), 355–364. doi:10.2307/2702029

Longmore, P. K. (1995). The second phase: From disability rights to disability culture. First published in *Disability Rag & Resource*, Sept./Oct. Retrieved from www.independentliving.org/docs3/longm95.html

Longmore, P. K. (2003). *Why I burned my book and other essays on disability*. Philadelphia, PA: Temple University Press.

Longmore, P. K., & Goldberger, D. (2000). The League of the Physically Handicapped and the Great Depression: A case study in the new disability history. *Journal of American History, 87*(3), 888–922. doi:10.2307/2675276

Lund, E. M., Nadorff, M. R., & Seader, K. (2016). Relationship between suicidality and disability when accounting for depressive symptomology. *Rehabilitation Counseling Bulletin, 59*(3), 185–188. doi:10.1177/0034355215586388

Lund, E. M., Nadorff, M. R., Winer, E. S., & Seader, K. (2016). Is suicide an option?: The impact of disability on suicide acceptability in the context of depression, suicidality, and demographic factors. *Journal of Affective Disorders, 189*, 25–35. doi:10.1016/j.jad.2016.05.001

Lupton, D. (2014). The pedagogy of disgust: The ethical, moral and political implications of using disgust in public health campaigns. *Critical Public Health, 25*(1), 4–14. doi:10.1080/09581596.2014.885115

Luria, A. R. (1966). *Higher cortical functions in man*. New York, NY: Basic Books.

Lyle, M. L., & Simplican, S. C. (2015). Elite repudiation of the r-word and public opinion about intellectual disability. *Intellectual and Developmental Disabilities, 53*(3), 211–227. doi:10.1352/1934-9556-53.3.211

Lynch, R. T., Thuli, K., & Groombridge, L. (1994). Person-first disability language: A pilot analysis of public perceptions. *Journal of Rehabilitation, 60*, 18–22.

Maciver, D., Prior, S., Forsyth, K., Walsh, M., Meiklejohn, A., Irvine, L., & Pentland, D. (2013). Vocational rehabilitation: Facilitating evidence based practice through participatory action research. *Journal of Mental Health, 22*(2), 183–190. doi:10.3109/09638237.2012.734659

Mackelprang, R. W., & Salsgiver, R. O. (2016). *Disability: A diversity model approach in human service practice* (3rd ed.). New York, NY: Oxford University Press.

Marcia, J. E. (1966). Development and validation of ego-identity status. *Journal of Personality and Social Psychology, 3*(5), 551–558.

Markel, K. S., & Barclay, L. A. (2009). Addressing the underemployment of persons with disabilities: Recommendations for expanding organizational social responsibility. *Employee Responsibilities and Rights Journal, 21*(4), 305–318. doi:10.1007/s10672-009-9125-3

Marks, B. (2007). Cultural competence revisited: Nursing students with disabilities. *Journal of Nursing Education, 46*(2), 70–74.

Marks, D. (1999). *Disability: Controversial debates and psychosocial perspectives*. London, UK: Routledge.

Marrone, S. R. (2012). Organizational cultural competence. In L. D. Purnell (Ed.), *Transcultural health care: A culturally competent approach* (4th ed., pp. 60–73). Philadelphia, PA: FA Davis Publishing Company.

McAdams, D. P. (2001). The psychology of life stories. *Review of General Psychology, 5*(2), 100–122. doi:10.1037/1089-2680.5.2.100

McAdams, D. P., & McLean, K. C. (2013). Narrative identity. *Current Directions in Psychological Science, 22*(3), 233–238. doi:10.1177/0963721413475622

McBryde Johnson, H. (2003). Unspeakable conversations. *New York Times. February, 16,* 2003.

McCarn, S. R., & Fassinger, R. E. (1996). Revisioning sexual minority identity formation: A new model of lesbian identity and its implications for counseling and research. *The Counseling Psychologist, 24*(3), 508–534. doi:10.1177/0011000096243011

McCarthy, H. (2003). The disability rights movement: Experiences and perspectives of selected leaders in the disability community. *Rehabilitation Counseling Bulletin, 46*(4), 209–223. doi:10.1177/00343552030460402

McCarthy, H. (2011). A modest festschrift and insider perspective on Beatrice Wright's contributions to rehabilitation theory and practice. *Rehabilitation Counseling Bulletin, 54*(2), 67–81. doi:10.1177/0034355210386971

McCoy, V. A., & DeCecco, P. G. (2011). Person-first language training needed in higher education. Retrieved from http://counselingoutfitters.com/vistas/vistas11/Article_05.pdf

McDermott, R., & Varenne, H. (1995). Culture as disability. *Anthropology & Education Quarterly, 26*(3), 324–348. doi:10.1525/aeq.1995.26.3.05x0936z

McDonald, G., & Oxford, M. (1995). History of independent living. Independent Living Research Utilization Program. Rehabilitation Services Administration, U.S. Department of Education. Retrieved from http://www.ilru.org/sites/default/files/History_of_Independent_Living.pdf

McDonald, K. E., & Raymaker, D. M. (2013). Paradigm shifts in disability and health: Toward more ethical public health research. *American Journal of Public Health, 103*(12), 2165–2173. doi:10.2105/ajph.2013.301286

McLean, K. C., & Syed, M. (2014). The field of identity development needs an identity. In K. C. McLean & M. Syed (Eds.), *The Oxford handbook of identity development* (pp. 1–11). New York, NY: Oxford University Press.

McMillen, J. C., & Cook, C. L. (2003). The positive by-products of spinal cord injury and their correlates. *Rehabilitation Psychology, 48*(2), 77–85. doi:10.1037/0090-5550.48.2.77

McRuer, R. (2006). *Crip theory: Cultural signs of queerness and disability.* New York, NY: New York University Press.

Meltzer, H., Brugha, T., Dennis, M. S., Hassiotis, A., Jenkins, R., McManus, S., . . . Bebbington, P. (2012). The influence of disability on suicidal behaviour. *ALTER - European Journal of Disability Research/Revue Européenne de Recherche Sur Le Handicap, 6*(1), 1–12. doi:10.1016/j.alter.2011.11.004

Meyer, I. H. (1995). Minority stress and mental health in gay men. *Journal of Health and Social Behavior, 38*–56. doi:10.2307/2137286

Miller, E., Chen, R., Glover-Graf, N. M., & Kranz, P. (2009). Willingness to engage in personal relationships with persons with disabilities: Examining category and severity of disability. *Rehabilitation Counseling Bulletin, 52*(4), 211–224. doi:10.1177/0034355209332719

Miller, P., Parker, S., & Gillinson, S. (2004). *Disablism: How to tackle the last prejudice.* London, UK: Demos.

Mingus, M. (2011). Changing the framework: Disability justice. *RESIST, 19*(6), 1–2. Retrieved from http://leavingevidence.wordpress.com/2011/02/12/changing-the-framework-disabilityjustice/

Minkler, M., Fadem, P., Perry, M., Blum, K., Moore, L., & Rogers, J. (2002). Ethical dilemmas in participatory action research: A case study from the disability community. *Health Education & Behavior, 29*(1), 14–29. doi:10.1177/109019810202900I004

Miralles, C., Garcia-Sabater, J. P., Andres, C., & Cardos, M. (2007). Advantages of assembly lines in sheltered work centres for disabled. A case study. *International Journal of Production Economics, 110*(1–2), 187–197. doi:10.1016/j.ijpe.2007.02.023

Misiaszek, J., Dooling, J., Gieseke, M., Melman, H., Misiaszek, J. G., & Jorgensen, K. (1985). Diagnostic considerations in deaf patients. *Comprehensive Psychiatry, 26,* 513–521. doi:10.1016/0010-440X(85)90018-5

Mitchell, D. A., & Lassiter, S. L. (2006). Addressing health care disparities and increasing workforce diversity: The next step for the dental, medical, and public health professions. *American Journal of Public Health, 96*(12), 2093–2097. doi:10.2105/ajph.2005.082818

Mitra, S. (2014). Reconciling the capability approach and the ICF: A response. *ALTER-European Journal of Disability Research/Revue Européenne de Recherche sur le Handicap, 1*(8), 24–29. doi:10.1016/j.alter.2013.11.005

Molloy, D., Knight, T., & Woodfield, K. (2003). *Diversity in disability: Exploring the interactions between disability, ethnicity, age, gender and sexuality* (No. 188). Leeds, UK: Corporate Document Services.

Morris, J. (2005). *Citizenship and disabled people: A scoping paper prepared for the Disability Rights Commission.* Leeds, UK: Disability Archive UK. Retrieved from http://disability-studies.leeds.ac.uk/files/library/morris-Citizenship-and-disabled-people.pdf

Mona, L. R., Cameron, R. P., & Clemency Cordes, C. (2017). Disability culturally competent sexual healthcare. *American Psychologist, 72*(9), 1000–1010. doi:10.1037/amp0000283

Mona, L. R., Syme, M. L., Cameron, R. P., Clemency Cordes, C., Fraley, S. S., Baggett, L. R., & Roma, V. G. (2014). Sexuality and disability: A disability-affirmative approach to sex therapy. In Y. M. Binik & K. Hall (Eds.), *Principles and practices of sex therapy* (5th ed., pp. 457–481). New York, NY: Guilford Press.

Mpofu, E., Chronister, J., Johnson, E. T., & Denham, G. (2012). Aspects of culture influencing rehabilitation and persons with disabilities. In P. Kennedy (Ed.), *The Oxford handbook of rehabilitation psychology* (pp. 543–553). New York, NY: Oxford University Press.

Nagraj, D., & Omar, H. A. (2015). Disability and suicide. In H. A. Omar (Ed.), *Youth suicide prevention: Everybody's business* (pp. 85–95). Hauppauge, NY: Nova Science Publishers.

Nario-Redmond, M. R., Gospodinov, D., & Cobb, A. (2017). Crip for a day: The unintended negative consequences of disability simulations. *Rehabilitation Psychology, 62*(3), 324–333. doi:10.1037/rep0000127

Nario-Redmond, M. R., Noel, J. G., & Fern, E. (2013). Redefining disability, re-imagining the self: Disability identification predicts self-esteem and strategic responses to stigma. *Self and Identity, 12*(5), 468–488. doi:10.1080/15298868.2012.681118

Nario-Redmond, M. R., & Oleson, K. C. (2016). Disability group identification and disability-rights advocacy: Contingencies among emerging and other adults. *Emerging Adulthood, 4*(3), 207–218. doi:10.1177/2167696815579830

National Association of the Deaf. (n.d.). *Position statement on schools for the Deaf.* Retrieved from https://nad.org/issues/education/k-12/position-statement-schools-deaf

National Council on Disability (NCD). (2012). Rocking the cradle: Ensuring the rights of parents with disabilities and their children. Retrieved from http://www.ncd.gov/publications/2012/Sep272012/

National Disability Rights Network. (n.d.). Guidelines for reporting and writing about people with disabilities. Retrieved from http://www.ndrn.org/images/Documents/Advocacy/Amicus_Activity/Guidelines_for_Reporting_and_Writing_about_People_with_Disabilities.pdf

National Federation of the Blind. (2009). *The Braille literacy crisis in America: Facing the truth, reversing the trend, empowering the blind.* Baltimore, MD: Jernigan Institute.

National Institute on Disability and Rehabilitation Research (NIDILRR). (2017). Administration for Community Living, Department of Health and Human Services. National Institute on Disability and Rehabilitation Research (NIDILRR) draft long-range plan for the period 2018–2023. Office of Special Education and Rehabilitative Services, Department of Education. Retrieved from https://www.acl.gov/sites/default/files/news%202017-05/NIDILRR-Long-Range-Plan-DRAFT.pdf

Naumann, L. P., Benet-Martínez, V., & Espinoza, P. (2017). Correlates of political ideology among US-born Mexican Americans: Cultural identification, acculturation attitudes, and socioeconomic status. *Social Psychological and Personality Science, 8*(1), 20–28. doi:10.1177/1948550616662124

Nelson, A. (2002). Unequal treatment: Confronting racial and ethnic disparities in health care. *Journal of the National Medical Association, 94*(8), 666–668.

Nelson, G., Ochocka, J., Griffin, K., & Lord, J. (1998). "Nothing about me, without me": Participatory action research with self-help/mutual aid organizations for psychiatric consumer/survivors. *American Journal of Community Psychology, 26*(6), 881–912. doi:10.1023/a:1022298129812

Nielsen, K. E. (2012). *A disability history of the United States.* Boston, MA: Beacon Press.

Nielsen, K. E. (2009). *The radical lives of Helen Keller.* New York, NY: New York University Press.

Niemeier, J. P., Burnett, D. M., & Whitaker, D. A. (2003). Cultural competence in the multidisciplinary rehabilitation setting: Are we falling short of meeting needs? *Archives of Physical Medicine and Rehabilitation, 84*(8), 1240–1245. doi:10.1016/s0003-9993(03)00295-8

Norcross, J. C. (2005). The psychotherapist's own psychotherapy: Educating and developing psychologists. *American Psychologist, 60*(8), 840–850. doi:10.1037/0003-066x.60.8.840

Nosek, M. A., Hughes, R. B., & Taylor, H. B. (2004). Violence against women with disabilities: The role of physicians in filling the treatment gap. In S. L. Welner & F. Haseltine (Eds.), *Welner's guide to the care of women with disabilities* (pp. 333–345). Philadelphia, PA: Lippincott, Williams, and Wilkins.

Nussbaum, M. C. (2009). *Hiding from humanity: Disgust, shame, and the law.* Princeton, NJ: Princeton University Press. doi:10.1515/9781400825943

Offergeld, J. (2012). Inclusion & civic participation, poverty and exclusion. UN Convention on the Rights of Persons with Disabilities. Retrieved from http://disabilityandhumanrights.com/2012/02/23/public-attitudes-towards- persons-with-disabilities-and-their-role-in-achieving-an-inclusive-society/

U.S. Office of the Surgeon General Office on Disability. (2005). *The Surgeon General's call to action to improve the health and wellness of persons with disabilities.* Rockville, MD: Author. Retrieved from https://www.ncbi.nlm.nih.gov/books/NBK44662/

Oliver, M. (2013). The social model of disability: Thirty years on. *Disability & Society, 28*(7), 1024–1026. doi:10.1080/09687599.2013.818773

Olkin, R. (1999). *What psychotherapists should know about disability.* New York, NY: Guilford Press.

Olkin, R. (2002). Could you hold the door for me? Including disability in diversity. *Cultural Diversity and Ethnic Minority Psychology, 8*(2), 130–137. doi:10.1037/1099-9809.8.2.130

Olkin, R. (2007). Disability-affirmative therapy and case formulation: A template for understanding disability in a clinical context (Case study). *Counseling and Human Development.* Retrieved from https://www.highbeam.com/doc/1G1-175350872.html

Olkin, R. (2017). *Disability-affirmative therapy.* New York, NY: Oxford University Press.

Olkin, R., & Pledger, C. (2003). Can disability studies and psychology join hands? *American Psychologist, 58*(4), 296. doi:10.1037/0003-066X.58.4.296

O'Neil, J. M., Egan, J., Owen, S. V., & Murry, V. M. (1993). The Gender Role Journey Measure: Scale development and psychometric evaluation. *Sex Roles, 282*(3–4), 167–185. doi:10.1007/bf00299279

Otieno, P. A. (2009). Biblical and theological perspectives on disability: Implications on the rights of persons with disability in Kenya. *Disability Studies Quarterly, 24*(4). doi:10.18061/dsq.v29i4.988

O'Toole, C. J., & Doe, T. (2002). Sexuality and disabled parents with disabled children. *Sexuality and Disability, 20*(1), 89–101. doi:10.1023/a:1015290522277

Owens, T., & De Than, C. (2015). *Supporting disabled people with their sexual lives: A clear guide for health and social care professionals.* London, UK: Jessica Kingsley Publishers.

Parens, E., & Asch, A. (Eds.). (2000). *Prenatal testing and disability rights.* Washington, DC: Georgetown University Press.

Patient Protection and Affordable Care Act, 42 U.S.C. § 18001 (2010).

Peers, D., Spencer-Cavaliere, N., & Eales, L. (2014). Say what you mean: Rethinking disability language in Adapted Physical Activity Quarterly. *Adapted Physical Activity Quarterly, 31*, 265–282. doi:10.1123/apaq.2013-0091

Pelka, F. (2012). *What we have done: An oral history of the disability rights movement.* Amherst, MA: University of Massachusetts Press.

Peterson, D., & Elliott, T. (2008). Advances in conceptualizing and studying disability. In R. Lent & S. Brown (Eds.), *Handbook of counseling psychology* (4th ed., pp. 212–230). New York, NY: Sage.

Pettigrew, T. F. (1998). Intergroup contact theory. *Annual Review of Psychology, 49*(1), 65–85. doi:10.1146/annurev.psych.49.1.65

Pettigrew, T. F., & Tropp, L. R. (2000). Does intergroup contact reduce prejudice? Recent meta-analytic findings. In S. Oskamp (Ed.), *Reducing prejudice and discrimination. The Claremont Symposium on Applied Social Psychology* (pp. 93–114). Mahwah, NJ: Lawrence Erlbaum.

Phillips, M. J. (1985). "Try harder": The experience of disability and the dilemma of normalization. *Social Science Journal, 22*(4), 45–57.

Phillips, M. J. (1990). Damaged goods: Oral narrative of the experience of disability in American culture. *Social Science Medicine, 30*(8), 849–855. doi:10.1016/0277-9536(90)90212-b

Phinney, J. S. (1990). Ethnic identity in adolescents and adults: Review of research. *Psychological Bulletin, 108*, 499–514. doi:10.1037/0033-2909.108.3.499

Phinney, J. S. (1996). When we talk about American ethnic groups, what do we mean? *American Psychologist, 51*(9), 918–927. doi:10.1037/0003-066x.51.9.918

Powers, L. E., Curry, M. A., Oschwald, M., Maley, S., Saxton, M., & Eckels, K. (2002). Barriers and strategies in addressing abuse: A survey of disabled women's experiences. *Journal of Rehabilitation, 68*, 4–13.

Price, C. C., & Eibner, C. (2013). For states that opt out of Medicaid expansion: 3.6 million fewer insured and $8.4 billion less in federal payments. *Health Affairs, 32*(6), 1030–1036. doi:10.1377/hlthaff.2012.1019

Prigatano, G. P. (1991). Disordered mind, wounded soul: The emerging role of psychotherapy in rehabilitation after brain injury. *Journal of Head Trauma Rehabilitation, 6*(4), 1–10. doi:10.1097/00001199-199112000-00004

Prout, H. T., & Browning, B. K. (2011). Psychotherapy with persons with intellectual disabilities: A review of effectiveness research. *Advances in Mental Health and Intellectual Disabilities, 5*(5), 53–59. doi:10.1108/20441281111180673

Pullin, D. (2002). Testing individuals with disabilities: Reconciling social science and social policy. In R. B. Ekstrom & D. Smith (Eds.), *Assessing individuals with disabilities in educational, employment, and counseling settings* (pp. 11–31). Washington, DC: American Psychological Association.

Putnam, M. (2005). Conceptualizing disability: Developing a framework for political disability identity. *Journal of Disability Policy Studies, 16*(3), 188–198. doi:10.1177/10442073050160030601

Radermacher, H., Sonn, C., Keys, C., & Duckett, P. (2010). Disability and participation: It's about us but still without us!. *Journal of Community & Applied Social Psychology, 20*(5), 333–346. doi: 10.1002/casp.1039

Radnitz, C. L., Bockian, N., & Moran, A. I. (2000). Assessment of psychopathology and personality in people with physical disabilities. In R. G. Frank & T. R. Elliott (Eds.), *Handbook of rehabilitation psychology* (pp. 287–309). Washington, DC: American Psychological Association.

Rao, S. (2004). Faculty attitudes and students with disabilities in higher education: A literature review. *College Students Journal, 38*, 191–198.

Rath, J. F., & Elliott, T. R. (2012). Psychological models in rehabilitation psychology. In P. Kennedy (Ed.), *The Oxford handbook of rehabilitation psychology* (pp. 32–46). New York, NY: Oxford University Press.

Ravindran, N., & Myers, B. J. (2012). Cultural influences on perceptions of health, illness, and disability: A review and focus on autism. *Journal of Child and Family Studies, 21*(2), 311–319. doi:10.1007/s10826-011-9477-9

Reed, G. M., Lux, J. B., Bufka, L. F., Trask, C., Peterson, D. B., Stark, S., et al. (2005). Operationalizing the International Classification of Functioning, Disability and Health in clinical settings. *Rehabilitation Psychology, 50*(2), 122–131. doi:10.1037/0090-5550.50.2.122

Reznick, J. S., Gambel, J., & Hawk, A. J. (2009). Historical perspectives on the care of service members with limb amputations. In P. Pasquina & R. A. Cooper (Eds.), *Care of the combat amputee* (pp. 19–40). Washington, DC: Office of the Surgeon General at TMM Publications, Borden Institute, Walter Reed Army Medical Center.

Robinson-Whelen, S., Hughes, R. B., Gabrielli, J., Lund, E. M., Abramson, W., & Swank, P. R. (2014). A safety awareness program for women with diverse disabilities: A randomized controlled trial. *Violence Against Women, 20*(7), 846–868. doi:10.1177/1077801214543387

Rogers-Adkinson, D. L., Ochoa, T. A., & Delgado, B. (2003). Developing cross-cultural competence: Serving families of children with significant developmental needs. *Focus on Autism and Other Developmental Disabilities, 18*(1), 4–8. doi:10.1177/10883576030180102

Rojahn, J., Komelasky, K. G., & Man, M. (2008). Implicit attitudes and explicit ratings of romantic attraction of college students toward opposite-sex peers with physical disabilities. *Journal of Developmental and Physical Disabilities, 20*(4), 389–397. doi:10.1007/s10882-008-9108-6

Rose, D. W. (2016). *Friends and partners: The legacy of Franklin D. Roosevelt and Basil O'Connor in the history of polio.* Cambridge, MA: Academic Press.

Rottenstein, A. (2014). *Survey on disability.* Unpublished raw data, University of Michigan, Ann Arbor.

Ruiter, R. A. C., Kessels, L. T. E., Peters, G. Y., & Kok, G. (2014). Sixty years of fear appeal research: Current state of the evidence. *International Journal of Psychology, 49*(2), 63–70. doi:10.1002/ijop.12042

Ruiz-Williams, E., Burke, M., Chong, V. Y., & Chainarong, N. (2015). "My Deaf is not your Deaf": Realizing intersectional realities at Gallaudet University. In M. Friedner & A. Kusters (Eds.), *It's a Small World: International Deaf Spaces and Encounters* (pp. 262–274). Washington, DC: Gallaudet University Press.

Russell, D., Turner, R. J., & Joiner, T. E. (2009). Physical disability and suicidal ideation: A community-based study of risk/protective factors for suicidal thoughts. *Suicide and Life-Threatening Behavior, 39*(4), 440–451. doi:10.1521/suli.2009.39.4.440

Saini, M. A. (2008). Evidence base of custody and access evaluations. *Brief Treatment and Crisis Intervention, 8*(1), 111–129. doi:10.1093/brief-treatment/mhm023

Sandoval, J. H., Frisby, C. L., Geisinger, K. F., Scheuneman, J. D., & Grenier, J. R. (1998). *Test interpretation and diversity: Achieving equity in assessment.* Washington, DC: American Psychological Association.

Sartor, A. (2000). WongDoody copywriter develops MADD campaign. Retrieved from http://www.allbusiness.com/marketing-advertising/4189378-1.html

Saunders, P. (2018). Neurodivergent rhetorics: Examining competing discourses of autism advocacy in the public sphere. *Journal of Literary & Cultural Disability Studies, 12*(1), 1–17. doi:10.3828/jlcds.2018.1

Savulescu, J., & Kahane, G. (2011). Disability: A welfarist approach. *Clinical Ethics, 6*(1), 45–51. doi:10.1258/ce.2011.011010

Saxton, M., Curry, M. A., Powers, L. E., Maley, S., Eckels, K., & Gross, J. (2001). "Bring my scooter so I can leave you": A study of disabled women handling abuse by personal assistance providers. *Violence Against Women, 7*(4), 393–417. doi:10.1177/10778010122182523

Saxton, M., McNeff, E., Powers, L., Curry, M., & Limont, M. (2006). We are all little John Waynes: A study of disabled men's experience of abuse by personal assistants. *Journal of Rehabilitation, 72*(4), 3–13.

Scharrón-del Río, M. R., & Aja, A. A. (2015). The case for "Latinx": Why intersectionality is not a choice. *Latino Rebels.* Retrieved from http://www.latinorebels.com/2015/12/05/the-case-for-latinx-why-intersectionality-is-not-a-choice/

Schmidt, A. H. (2018). *Does person-first language increase empathy and feelings of closeness for those with HIV and cancer?* (Unpublished master's thesis). Georgia Southern University, Statesboro, GA.

Schultz, I. Z., & Stewart, A. M. (2008). Disentangling the disability quagmire in psychological injury and law: Evolution of disability models: Conceptual, methodological and forensic practice issues. *Psychological Injury and Law, 1*(2), 103–121. doi:10.1007/s12207-008-9007-2

Schweik, S. M. (2009). *The ugly laws: Disability in public.* New York, NY: New York University Press.

Scotch, R. (2002). Paradigms of American social research on disability: What's new?. *Disability Studies Quarterly, 22*(2), 23–34. doi:10.18061/dsq.v22i2.342

Section 504 of the Rehabilitation Act. Pub. L. No. 93-122. (1973).

Section 504 of the Rehabilitation Act of 1973, amended. Pub. L. No. 93-112. (1989).

Seligman, M. E. P., Park, N., & Peterson, C. (2004). The Values in Action (VIA) classification of character strengths. *Ricerche di Psicologia, 27*(1), 63–78.

Serafini, G., Pompili, M., Forte, A., Amore, M., & Girardi, P. (2014). Suicide behavior in multiple sclerosis. *Neurology, Psychiatry and Brain Research, 20*(1), 23. doi:10.1016/j.npbr.2014.01.169

Serlin, D. (2015). Constructing autonomy: Smart homes for disabled veterans and the politics of normative citizenship. *Critical Military Studies, 1*(1), 38–46. doi:10.1080/23337486. 2015.1005392

Shakespeare, T. (1996). Disability, identity and difference. In C. Barnes & G. Mercer (Eds.), *Exploring the divide* (pp. 94–113). Leeds, UK: Disability Press.

Shakespeare, T. (Ed.). (1998). *Disability reader: Social sciences perspectives.* London, UK: Cassell.

Shakespeare, T. (2013). *Disability rights and wrongs revisited.* Abington, UK: Routledge.

Shakespeare, T., Gillespie-Sells, K. and Davies, D. (1996). *The Sexual Politics of Disability: Untold Desires.* London: Cassell.

Shakespeare, T., & Watson, N. (1997). Defending the social model. *Disability & Society, 12,* 293–300. doi:10.1080/09687599727380

Shalev, A. Y., Schreiber, S., Galai, T., & Melmed, R. N. (1993). Post-traumatic stress disorder following medical events. *British Journal of Clinical Psychology, 32*(2), 247–253. doi:10.1111/j.2044-8260.1993.tb01052.x

Shannon, C. D., Tansey, T. N., & Schoen, B. (2009). The effect of contact, context, and social power on undergraduate attitudes toward persons with disabilities. *Journal of Rehabilitation, 75*(4), 11–18.

Shapiro, A. (2003). *Everybody belongs: Changing negative attitudes toward classmates with disabilities.* Abington, UK: Routledge.

Shapiro, J. P. (1994). *No pity: People with disabilities forging a new civil rights movement.* New York, NY: Three Rivers Press.

Sheppard, K., & Badger, T. (2010). The lived experience of depression among culturally Deaf adults. *Journal of Psychiatric and Mental Health Nursing, 17*(9), 783–789. doi:10.1111/j.1365-2850.2010.01606.x

Shontz, F. C. (1977). Six principles relating disability and psychological adjustment. *Rehabilitation Psychology, 24*(4), 207. doi:doi.org/10.1037//0090-5550.24.4.207

Siebers, T. (2003). What can disability studies learn from the culture wars? *Cultural Critique, 55*(1), 182–216. doi:10.1353/cul.2003.0051

Silverman, A. M., Gwinn, J. D., & Van Boven, L. (2015). Stumbling in their shoes: Disability simulations reduce judged capabilities of disabled people. *Social Psychological and Personality Science, 6*(4), 464–471. doi:10.1177/1948550614559650

Sinclair, L. B., Lingard, L. A., & Mohabeer, R. N. (2009). What's so great about rehabilitation teams? An ethnographic study of interprofessional collaboration in a rehabilitation unit. *Archives of Physical Medicine and Rehabilitation, 90*(7), 1196–1201. doi:10.1016/j.apmr.2009.01.021

Sins Invalid. (2016). Skin, tooth, and bone: The basis of a movement is our people: A disability justice primer. *Reproductive Health Matters, 25*(50), 149–150.

Sireci, S. G., Li, S., & Scarpati, S. (2003). The effects of tests accommodations on test performance: A review of the literature. Commissioned paper by the National Academy of Sciences/ National Research Council's Board on Testing and Assessment.

Slayter, E. (2009). Intimate partner violence against women with disabilities: Implications for disability service system case management practice. *Journal of Aggression, Maltreatment & Trauma, 18*(2), 182–199. doi:10.1080/10926770802675668

Smith, T., & Eikeseth, S. (2011). O. Ivar Lovaas: Pioneer of applied behavior analysis and intervention for children with autism. *Journal of Autism and Developmental Disorders, 41*(3), 375–378. doi:10.1007/s10803-010-1162-0

Snyder, S. L., & Mitchell, D. T. (1996). *Vital signs: Crip culture talks back.* Boston, MA: Fanlight Distributors.

Sobsey, D. (2014). Violence and disability. Retrieved from http://eugenicsarchive.ca/discover/ encyclopedia/535eee9d7095aa0000000262

Sofair, A. N., & Kaldjian, L. C. (2000). Eugenic sterilization and a qualified Nazi analogy: The United States and Germany, 1930–1945. *Annals of Internal Medicine, 132*(4), 312–319. doi:10.7326/0003-4819-132-4-200002150-00010

Solvang, P. K. (2012). From identity politics to dismodernism? Changes in the social meaning of disability art. *ALTER-European Journal of Disability Research/Revue Européenne de Recherche sur le Handicap, 6*(3), 178–187. doi:10.1016/j.alter.2012.05.002

Somerfield, M. R., & McCrae, R. R. (2000). Stress and coping research: Methodological challenges, theoretical advances, and clinical applications. *American Psychologist, 55*(6), 620–625. doi:10.1037/0003-066x.55.6.620

Stets, J. E., & Burke, P. J. (2000). Identity theory and social identity theory. *Social Psychology Quarterly, 63*(3), 224–237. doi:10.2307/2695870

Stibe, A., & Cugelman, B. (2016). Persuasive backfiring: When behavior change interventions trigger unintended negative outcomes. *Lecture Notes in Computer Science, 9638*, 65–77. doi:10.1007/978-3-319-31510-2_6

St. Louis, K. O. (1999). Person-first labeling and stuttering. *Journal of Fluency Disorders, 24*(1), 1–24. doi:10.1016/s0094-730x(98)00024-2

Stodden, R. A., Stodden, N. J., Kim-Rupnow, W. S., Thai, N. D., & Galloway, L. M. (2003). Providing effective support services for culturally and linguistically diverse persons with disabilities: Challenges and recommendations. *Journal of Vocational Rehabilitation, 18*(3), 177–189.

Story, M., Mueller, J., & Mace, R. (1998). The universal design file: Designing for people of all ages and abilities. North Carolina State University Center for Universal Design, Raleigh, NC. Retrieved from https://files.eric.ed.gov/fulltext/ED460554.pdf

U.S. Substance Abuse and Mental Health Services Administration. (2014). *Improving cultural competence.* Treatment Improvement Protocol (TIP) Series No. 59. HHS Publication No. (SMA) 14-4849. Rockville, MD: Substance Abuse and Mental Health Services Administration.

Sue, D. W. (2001). Multidimensional facets of cultural competence. *Counseling Psychologist, 29*(6), 790–821. doi:10.1177/0011000001296002

Sue, D. W., Capodilupo, C. M., Torino, G. C., Bucceri, J. M., Holder, A., Nadal, K. L., & Esquilin, M. (2007). Racial microaggressions in everyday life: Implications for clinical practice. *American Psychologist, 62*(4), 271–286. doi:10.1037/0003-066x.62.4.271

Sue, S. (1998). In search of cultural competence in psychotherapy and counseling. *American Psychologist, 53*(4), 440–448. doi:10.1037/0003-066x.53.4.440

Sullivan, L. W. (2004). Missing persons: Minorities in the health professions. Report of the Sullivan Commission on Diversity in the Healthcare Workforce.

Tannenbaum, M. B., Hepler, J., Zimmerman, R. S., Saul, L., Jacobs, S., Wilson, K., & Albarracín, D. (2015). Appealing to fear: A meta-analysis of fear appeal effectiveness and theories. *Psychological Bulletin, 141*(6), 1178–1204. doi:10.1037/a0039729

Tate, D. G., & Pledger, C. (2003). An integrative conceptual framework of disability: New directions for research. *American Psychologist, 58*(4), 289–295. doi:10.1037/0003-066x.58.4.289

Taylor, B., & Davis, S. (2007). The extended PLISSIT model for addressing the sexual wellbeing of individuals with an acquired disability or chronic illness. *Sexuality and Disability, 25*(3), 135–139. doi:10.1007/s11195-007-9044-x

Taylor, P., Lopez, M. H., Martínez, J. H., & Velasco, G. (2012). *When labels don't fit: Hispanics and their views of identity*. Washington, DC: Pew Hispanic Center.

Tengland, P. (2012). Behavior change or empowerment: On the ethics of health-promotion strategies. *Public Health Ethics, 5*(2), 140–153. doi:10.1093/phe/phs022

Tervalon, M., & Murray-Garcia, J. (1998). Cultural humility versus cultural competence: A critical distinction in defining physician training outcomes in multicultural education. *Journal of Health Care for the Poor and Underserved, 9*(2), 117–125. doi:10.1353/hpu.2010.0233

Teuber, H. L. (1969). Neglected aspects of the posttraumatic syndrome. In A. E. Walker, W. F. Caveness, & M. Critchley (Eds.), *The late effects of head injury* (pp. 13–14). Springfield, IL: Charles C Thomas.

Thomson, R. G. (1996). Introduction: From wonder to error—A genealogy of freak discourse in modernity. In R. G. Thomson (Ed.), *Freakery: Cultural spectacles of the extraordinary body* (pp. 1–19). NYU Press.

Tilley, E., Walmsley, J., Earle, S., & Atkinson, D. (2012). "The silence is roaring": Sterilization, reproductive rights and women with intellectual disabilities. *Disability & Society, 27*(3), 413–426. doi:10.1080/09687599.2012.654991

Torre, M. E., Fine, M., Stoudt, B. G., & Fox, M. (2012). Critical participatory action research as public science. In H. Cooper, P. M. Camic, D. L. Long, A. T. Panter, D. Rindskopf, & K. J. Sher (Eds.), *APA handbook of research methods in psychology*, Vol. 2. *Research designs: Quantitative, qualitative, neuropsychological, and biological* (pp. 171–184). Washington, DC: American Psychological Association.

Torres, L., & Taknint, J. T. (2015). Ethnic microaggressions, traumatic stress symptoms, and Latino depression: A moderated mediational model. *Journal of Counseling Psychology, 62*(3), 393–401. doi:10.1037/cou0000077

Turner, A. P., Hartoonian, N., Sloan, A. P., Benich, M., Kivlahan, D. R., Hughes, C., . . . Haselkorn, J. K. (2016). Improving fatigue and depression in individuals with multiple sclerosis using telephone-administered physical activity counseling. *Journal of Consulting and Clinical Psychology, 84*(4), 297–309. doi:10.1037/ccp0000086

Turner, J. A., Holtzman, S., & Mancl, L. (2007). Mediators, moderators, and predictors of therapeutic change in cognitive–behavioral therapy for chronic pain. *Pain, 127*(3), 276–286. doi:10.1016/j.pain.2006.09.005

United Spinal Association. (2011). Disability etiquette. Retrieved from http://www.unitedspinal.org/pdf/DisabilityEtiquette.pdf

U.S. Holocaust Memorial Museum. The murder of the handicapped. *Holocaust Encyclopedia.* Retrieved from https://www.ushmm.org/outreach/en/article.php?ModuleId=10007683

Valdeón, R. A. (2013). Hispanic or Latino: The use of politicized terms for the Hispanic minority in US official documents and quality news outlets. *Language and Intercultural Communication, 13*(4), 433–449. doi:10.1080/14708477.2012.740047

Vanderploeg, R. D. (2000). The interpretation process. In R. D. Vanderploeg (Ed.), *Clinician's guide to neuropsychological assessment* (pp. 111–154). Mahwah, NJ: Lawrence Erlbaum Associates.

Virues-Ortega, J. (2010). Applied behavior analytic intervention for autism in early childhood: Meta-analysis, meta-regression and dose-response meta-analysis of multiple outcomes. *Clinical Psychology Review, 30*(4), 387–399. doi:10.1016/j.cpr.2010.01.008

Voh, J. (1993). On belonging: A place to stand, a gift to give. In A. P Turnbull, J. A. Patterson, S. K. Behr, D. L. Murphy, J. G. Marquis, & M. J. Blue-Banning (Eds.), *Cognitive coping, families, and disability* (pp. 51–67). Baltimore, MD: Paul H. Brookes Publishing.

Wang, P. P., Badley, E. M., & Gignac, M. (2006). Exploring the role of contextual factors in disability models. *Disability and Rehabilitation, 28*(2), 135–140. doi:10.1080/09638280500167761

Watermeyer, B., & Swartz, L. (2016). Disablism, identity and self: Discrimination as a traumatic assault on subjectivity. *Journal of Community & Applied Social Psychology, 26*(3), 268–276. doi:10.1002/casp.2266

Wechsler, D. (2014). *Wechsler adult intelligence scale–fourth edition (WAIS–IV).* San Antonio, TX: Psychological Corporation.

Weeber, J. E. (2004). *Disability community leaders' disability identity development: A journey of integration and expansion* (Unpublished doctoral dissertation). North Carolina State University, Raleigh, NC.

Wehmeyer, M. L. (Ed.). (2013). *The Oxford handbook of positive psychology and disability.* New York, NY: Oxford University Press.

Whatley, S. (2010). The spectacle of difference: Dance and disability on screen. *International Journal of Screendance, 1*(1), 41–52. doi:10.18061/ijsd.v1i0.6144

White, M. J., Jackson, V., & Gordon, P. J. (2006). Implicit and explicit attitudes toward athletes with disabilities. *Journal of Rehabilitation, 72*(3), 33–40.

Whyte, A., Aubrecht, A., McCullough, C., Lewis, J., & Thompson-Ochoa, D. (2013). Understanding Deaf people in counseling contexts. *Counseling Today, 56*(4), 38–45.

Williams, J., & Colvin, L. (2016). Coming together to end violence against women and girls with disabilities. In S. Miles-Cohen & C. Signore (Eds.), *Eliminating inequities for women with disabilities: An agenda for health and wellness* (pp. 243–262). Washington, DC: American Psychological Association. doi:10.1037/14943-000

Willner, P. (2005). The effectiveness of psychotherapeutic interventions for people with learning disabilities: A critical overview. *Journal of Intellectual Disability Research, 49*(1), 73–85. doi:10.1111/j.1365-2788.2005.00633.x

Winter, J. A. (2003). The development of the disability rights movement as a social problem solver. *Disability Studies Quarterly, 23*(1). doi:10.18061/dsq.v23i1.399

Wolbring, G. (2008). The politics of ableism. *Development, 51*(2), 252–258. doi:10.1057/dev.2008.17

Wong, D. W., Chan, F., Da Silva Cardoso, E., Lam, C. S., & Miller, S. M. (2004). Rehabilitation counseling students' attitudes toward people with disabilities in three social contexts: A conjoint analysis. *Rehabilitation Counseling Bulletin, 47*(4), 194–204. doi:10.1177/ 00343552040470040101

World Health Organization. (1980). *International classification of impairments, disabilities and handicaps.* Geneva, Switzerland: Author.

World Health Organization. (2001). *International classification of functioning, disability, and health.* Geneva, Switzerland: Author.

World Health Organization (WHO). (2002). *Towards a Common Language for Functioning, Disability and Health.* ICF. Geneva, Switzerland: Author.

World Health Organization. (2006). *Defining sexual health: Report of a technical consultation on sexual health.* Geneva, Switzerland: Author.

World Health Organization. (2013). *How to use the ICF: A practical manual for using the International Classification of Functioning, Disability and Health (ICF). Exposure draft for comment.* Geneva, Switzerland: Author.

Wright, B. (1983). *Physical disability: A psychosocial approach* (2nd ed.). New York, NY: Harper & Row. doi:10.1037/10589-000

Wright, B. A. (1988). Attitudes and the fundamental negative bias: Conditions and corrections. In H. E. Yuker (Ed.), *Attitudes toward persons with disabilities* (pp. 3–21). New York, NY: Springer.

Wright, B. A. (1991). Labeling: The need for greater person-environment individuation. In C. R. Snyder & D. R. Forsyth (Eds.), *Handbook of social and clinical psychology: The health perspective* (pp. 469–487). New York, NY: Pergamon Press.

Young, S. (2012). "We're not here for your inspiration." The Drum, July 3. Retrieved from http:// www.abc.net.au/news/2012-07-03/young-inspiration-porn/4107006

Yuen, E. (1997). Social movements, identity politics and the genealogy of the term "people of color." *New Political Science, 19*(1–2), 97–107. doi:10.1080/07393149708429789

Yuker, H. E. (1994). Variables that influence attitudes toward persons with disabilities: Conclusions from the data. *Journal of Social Behavior and Personality, 9*(5), 3–22.

Yuker, H. E., Block, J. R., & Campbell, W. J. (1960). *A scale to measure attitudes towards disabled persons.* Albertson, NY: Human Resources Center.

Zhang, L., & Haller, B. (2013). Consuming image: How mass media impact the identity of people with disabilities. *Communication Quarterly, 61*, 319–334. doi:10.1080/01463373.2013.776988

# Index

Tables, figures, and boxes are indicated by *t*, *f*, and *b* following the page number

*For the benefit of digital users, indexed terms that span two pages (e.g., 52–53) may, on occasion, appear on only one of those pages.*